Asian American Sexual Politics

Asian American Sexual Politics

The Construction of Race, Gender, and Sexuality

Rosalind S. Chou

ROWMAN & LITTLEFIELD PUBLISHERS, INC.
Lanham • Boulder • New York • Toronto • Plymouth, UK

Published by Rowman & Littlefield Publishers, Inc.
A wholly owned subsidary of The Rowman & Littlefield Publishing Group, Inc.
4501 Forbes Boulevard, Suite 200, Lanham, Maryland 20706
www.rowman.com

10 Thornbury Road, Plymouth PL6 7PP, United Kingdom

British Library Cataloguing in Publication Information Available

Library of Congress Cataloging-in-Publication Data

Chou, Rosalind.
Asian American sexual politics : the construction of race, gender, and sexuality / Rosalind S. Chou.
p. cm.
Includes index.
ISBN 978-1-4422-0924-4 (cloth : alk. paper) -- ISBN 978-1-4422-0926-8 (electronic)
1. Asian American women--Sexual behavior. 2. Asian Americans--Social conditions. I. Title.
HQ29.C47 2012
306.76089'95073--dc23
2012012097

Printed in the United States of America

This book is dedicated to my parents, Charlie and Snow Chou.

I also dedicate it to the life and memory of Stuart J. Hysom (1964 - 2011)

Contents

Preface

In the spring of 2009, I had to take my doctoral comprehensive exams. These exams are as close to "hazing" as you can get in academia. I had just completed three 14-hour writing days discussing the history of racialized and gendered oppression in the United States. I was mentally and physically exhausted. Just halfway through the weeklong exam, a day was built in the middle for rest. In the "day off" from exams, I attended a graduate student happy hour gathering in Austin, Texas. After spending three days deeply immersed in gender and race research, I was happy to enjoy some time away from my books and to see some friendly faces. However, my evening was quickly spoiled by an interaction with a bartender. My white friend and I walked up to the bar, and before I could even order anything, the bartender greeted me with mock Asian language and accent, delivering a statement about female anatomy that was reminiscent of early media portrayals of Asian prostitutes in war-torn countries soliciting soldiers with "me so horny, me love you long time."

Although I should be used to this by now, I was caught off guard. I very calmly told him that I was not particularly fond of the "underlying racialized tone" of his comments. Instead of apologizing, he completely dismissed my request to "knock it off" and repeated his statement, word for word. I looked at my friend, who has unfortunately witnessed similar instances like this with me before, and I suggested that we leave this place of business. My night was spoiled, and I turned in early. My friend, who was also upset about the incident, was able to carry on with other friends into the early morning. The incident still felt like a heavy weight for me the following morning, making it more difficult for me to concentrate on my responsibilities. The clock was ticking to finish my exams and I had less than 36 hours left. The incident from the night before left me debilitated, and I could not write a word.

The incident led me to "waste" almost twenty-four hours being upset about what took place. I had been using up my emotional energy dealing with the incident, jeopardizing the future of my PhD. Even worse, I was beating myself up about how I handled it. In true "model minority" fashion, I was polite, calm, and almost cordial to the bartender. However, this morning, I allowed my suppressed emotions to be released. I had to deal with my sadness, anger, and tears at the most inconvenient time. I am actually a more tender person than my outward appearance and presentation suggest, but I usually manage these things without such emotional distress. This incident was the icing on the cake because it was the fourth racist incident in Austin in four months. I replayed the incident over and over, making excuses for the bartender, accusing myself of being too sensitive. The most absurd part of the whole story is that the bartender is a gay man, and I am a lesbian woman. This happened in a gay bar, so his performance was not an actual sexual proposition. He was pulling from a racial script already set in place, one that constructs Asian women as "tasty treats" to be consumed (I am paraphrasing his comments).

I wondered to myself if the fact that I am an Asian American woman opened the door for more public taunting in this self-proclaimed "liberal" island of Texas. The stereotype surrounding Asian Americans as "model minorities"—hard-working, diminutive, passive people—gives license to these incidents because there is no perceived threat of resistance. I share this story because the racialized and gendered constructions of Asian Americans may precipitate this type of taunting with very few anticipated consequences. In that instance, my body was both racialized and sexualized in a particular fashion where controlling images of Asian American women's bodies were evoked. To the bartender, it was merely a joke or a way to interact with me. I felt demeaned and belittled and wish I could have conveyed that in an effective manner. I often joke with my friends that next time, they need to be ready to haul me out of the establishment because I'm breaking a beer bottle on the countertop and doing everything I can to create an image so entirely opposite of the passive, submissive Asian woman who just allows people to talk to her like a piece of meat. While breaking a beer bottle is honestly not the most logical choice in that situation, it really exemplifies the physical and emotional management that is expected from people of color when they are mistreated. I would be stepping out of my gendered box to aggressively demand that I be treated as a whole human being. In many cases, African Americans are quickly and erroneously accused of being "angry" and "out of control" if they speak up and speak out about racism. The need for this kind of emotional management on the part of people of color is a consequence of white supremacy.

My interaction with the bartender and the way I was gendered, racialized, and sexualized in that moment cemented why I needed to write this book. The incident and the many others described by my interview respondents illustrate how Asian Americans are uniquely affected by interlocking systems of oppression. Asian American intersections of race, gender, and sexuality have not been thoroughly explored and discussed in this manner. In the following chapters, sixty Asian Americans share their stories and my hope is that I can contribute to the understanding of how interlocking systems of oppression such as racial domination, colonialism, hegemonic masculinity, and heterosexism interact in and affect the lives of Asian Americans.

Acknowledgments

First and foremost, I must thank my parents Chuen Cheng and Li-Hsueh Chou. My parents were thrilled about the possibilities to come. To them, America was the land of opportunity, a place where dreams come true, and they were told that the streets were lined with gold. I think about the sacrifices made by my two loving parents. They left all of their family, friends, everything familiar, to start a new life. I am grateful for the opportunities they provided for me. I am so thankful for my two older sisters, Nina Sickler and Alice Chou. They have always been incredible role models to me.

I am a sociologist because of my wonderful high school history/sociology teacher John Dunn. He presents American history with a critical lens and opened my eyes to the sociological world. I want to also thank my friends from high school, Joshua Adrian, Greg Wolfson, Michael Peluso, and Andrew Tirrell. I must also thank Coach Regina Dooley and Julie DeMar.

My work at Camp E-Nini-Hassee changed my life. I received great mentorship from Gale Wire and Jo Lynn Smith. My appreciation goes out to my friends whom I work alongside: Deb Long, Charlene Whitney, Lynn Player, Kirsen Rostad, Cherri Baker, Remi Davis Wingo, Maribeth Pierce, Stacy Breton, Kelly Theodore, Aleisha Kraft, and Kodi McCarson.

I have received wonderful scholarly guidance from the invaluable relationships during my graduate training. Special thanks to Kristen Lavelle, Jennifer Mueller, Glenn Bracey, Lorena Murga, Elyshia Aseltine, Daniel Delgado, Ruth Thompson-Miller, Christopher Chambers, Michelle Christian, Joe R. Feagin, Wendy Leo Moore, W. Alex McIntosh, Marian Eide, Stuart J. Hysom, Jane Sell, Ashley Currier, Eduardo Bonilla-Silva, Kerry L. Haynie, Paula D. McClain, and two wonderful students I met during my time at Duke, Simon Ho and Kristen Lee.

I like to pride myself on having a balanced life and dedicating a sizeable portion of my life to things outside of scholarship. I am indebted to my incredible network of rugby friends: Stephanie Dorsey, Rachel Kraft, Kelly Frazer, Meredith Bagley, Marinda Reynolds, Tiffany Hall, Alex Davenport, Rachel Suniga Osborn, Emily Smith, and Suzanne "Cupcake" Uchneat.

ONE

Why Asian American Sexual Politics?

In 2000, two white men and a white woman in Spokane, Washington, specifically targeted Japanese women in an elaborately planned scheme to kidnap, rape, sodomize, and torture them and to videotape the whole ordeal. According to police reports, the rapists had a sexual fantasy about and fixation with young Japanese women. The three assailants believed that the Japanese women were submissive.[1] In just one month, the predators abducted five Japanese exchange students, ranging in age from eighteen to twenty. Motivated by their sexual biases about Asian women, all three used both their bodies and objects to repeatedly rape—vaginally, anally, and orally—two of the young women for over seven hours.[2] One of the attackers immediately confessed to searching only for Japanese women to torture and rape; eventually, all pled guilty and were convicted.[3]

In 2004, *American Idol,* the most watched TV series in the Nielsen ratings and the only program to have been number one for seven consecutive seasons,[4] premiered the season with an episode that showcased twenty-one-year-old William Hung singing a rendition of Ricky Martin's "She Bangs." The episode was a collection of the most "talentless" of those who auditioned, and it was if Hung was crowned the "king." His inability to carry a tune, dance to the beat, or exude any sex appeal made the video go viral on the Internet, and viewers were laughing at him, not with him. He was a perfect fit for the unflattering racial stereotype of the asexual, nerdy Asian American man. Across the blogosphere, race scholars and Asian American men were bemoaning the perpetuation of the racist stereotyping and yet another instance where Asian American men are emasculated in American media.

These two examples demonstrate the racial stereotyping of Asians and Asian Americans. The perpetrators in Spokane, Washington, used

1

racist stereotypes to pick their targets. While both being racially "othered," Asian and Asian American women have been constructed as sexually exotic docile bodies while men have been racially "castrated." These constructions created a complicated racialized Asian American sexual politics affected by racist-gendered constructions but also "home-culture" expectations. The vignettes and analysis shared in this book are an attempt to look at the nuanced way that constructions can operate in the lives of some Asian Americans.

Feminist scholars argue that women's sexuality is socially shaped in ways that sustain men's social and political dominance. I extend this feminist scholarship and argue that Asian American sexuality is socially shaped in ways that maintain social and political dominance for whites, particularly white men. I want to set this stage with the assertions made by Patricia Hill Collins in her seminal work, *Black Sexual Politics*.[5] Collins defines sexual politics as "a set of ideas and social practices shaped by gender, race, and sexuality that frame all men and women's treatment of one another, as well as how individual men and women are perceived and treated by others."[6] Collins brilliantly asserts that the oppression of African Americans extends beyond race. Controlling and enforcing the gender and sexuality of African Americans maintains white supremacy. Similarly, Asian Americans have their own unique sexual politics as they face gendered and sexualized racial stereotyping and discrimination. However, there is also dissimilarity.

Collins notes the hypersexualization of African American men and women within the outwardly appearing "sexually repressive" nature of the United States.[7] She extends her analysis to other people of color, but the sexualization of Asian Americans is somewhat different. Asian Americans come from nations with different sexual mores than the United States, and their experiences cannot be explained in the same fashion. Within those nations of origin, there are differences in gender oppression and homophobia that should be taken into account when understanding Asian American femininity, masculinity, and sexuality. In later chapters, these differences in nationhood and origin are explored to help explain the unique experiences of Asian Americans.

In my narrative analysis, it is apparent that the maintenance of white supremacy through controlling images and stereotypes of Asian Americans as gendered and sexualized bodies is a sobering reality for my respondents. While all people go through a gendered and sexualized process in this society, the intersecting racial identity for people of color introduces racial domination into the mix. The additional struggle with defining one's own racial identity is difficult enough as a man, woman, gay, straight, bisexual, or trans person. There are societal forces constantly imposing identity on us all based on gender, sexuality, class, race, age, ability, religion, and so on. However, consideration of *power* and *domination* must constantly be centralized in the analysis to get a clear picture of how oppression is operating. Asian Americans, while perhaps seen as "nearly white,"[8] are not free from gendered, racialized treatment. This racialized and gendered process is not static. The sexual stereotyping of people of Asian descent has mutated throughout American history, changing based on the needs and interests of whites. Interview respondents share in great detail the present-day gendered and racialized process they face as Asian Americans.

Structural factors based on race, class, gender, and sexuality have an effect on the lives of Asian Americans. I would be naïve if I believed my own attraction to others was solely based on internal "animal instinct." However, research in the life sciences and psychology factor in a biological basis for sexual desires. Pheromones,[9] ovulation patterns,[10] symmetry of facial features,[11] and chest-waist-hip ratios[12] have been determined as legitimate scientific indicators of what is attractive and beautiful. However, these factors are socially constructed categories of significance.[13] Historically, science has been used to justify social systems of inequality and oppression.[14] While examining sex, sexuality, gender, and race, it would be unwise to believe that biases fail to exist in these studies. Numerous studies have indicated that racial stereotyping can affect perceptions of others and the self, the most influential and famous case being the Kenneth Clark study used during *Brown v. Board of Education*.[15]

The terms *sex* and *sexuality* have become intertwined with our cultural understanding of gender. Race is not so intimately wed to a layman's understanding of sex, sexuality, and gender. However, race is central to how sex, sexuality, and gender can be understood in the lives of Asian Americans. While functioning in both similar and different ways for Asian American men and women, gender and sexuality act as fundamental mechanisms in maintaining white supremacy and white hegemonic ideals. Racial stereotypes crawl into bed with people of all races. White hegemonic ideologies of masculinity and femininity determine who gets to have sex with whom and the characteristics of those sexual and romantic partners. The selection and vetting process of potential sexual or romantic partners is not happening outside of our social world. We do not make choices of attraction in a vacuum. Whether we are conscious or not, ideas of masculinity, femininity, and race influence our decisions for potential partners. Our world shapes our "wants" and "choices" of whom we sleep with or take home to introduce to our families. Hegemonic ideology becomes our commonsense notions. When we believe we find someone attractive, there is a socializing element that comes into play.

This research is a call to scholars, educators, policy makers, journalists, and any person concerned with issues of race, gender, and sexuality to pay attention to Asian Americans. Their experiences speak more broadly to issues of racism, sexism, and homophobia in the United States, and we can learn a great deal about the tangled web of social structures through this narrative analysis. Our identities are so complexly intertwined, and the numerous social norms and hegemonic common-sense programming pulls individuals in a number of directions. This book is an attempt to begin to capture and decipher the complexity. Through the words of respondents, hopefully we can learn how to talk about how someone is sexualized and gendered while being simultaneously racialized.

These identities do not always become salient at the same time or with equal force. The complexity of intersecting identities is how their salience shifts and alters from situation to situation. Larger social structures and hierarchies remain omnipresent, but there are instances when stereotyping may seem "positive" or "negative." Whether the difference in stereotyping awards an individual with actual structural power is contestable and may remain to be seen. This book is an effort to begin to ask these questions and start to define and discuss the sexual politics of Asian Americans.

WHY ASIAN AMERICAN SEXUAL POLITICS?

Why should we study Asian American sexual politics? By evaluating constructions of Asian American gender and sexuality, it informs us on how racism, specifically white supremacy, works in the United States. The externally imposed meanings placed upon Asian and Asian American bodies unveil the new racism in this supposed postracial United States.

One thing I recognize and acknowledge is that many of us do not like to be told whom we should and should not love. Love and relationships, whether in fairy tales or Hollywood blockbusters, is not romantic if thought of as a calculated political move, but all love is shaped by sociohistorical factors.[16] Whether a relationship is intra- or interracial, same or opposite sex, there are negotiations and choices to be made, conscious and unconscious. This book gives us a look into the lives of sixty Asian Americans and how they negotiate their racialized gender, sexuality, and relationships.

The goal of this book is to not only share the experiences of my respondents but continue the dialogue that other scholars have already begun about the intersection of race, ethnicity, gender, and sexuality. Social forces shape our lives. Ideas are normalized about our identities that may influence our thoughts, feelings, and actions. I am not writing this book to tell people whom they should and should not find attractive. Most important, I hope my readers begin to recognize the role of power and privilege and to see white hegemonic masculinity[17] in its various forms and the way it shapes how we see the world. As a result of normalized hegemonic ideology, we can fail to deconstruct our world, motivations, preferences, and "choices." My Asian American respondents see the world through "frames." They can be "multiframers" who possess ideology from a "white racial frame" and simultaneously draw from "counter-frames" that are in conflict with each other.[18] Individuals make sense of their world through these frames and are either shaped by white social structure or at odds with oppressive powers.

METHODOLOGY: STANDPOINT EPISTEMOLOGY, EXTENDED CASE METHOD, AND NARRATIVE ANALYSIS

There are three key elements to my methodological approach for this project: standpoint epistemology, extended case method, and narrative analysis. Among my sixty interview participants, thirty-two self-identify as women, twenty-seven as men, and one as "female-bodied gender queer." Ethnically, the respondents self-identify as Taiwanese, Chinese, Indian, Filipino, Korean, Malaysian, Vietnamese, Hmong, Pakistani, Bangladeshi, Japanese, Thai, and multiracial Americans. The umbrella term "Asian American" is used to describe the participants.[19] The age range is eighteen to seventy-one years of age. The respondents come from varying geographic regions around the country.[20] The sample is overly educated, with 90 percent of the respondents having bachelor degrees.[21]

I begin my research with standpoint epistemology, where the voice of the "marginal" is the starting point. Specific to feminist theory, the focus lies on power differentials that exist in gender relations; I am extending the feminist theory to include racial marginalization. Harding asserts, "The activities of those at the bottom of such social hierarchies can provide starting points for thought—for *everyone's* research and scholarship—from which humans' relations with each other and the natural world can become visible."[22] My research addresses intersecting identities placed in overlapping hierarchies, so it will be a delicate task to describe how they operate separately and in combination. Power has been centered in scholarship from the top of hierarchy, so standpoint epistemology creates knowledge from a different perspective. The research is situated where one stands in a marginal position and investigates how a person "comes to know." However, a person in a more powerful position in a hierarchy can also contribute, as long as standpoint position is acknowledged. The goal is to provide a look from the "bottom up."[23]

Standpoint epistemology acknowledges situatedness instead of labeling itself as an objective point of view" because the whole notion of "objectivity" is interrogated. Feminist scholars assert that history and knowledge labeled as "objective" produced by academics has largely been "phallocentric."[24] Harding contends:

Thus the standpoint claims that all knowledge attempts are socially situated and that some of these objective social locations are better than others as starting points for knowledge projects [that]challenge some of the most fundamental assumptions of the scientific world view and the Western thought that takes sciences as its model of how to produce knowledge.[25]

Sandra Harding asserts, "one can see these sexist and or androcentric practices in the discipline."[26] Much of the knowledge that has been produced has come from the standpoint of privileged white men. The situatedness of standpoint epistemology can elaborate on the experiences and contributions made by women.[27] The standpoint approach works to "eliminate dominant group interests and values of *successfully colonized* minorities."[28] My research is an exercise in elaborating on the situated experiences of Asian American men and women and offers perspectives that may counter the historically white, androcentric dominant view.

Qualitative methods are used to make meaning of social phenomenon at the micro level and highlight the relationship of these interactions to the macro level.[29] While quantitative methods illuminate shifts or movement of group trends, such as Asian American intermarriage rates, qualitative methods can help to explain the phenomenon.In this research, I rely on the use of the extended case method (ECM)because it elucidates the link between the micro and macro by placing "everyday life in its extralocal and historical contexts."[30] In this case, extended case method informs us how external forces shape the lives of Asian American men and women.[31]

Narrative analysis takes as its starting point the belief that, as human beings, we understand our experiences and ourselves by telling stories. These can be as specific as accounts of particular events, or as broad as an entire life story. Meaning-making involves storytelling as interview participants attempt to make sense of their experiences. My task during narrative analysis is to understand those stories, examining not only their content but also their structure. Analyzing content is fundamental to any mode of qualitative research; what narrative analysis offers is a chance to expand our understanding of informants by examining how they tell us what they want us to know. Narrative structure is both holistic (the form the story takes) and particular (the language used to tell it). Narrative analysis, then, addresses both the content and the form of interview data. Although individuals are sharing these narratives, other elements of social life affect their experiences. Their storytelling will incorporate larger ideologies of placement in social structure, media discourse, and cultural values.

THEORETICAL PERSPECTIVES ON RACE, GENDER AND SEXUALITY

First and foremost, I treat *race, sexuality, and gender* as sociohistorical constructions. Omi and Winant explain that "Racial categories and the meaning of race are given concrete expression by the specific social relations and historical context in which they are embedded. Racial meanings have varied tremendously over time and between societies."[32] I define *gender* as a "social status, a legal designation, and a personal identity" and "through social processes of gendering, gender divisions and their accompanying norms and role expectations are built into the major social institutions of society."[33] While I use the terms "men," "women," "boys," and "girls" I want to clarify that I find problems with the terminology. The terms are constructed as a binary and restrict gender to just two categories. Because of the restrictive boundaries to this language, please note that my usage of gender pronouns are understood as constructed categories that are problematic. There are male-bodied and female-bodied respondents that may have different gender presentations then what present language may allow. When a respondent self-identified as something else outside of this binary gender paradigm, such as butch, boi, or trans, it is stated, and the pronoun they prefer is used.

Second, I define *sexuality* as "lustful desire, emotional involvement, and fantasy, as enacted in a variety of long- and short-term intimate relationships.[34] I do find the terms *homosexual* and *heterosexual* problematic because the origin of the terms arises from the early discipline of sexology that created a legal and medical discourse that stigmatized any sexual practices that deviated from monogamous heterosexual relationships.[35] Jeffrey Weeks asserts that through the use of medical terminology differentiating homosexuality from heterosexuality, stigma has been attached to same-sex loving sexualities.[36] The mere act of labeling homosexuality as a practice creates a discourse of deviant behavior that strays from the "norm," heterosexuality. Similarly, laws construct a discourse surrounding sexual acts, dividing them into acceptable and unacceptable categories.

Systemic Racism, the White Racial Frame, and Counter-Frames

I use a systemic racism approach to view racial oppression as a foundational and persisting underpinning of U.S. society. From the beginning, powerful whites have designed and maintained the country's economic, political, and social institutions to benefit, disproportionately and substantially, their own racial group. For centuries, unjust impoverishment of Americans of color has been linked to unjust enrichment of whites, thereby creating a central racial hierarchy and status continuum in which whites are generally the dominant and privileged group.[37]

Since the earliest period of colonization, European Americans have sustained this hierarchical system of unjust material enrichment and unjust material impoverishment with legal institutions and a strong white racial *framing* of this society. Whites have combined within this pervasive white frame many racist stereotypes (the cognitive aspect), racist concepts (the deeper cognitive aspect), racist images (the visual aspect), racialized emotions (feelings), and inclinations to take discriminatory action.[38] This white racial frame is old, enduring, and oriented to assessing and relating to Americans of color in everyday situations. Operating with this racial frame firmly in mind, the dominant white group has used its power to place new non-European groups, such as Asian immigrants and their children, somewhere in the racial hierarchy that whites firmly control—that is, on a white-to-black continuum of status and privilege with whites at the highly privileged end, blacks at the unprivileged end, and other racial groups typically placed by whites somewhere in between.[39] This white racist framing is centuries old and continues to rationalize racism that has been systemic in this society.

Understanding framing is essential to understanding how racism persists today and is disguised in institutions and color-blind discourse. Eduardo Bonilla-Silva asserts that whiteness is normalized by "white habitus."[40] "White habitus" is defined as a "racialized uninterrupted socialization process that conditions and creates whites' racial tastes, perceptions, feelings, and emotions and their views on racial matters."[41] The socialization process of whites that shapes their racial tastes, perceptions, and feelings can also have the same affect on people of color. Feagin's definition of framing allows for the inclusion of people of color in the adoption of these racist ideologies. Scholarship in gender and sexuality would use terms like "hegemonic masculinity" to discuss the powerful ideology of domination and how the ideas become normalized. In terms of race, "white habitus" can exist outside of white spaces and the meanings can be adopted by people of color and, in this case, Asian Americans.

In opposition to the white racist framing and hegemonic framing of masculinity are three types of counter-frames: (1) a white-crafted "liberty and justice" frame; (2) the anti-oppression counter-frames of Americans of color; and (3) the home-culture frames that Americans of color have drawn on in developing their counter-frames.[42] Asian Americans, collectively, have very few counter-frames from which to view alternative constructions of Asian American masculinity, femininity, or sexuality. The externally imposed identity of "Asian American" represents many different cultures which would provide a splintered or quilted "home-culture" frame with some overlap but a great deal of diversity of meanings and practices. Additionally, with more than half of Asians in the United States being newer immigrants, there are complications in identifying racist structure and oppression, which serves as another obstacle for developing strong anti-oppression counter-frames.

Whether the scholars choose to use "white racial framing," "white habitus," or racial "hegemony" to explain the persistence of racist thoughts, feelings, and practices, white supremacist ideology persists and comes in various forms embedded in institutions and in the psyches of whites and people of color alike. Racist ideology is passed along subconsciously through "colorblind discourse" in the era of the "new racism."[43] Asian Americans in this study have been socialized in a society where whiteness is normalized.

Asian American Masculinity and Femininity

While the racial demographics of the United States have shifted and continue to shift over time, they are not necessarily "naturally" occurring changes. The law has played a central role in the "racial morphology" of the country.[44] Asians in the United States comprise just over 4 percent of the population. This is by white supremacist design. Legislation, both racist and sexist in nature, has played a significant role in the lives of Asian Americans. These laws have shaped their racial and gendered experiences. These imposed gendered meanings faced by Asian Americans have operated to support white supremacy, the white racial frame, and hegemonic masculinity. Asian American men and women share some of the same racialized experiences; however, the racialized experiences can manifest differently for people based on gender, class, and sexuality. Asian American women have consistently been constructed as sexually available to white men. Asian American men have seen a different shift in gender stereotyping that is unlike other men of color in the United States because they, exclusively, have gone through an emasculating, castrating process.[45]

Who Moved My Manhood? The Evolution of Asian American Masculinity

Dana Takagi argues, "As Asian Americans, we do not think in advance about whether or not to present ourselves as 'Asian American,' rather that is an identification that is worn by us, whether we like it or not, and which is easily read off of us by others."[46] Asian Americans have specific racial stereotypes imposed upon them by others, but that identity does not stand alone. Race intersects gender and sexuality in a particular way. Racial stereotypes can and do change over time, but the meaning remains the same—people of color are inferior to whites. Antiblack stereotypes remain from the slavery era, but in our "colorblind" society, these stereotypes are coded or rephrased to seem less overtly racist.[47] However, this relatively constant stereotyping of African Americans as aggressive, dangerous, and oversexed varies greatly from the ideological transition of Asian American manhood. Historian Ronald Takaki describes the stereotyping of early male Chinese immigrants that was very similar to past and current constructions of African American men:

> The language used to describe the Chinese had been employed before: Racial qualities that had been assigned to blacks became Chinese characteristics. Calling for Chinese exclusion, the editor of the *San Francisco Alta* claimed the Chinese had most of the vices of the African: "Every reason that exists against the toleration of free blacks in Illinois may be argued against that of the Chinese here." Heathen, morally inferior, savage and childlike, the Chinese were also viewed as lustful and sensual.[48]

Chinese men and women faced stereotypes quite similar to African Americans. Takaki asserts that they went through a "Negroization" process as they settled into this country. The sexual stereotypes were uncannily the same. Chinese men were denounced as sexual threats to white women. White parents were advised not to send their daughters on errands to the Chinese laundry where horrible things happened to white girls in the back rooms.[49]

Also mirroring the stereotypes of American Indian and African American men, Chinese men were accused of having a special appetite for white women and girls. If a white woman married a Chinese man, it was considered an act that threatened "white racial purity." The association with African Americans was so close that the Chinese were called "nagurs" and the "new barbarians.[50] "

This stereotyping of Asian American men has disappeared from the discourse and, like a pendulum, has swung to the opposite of end of the spectrum where they are seemingly castrated and devoid of all things "manly." Even Asian American men as martial artists serve as targets for mocking.[51] Early immigrants to the United States such as the Irish and Italian were negatively stereotyped when they arrived. As they melted into the collective "whiteness," these men retained their manhood in the discourse, unlike Asian American men.[52]

Scholars have noted that the types of labor assigned to early Asian immigrants in the United States were "feminizing" occupations.[53] Asian American men worked in a more domestic realm, doing laundry and restaurant work. This type of labor is often labeled "women's work," but many Asian immigrant men were doing agricultural farming and construction work as well (specifically, with the railroad).[54] These types of segmented labor were also assigned to African and Latino American men. The feminized labor argument does not fully explain the shift in gender ideology of Asian American men because all of these men of color have historically shared the same gendered labor.

Asian American Femininity

The stereotyping of Asian American women has been relatively consistent throughout U.S. history compared to the shifts felt by their male counterparts. Research interrogating the sexualization of Asian women in the United States shows that the images have remained stable over time.[55] The images of Asian women as sexually available have been globalized, though these images are centered mainly on women of East Asian descent, with very little representation of women of South or Southeast Asian descent. South Asian women are often invisible or lack sexuality. My respondents of South and Southeast Asian descent speak openly about their lack of representation in the media.

Some scholars agree that femininity is undertheorized in the current literature,[56] but there are some definitions of femininity that have been. Pyke, Johnson, and Schippers use the term *hegemonic femininity* while Connell chooses the term *emphasized femininity* to describe what is usually equated with white, heterosexual, middle-class women.[57] Pyke and Johnson, however, conceptualize hegemonic femininity in an entirely different way than Schippers. *Subordinate(d)* or *pariah femininities* are femininities associated with sexually transgressive women, such as lesbian, bisexual, and nonmonogamous women.[58] *Marginalized femininities* are femininities associated with women of color or poor or working-class women.[59] Using either theoretical terminology, Asian American women are either the "de-emphasized" or "marginalized" femininity. Asian American femininity is seen as attractive to men because of the stereotyping as passive or docile, but these stereotypes have different meanings in a hierarchy of women.

Intersections of Race, Gender, Sexuality, and Nationality

"Orientalism" is a useful descriptive term developed by Edward Said to describe white racism against Asians and Asian Americans.[60] He uses the term to describe how whites associate with East with being "static and unfree," and Western civilization with being "dynamic and free."[61] Vijay Prashad insists that "Orientalism" is a method that whites use to negatively stereotype Asian Americans as exotic, barbaric, and primitive.[62]

Theorists argue that Orientalism is the root of Asian emasculation. It is the ideology established during colonialism that the West is the protector of the East.[63] A binary ideology exists which describes the West as "masculine" and the East as "feminine." Orientalism is Eurocentric in notion and serves to "exoticize" what is seen as Eastern culture in a patronizing way. It works to create difference between East and West with power and dominance being associated with the West. However, Takaki's historical evidence that Asian American men were initially feared like African and Latino American men complicates this theory. Asian Americans were often seen as "shifty," "untrustworthy," and "filthy," but even as early immigrants they were classified as "intelligent" compared to other people of color.[64] This early "model minority" stereotyping was not dominant in the discourse. World War II played a pivotal role in launching the "model minority" stereotype into mainstream discourse.[65] Japanese Americans were seen as a threat to national security and the response of the interned Nisei[66] generation was a systematic attempt to combat future racial assaults by pushing their Sansei children to do well in school. A dramatic shift in discourse can be traced to the relative financial and academic success of Asian Americans during this time period after World War II.[67] As a threat to white power and privilege by these "model minorities" became seemingly more realistic, the stereotypes of Asian American men as hypersexual, violent, and dangerous seemed to subside.

Gender, race, and class intersect in a unique way.[68] The white racist structure has had effects on the class mobility and divisions of labor for African American men and women.[69] Similarly, Asian Americans have faced specific labor barriers that have been gendered.[70] The historical and contemporary oppression of Asians in the United States has (re)structured the balance of power between Asian American women and men.[71] Race, gender, and class, as categories of difference, are not parallel to but intersect with and confirm one another.

Joane Nagel contends that sex is a core element of "race, ethnicity, and the nation, and that race, ethnicity, and nationalism are crucial components of sexual and moral boundaries and systems."[72] Where Feagin identifies racist images as a key component in the white racial frame, Nagel adds that *sexual* images and stereotypes are imbedded in ethnic images and stereotypes.[73] There is also an emotional aspect to ethnosexuality. Nagel asserts, "Sexual fears and loathing are endemic to racial terror and hatred." Similar to Feagin's conception of the white racial frame, strong emotive reactions from whites fearing the sexuality of people of color is fundamentally tied to racial domination. This white fear, especially of Asian American men, becomes apparent through participant narratives in later chapters.

Intersectional scholars have argued that oppressions of race, class, gender, sexuality, and nation are interconnected; black women have often been restricted because of external definitions of black womanhood expressed through controlling images, and black women have created worldviews out of a need for self-definition and to work on behalf of social justice.[74] I extend these points to Asian Americans. Theorizing the intersection of race and gender is a complex task. Intersectional paradigms view race, class, gender, sexuality, ethnicity, and age, among others, as mutually constructing systems of power. Because these systems permeate all social relations, untangling their effects in any given situation or for any given population remains difficult.[75]

Patricia Hill Collins suggests that because of intersecting identities, African American women and men are engaged in unique "Black sexual politics." These politics are defined

> as a set of ideas and social practices shaped by gender, race, and sexuality that frame all men and women's treatment of one another, as well as how individual men and women are perceived and treated by others. Because African Americans have been so profoundly affected by racism, grappling with racism occupies a prominent place within Black sexual politics.[76]

Similarly, Asian Americans have been affected by racism. The affects of this racism remain relatively invisible in the dominant racial discourse, even among academics.[77] Collins contends that "such politics lie at the heart of beliefs about Black masculinity and Black femininity, of gender-specific experiences of African Americans, and of forms that the new racism takes in the post-civil rights era."[78] As demonstrated by my respondents, gender-specific experiences are a reality for Asian Americans in this now "post-racial" society four decades after the civil rights movement.

Race, class, and gender intersect and affect the lives of African American men and women in many different ways, but with similarly oppressive results.[79] A narrow sexual politics based on American ideas, ideals of masculinity and femininity, and the appropriate expression of sexuality work to repress gay and straight, male and female.[80] The hegemonic racial and gender ideologies repress Asian Americans, but there are diasporic factors to consider that differ from the African American experience. Colonialism and Orientalism have a unique effect on the construction of Asian American gender and sexuality. Hung Cam Thai's work in *For Better or for Worse* demonstrates the complicated nature racist relations can have on a global transnational scale.[81] While Vietnamese American men may face obstacles being viewed as "unmarriageable" in the United States because of the way class intersects race, their "Americanness" is a commodity for them in Vietnam.[82] The Westernization of these men appeals to women in Vietnam, and the men improve their social standing and regain a sense of dignity by finding a bride.[83] This convertibility of social capital was evident for some of my respondents as well, even if they were high wage earners in the United States. The constructions of Asian masculinity often put them in the lower rungs of the male hierarchy so that it was "easier" for them to find partners that were less Americanized; specifically, they either sought out their wives in Asian countries or married very recent immigrants to the United States.

Intersectional paradigms are important to understanding intersectionality because they stimulate new interpretations of experiences of various identities working simultaneously. They untangle relationships between knowledge and empowerment because they shed new light on how domination is organized.[84] Collins utilizes the concept of a "matrix of domination" to better address the analytical dilemma raised by intersecting identities. Collins's matrix is a mechanism to explain how power and dominance work structurally in intersecting systems. Collins states, "All contexts of domination incorporate some combination of intersecting oppressions, and considerable variability exists from one matrix of domination to the next as to how oppression and activism will be organized."[85] However, while there is variability from one matrix to another, they all share common elements. They all have at work the same four "domains of power": structural, disciplinary, hegemonic, and interpersonal.

The structural domain of power "encompasses how social institutions are organized to reproduce Black women's subordination over time. One characteristic feature of this domain is its emphasis on large-scale, interlocking social institutions."[86] This domain of power includes institutions such as the legal system, labor markets, housing, and banking. African American women will have a different experience with these institutions than white women or black men. Similarly, Asian American women will have different experiences than white women or Asian American men.

The hegemonic domain of power deals with "ideology, culture, and consciousness."[87] In order for hegemony to operate, coercive force must become consensual by controlling ideology and making the thoughts, feelings and values of the dominant group appear to be "common sense."[88] The hegemonic domain of power dangerously reinforces the form of power, structural and disciplinary, because it "aims to justify the practices in these domains of power" without force.[89] Collins contends, "By manipulating ideology and culture, the hegemonic domain acts as a link between social institution (structural domain), their organizational practices (disciplinary domain), and the level of everyday social interaction (interpersonal domain). . . . In the United States, hegemonic ideologies concerning race, class, gender, sexuality, and nation are often so pervasive that it is difficult to conceptualize alternatives to them."[90] Media play a major role in the dissemination of hegemonic ideals, normalizing them. The interpersonal domain of power is the place where an individual finds a microlevel of agency. Resistance to the other domains of power comes from this interpersonal domain. The resistance can take various forms, not just widespread political action, but also in the day-to-day practices of creating new self-definition.

Collins's assertion of the universality of the four domains of power allows for all standpoints to be recognized and evaluated in social science research. The matrix acknowledges the situatedness of individuals living in complex intersecting social structures. Collins also accounts for the transformative and mutating nature of oppression. She asserts "because oppression is constantly changing, different aspects of an individual U.S.

Black woman's self-definitions intermingle and become more salient: Her gender may be more prominent when she becomes a mother, her race when she searches for housing."[91] This is true for other marginalized people as well. The salience of an identity may change over time and place, but the focus remains on the position of power and dominance. Collins's matrix of domination extends earlier feminist standpoint epistemology to incorporate intersectionality.

Collins argues that African American men and women have unique sexual politics because of their particular situatedness in U.S. history. Similarly, Asian Americans have also experienced a unique history where immigration, land laws, and labor laws had an effect on gender relations.[92] Asian Americans also have a different relationship to nationhood in the United States compared to whites and African Americans because they face continual struggles with being perceived as foreign.[93] This can cause of clash of ideologies with the dominant "white racial" frame and "home-culture" frames.

David Eng argues that racial analysis of Asian Americans is inadequate without the consideration of how their sexuality has been constructed.[94] Eng's point becomes clearly apparent with the unique experience of my respondent narratives. Asian American men face a particular placement on a gendered hierarchy and deal with battles against hegemonic masculinity that operate differently than masculinity has for their Latino or African American male counterparts. Asian American women also have different perspectives and life experiences than white women and other women of color.[95] While Asian American men and women may share similar experiences facing white hegemony, their gender identity may cause differences in how that racism manifests.

THE SOCIAL CONSTRUCTION OF ASIAN AMERICAN GENDER AND SEXUALITY: 1800S TO WORLD WAR II

While there is a record of Asians in the United States dating back to the late 1700s, the first sizeable groups did not immigrate to the U.S. and its territories until the 1850s. In Hawaii, laborers were needed to work on sugar plantations; Chinese men filled that role. Chinese labor was also used for mining during the gold rush in California, with 20,000 individuals entering the United States in 1852 alone. Other Asian laborers were coming from nations including Korea, the Philippines, Japan, and India. Chan asserts, "Although these five Asian groups came under different sets of circumstances all were recruited as workers by U.S. capitalists to meet the need for inexpensive and manipulable labor in the still-developing U.S. capitalist economy."[96] The growing strength of the United States as a nation was dependent on the stolen land of indigenous people and the free and cheap labor of people of color. Asians fulfilled the same labor needs as Africans had on plantations. The interests of the white elites who ruled the nation were to continue to find cheap labor. Asian immigration was restricted because white ruling elites had no interest in having them become citizens; it was about capitalist exploitation that was racialized in nature.

Seen as laborers, not as humans, the policies in place to restrict families, more specifically the entrance of women and children, had a profound effect on the Asian men that entered the country. Asian men had no kinship networks and no access to intimate heterosexual partners. These men formed "bachelor societies," creating friendships with other men as replacement families and kinship networks. Since there were no women in these arrangements to do domestic, reproductive labor, these men learned to cook and do dishes and laundry. The homosocial elements of the bachelor communities and the domestic practices of men living in them had an emasculating effect on the racial discourse.

During this time, there was a small population of Asian immigrant women, but the majority worked as prostitutes.[97] In 1870, women made up 7.2 percent of Chinese immigrants.[98] There was fear that Chinese prostitutes would bring in "especially virulent strains of venereal diseases, introduce opium addition, and entice young white boys to a life of sin."[99] The Page Act was introduced to decrease the number of women because they were assumed to be amoral, disease-carrying prostitutes. Once this law was enacted in 1875, the sex ratio among Chinese immigrants became even more skewed, reaching its peak in 1890 at a rate of 27 men to 1 woman. There were similar trends in sex ratios for Asian Indian, Korean, Filipino, and Japanese Americans.[100] Donald Goellnicht suggests that the targeted exclusion of Chinese women was a "deliberate agenda by mainstream (white) culture to "prevent any increase in the Chinese American population and to undermine the virility of Chinese and Chinese American men."[101]

The law was used as a mechanism to control the sexuality of Asian American men. Asian men were constructed as impotent and their women as "whores." Controlling sexuality and creating controlling images of Asians in the United States reifies white supremacy, and these images become embedded into the white racial frame.[102] These images are both racialized and gendered; thus, hegemonic masculinity is also reinforced. The U.S. government (namely the white actors who ran it) played a central role in creating an environment of state-controlled sexuality for Asian Americans. The laws determined whether and with whom Asian American men could have heterosexual relationships. In some states, antimiscegenation laws made it impossible for Asian men to marry white women. Thus, Asian men had to create their kinships with each other; "institutionally barred from normative (hetero)sexual reproduction and nuclear family formations," many of these Chinese men had to "sustain themselves in a hostile society, often by redefining and extending the concept of "family" to include new forms of "queer domesticity."[103]

With small numbers, single Chinese women in the United States became highly prized and were thus empowered with some bargaining tools to pick the most financially sound bachelors. Chinese women who were sex workers received offers of marriage, which allowed them to escape their exploitative work for the chance of matrimony and raising a family.[104]

Men who were married before immigrating had the responsibility of sending back wages to their families overseas. The restrictive immigration laws in the United States were impacting couples and families transnationally, and "split households" left women in Asia caring for their families without the help of their husbands. Espiritu asserts, "The split-household arrangement, enforced and maintained by racist and gendered U.S. immigration policies, made possible the maximum exploitation of male workers."[105] The Asian male workers could be bought cheaply, and they were obligated to support families overseas. As they toiled in mines and laid railroad tracks, their wives were raising the next generation of laborers, many of whom would work in the United States. While Asian men in the United States were being exploited for their labor, they were facing contradictory stereotyping. On the one hand, they were painted as ruthless, hypersexed, violent, and dangerous with strong appetites for white women.[106] Media warned of the "Yellow Peril," worried that the "shifty" Asian man may attack at any moment. The Chinese became so detested that the Chinese Exclusion Act was passed in 1882 and the Gentlemen's Agreement with Japan served a similar purpose. On the other hand, at the opposite end of the spectrum, racist and sexist legislative moves were creating new stereotypes of Asian American men as impotent and asexual. Asian women in the United States, although exploited as sex workers, were gaining some independence from the disproportionate sex ratios.

Asian men were constructed in the media as hypersexual and threatening to white women roughly from 1850 to 1940.[107] But the restrictive labor market limited types of work available to Asian American men that were often "feminized" types of employment.[108] For example, Chinese "houseboys" became symbols of the upper class in San Francisco.[109] The "houseboy" labor further feminized the Asian male laborers as they performed "women's work."[110] Asian men working in the domestic realm were also of Korean, Filipino, and Japanese descent. The emasculating process became cyclical as domestic labor put Asian and Asian American men in subordinate positions to both white men and white women. White women who lived in households that could afford a "houseboy" would then exercise power over him as her servant, compounding the emasculating effects.

THE SOCIAL CONSTRUCTION OF ASIAN AMERICAN GENDER AND SEXUALITY: WORLD WAR II TO THE PRESENT

A more obvious change in the lives of Japanese Americans during World War II was wartime internment. Japanese Americans experienced unique racialized oppression and shifts in gender relations during internment. Relative to Japanese Americans, other Asian American groups saw somewhat improved lives, specifically with access to education and new work opportunities in manufacturing and professional arenas.[111] Despite different experiences among Asian American groups during the war and immediately after the war, all Asian Americans faced similar imposed racial and gendered stereotyping.

The incarceration of Japanese Americans began almost immediately after the bombing of Pearl Harbor. Executive Order 9066 had been signed, and 120,000 persons of Japanese ancestry were placed into concentration camps. The camps caused great disruption of the family structure. The male patriarchal figure in the Japanese American households lost authority over his wife and children.[112] Women did not have to cook and clean up meals because the meals were prepared communally and there was rarely running water or cooking facilities. This allowed women to spend time independent of men, enhancing their friendship networks and being involved in adult education classes and other activities. The Nisei[113] began to spend time with peers as opposed to their own families. Many Nisei were sent away from internment camps to finish their college educations in the Midwest and East. This was significant because 40 percent of the relocated students were women.

Women's newfound independence was one major shift in the gender structure for Japanese Americans at the cost of family structure and Issei men's manhood. The Nisei men suffered as well with high rates of alcohol abuse, and 40 percent did not reach the age of fifty-five.[114] The loss of prime farmland worsened the situation after internment. Fathers could not pass on their land to their sons, and Issei men and women who had previously owned successful farms or businesses were relegated to toiling in service work. Men worked "as gardeners, janitors, kitchen helpers, and handymen; their wives as domestic servants, garment workers, and cannery workers."[115] The Nisei, who had greater educational opportunities than their parents, still struggled with postwar anti-Japanese sentiment. They faced difficulty entering the workforce of their choice. Internment proved to further emasculate Japanese American men.

While Japanese Americans faced overt racial discrimination, people of Chinese, Korean, Filipino, and Asian Indian ancestry experienced a relatively different treatment. Their countries of origin were U.S. allies; so many men and some women joined the World War II military effort, which "dramatically changed American public attitudes toward these groups."[116] There was also a great need for labor in manufacturing that allowed Asian American men and women to get higher-salaried jobs than their service industry work.[117] Nevertheless, these better wages were still not on par with white workers'; Asian American women remained the lowest paid of the bunch. Even with lower wages relative to their white counterparts, the earnings from World War II manufacturing sparked the beginning of an Asian American middle class.

World War II was the beginning of a long string of wars with countries in Asia. As a result, a large population of "war brides" immigrated to the United States. Many Chinese Americans serving during World War II were eligible for citizenship. These men were also allowed to bring over wives with the passage of the War Brides Act of 1945. Women made up 89 percent of Chinese immigrants to the United States from 1945 to 1953. This was also the trend for many other Asian Americans, creating more gender parity. However, this immigration of Asian women to the United States was not without problems. The U.S. immigration service commonly detained Asian, mostly Chinese, women who were the wives of Chinese American husbands because they were assumed to be prostitutes.[118] The racial stereotyping of these women was taken directly from images from the white racial frame. With the influx of these women, there was a Chinese American baby boom. Patriarchal Chinese culture promotes a dominant ideology that prefers sons to daughters; thus, the young women of the second generation

> also had to combat sexist stereotypes of Asian American women, particularly the image of the sexy, submissive prostitute popularized by Nancy Kwan in the 1960 film *The World of Suzie Wong*. Besieged by mass media images that constructed and reinforced U.S. standards of beauty as "blond, blue eyed, and big breasted," young Chinese American women of the 1950s received a message of inferiority from the larger society as strong as that which they received at home.[119]

Within Chinese American households, and many other Asian American groups, gender scales tipped in favor of men. Outside the home, these women continued to face sexually exploitative and controlling images stemming from the white racial frame, further supporting white supremacy and hegemonic masculinity. Women were painted as perpetually sexually available to white men while Asian American men were constructed as castrated or impotent, which further reified the hierarchical racial and gender structures.

From 1952 to the present, a split-immigration pattern has caused an ethnic and class bifurcation of Asian Americans. A mass "intellectual migration" began in the 1950s, bringing highly educated and skilled middle- to upper-class East and South Asians to the United States for work in professional industries. East and South Asian Americans are often deemed "model minorities" and have higher household incomes than all other racial groups, including whites. For these more successful Asian Americans, patriarchal authority is challenged, but there is greater equity division of labor in the home with both spouses working in highly skilled jobs or owning their own businesses. Although there is more independence for women in these homes, they still do more of the domestic labor.

Among Asians immigrating as refugees, a high concentration of which come from Southeast Asia, the men have a greater loss of status. They do not have the same educational background, skill set, or access to resources.[120] With the ability to exploit female Asian labor because it is cheaper than male labor, capital interest further disrupts the family structure and gender relations in these homes. The lack of employability of lower-classed Asian American men further complicates the sexual politics of Asian Americans. While I have given much historical evidence of structural factors that have shaped the racialized and gendered lives of Asian Americans, these institutionalized practices also affect ideology. One aspect of the white racial frame is the ability for it to create alienating social relationships.[121] Through racist and sexist laws and practices, Asian Americans experience not only alienating relationships in relation to other racial groups but within their own relationships as men and women.

White anti-Asian sentiment has persisted since early colonial conquests. The historical background I provide denotes a pattern of policies by white lawmakers targeting various Asians in the United States. While these policies were targeting specific ethnic groups, they intersect with the constructed racial category "Asian American" and consequently provide new gendered and sexualized meanings. Policies that at first glance affect laborers did much more to shape and reshape families, bodies, and the gendered hierarchy. As seen with other Americans of color, policies and practices that are racialized, such as slavery, can have profound, long-lasting effects not only on individuals but on couples, families, and communities.

OVERVIEW

There is great variation within masculinity and femininity, even though the mainstream media often presents a narrowly defined hegemonic ideal. Any variation from the white, middle-upper-class, heterosexual standards occupy subordinate positions of interlocking social hierarchies. Race intersects these constructions of genders. For Asian Americans this is further complicated by the various ethnicities that are incorporated under the umbrella term. Asian American masculinity and femininity are also quite varied. There are many different stereotypes of Asian American men and women based on perceived country of origin, class, education, religion, and sexuality. There are also variations in terms of physical body—that is, height, weight, and skin tone. I do not contend that this is a completely exhaustive volume addressing all the variations. This work is an introduction to the conversation about Asian American gender and sexuality and how it is shaped by white racial ideology.

Coupled with white racial ideology and controlling media images, all Asian Americans face a reality of imposed stereotyping regardless of nation of ancestry, class, sexuality, or gender. In film, "Asian males yield to the sexual superiority of the white males who are permitted filmically to maintain their sexual dominance over both white women and women of color."[122] This is eerily parallel to the social reality of Asian American men. Among all other races and genders, Asian American women have the highest outmarriage rates. The majority of Asian American women who outmarry have white male partners.[123] There is a strained relationship between Asian American women and men as the media construct and portray the men as the most undesirable and incapable sexual partners.

Western film and literature constructs Asian women in a dichotomous fashion, as either the cunning "Dragon Lady" or a servile "Lotus Blossom."[124] Both of these constructions erotize Asian women, while Asian men are simultaneously "castrated" or denied manhood.[125] These omnipresent controlling images in the media exacerbate the oriental fetishism that Asian and Asian American women face.[126] Controlling images affecting both Asian American men and women exist "to define the white man's virility and the white man's superiority."[127] At the core of this imaging is hegemonic whiteness and masculinity. Defining white male virility and superiority through demeaning images of Asian Americans is essential in retaining white supremacy. These images are not contemporary inventions of Hollywood. In the United States, Asian Americans have faced 150 years of imposed identities through racialized and gendered projects. My hope is that through my participant narratives, we may begin to understand how these sociohistorical exercises of white supremacy may be affecting Asian American men and women today.

Chapters

In chapter 2, I introduce my key concepts and highlight the presence of the home-culture frames in the lives of my respondents. For first-generation Asian Americans, the "home-culture" frames play a central role in how gender and sexuality are constructed in their lives. For second-generation Asian Americans, the lessons from their parents may conflict with the white racial frame and definitions of Western masculinity, femininity, and sexuality. Subsequent generations of Asian Americans must negotiate the meanings of ethnic, racial, gender, and sexual identity.

In chapter 3, I focus primarily on messages my respondents received from external forces, in school, from peer groups, and in the media. Their narratives show how the white racial frame is used as a policing tool for racialized gender and sexuality. With the use of respondent narratives, I detail how Asian American masculinity and femininity is constructed and how it operates in a racial hierarchy. The male respondents share experiences that highlight how "racial castration" occurs in the socialization of Asian American men. Constructions of gender and sexuality are sometimes at odds with their "home-culture" frames and can leave lasting impressions on how they should act as boys and girls. A clear theme emerged in regard to masculinity; a hegemonic white ideology of masculinity was prevalent and pervasive. Respondents detail ways in which they were pressured or influenced to meet certain gendered racialized or sexualized expectations. Questions addressed in this chapter are: What methods are used to enforce these gendered and racialized stereotypes? How does gender socialization push Asian Americans into an intersected racial hierarchy? How are the experiences of men and women different?

Chapter 4 addresses the short- and long-term consequences of gendered and sexualized racist treatment for Asian American women. I analyze narratives that discuss how intersected racial and gender identity affects self-image and self-esteem. The women share their experiences as ethnosexualized beings, dealing with exotification and fetishism. Asian American women are met with an exotification and orientalization as sexual bodies but do not face the threat of physical bullying like their male counterparts. The women discuss psychological and emotional well-being relative to racial and gender identities. Respondents discuss how femininity has specifically been shaped by racial identity.

Chapter 5 details how the gendered and sexualized racialization process and racial castration has impacted Asian American men. Violence is a prevalent theme in gendered and racial formation. Asian American men begin as targets of violence and sometimes become perpetrators. In their own words, Asian American male respondents detail how they have internalized messages about their own physical attractiveness or lack thereof. Respondents address issues of self-image and dating. Male respondents make statements such as, "We're the ugly ones, and our women are hot," and, "I might as well not have a penis." Gay respondents discuss facing similar difficulties with emasculation in gay spaces. When these Asian American men resist their emasculating racism, it often mimics the hegemonic masculine image of powerful white male counterparts. They immerse themselves in activities such as sports to increase physical strength and join and create all-Asian groups, like fraternities, to create support networks.

Chapter 6 explores sexual and romantic relationships and examines the dynamics of Asian American intraracial and interracial relationships. Respondents balance messages from their families and external forces.

There is a hierarchy of partners based on race, ethnicity, class, and gender. Respondents discuss relationship hardship and success. I summarize my findings and discuss their implications, drawing larger conclusions about how race and gender operate in the lives of Asian Americans.

Chapter 7 addresses the question, "What now?" In this chapter I share resistance strategies my respondents use to confront racism, sexism, and homophobia in their daily lives and offer additional strategies. Many of my respondents lacked guidance from family, friends, or their community on how to cope with discrimination. Chapter 7 will hopefully be thought-provoking and facilitate discussions about race, racism, and how it relates to other systems of oppression. In greater detail, I conclude by offering both individual and structural-level strategies to cope with and combat racism and sexism.

There has been exceptional scholarship on Asians and Asian Americans regarding, race, ethnicity, gender, and sexuality. I am writing this book to extend the scope of existing work and to give an opportunity for Asian Americans to feel validated in their experiences and for others to be enlightened. This is part of the process of recovery and discovery. This is for individuals to share their experiences and for us to continue our conversations about oppression and how Asian Americans can simultaneously be a target group of oppression and can play a role in maintaining the racial status quo. This book aims to critique white supremacy and colonialism and to comment on the collision of these social forces with the unique Asian American experience.

I posed the question "why should we study Asian American sexual politics" earlier in this chapter, and when I first embarked on my research I did not have the answer. This project was born out of my first book in which I focused primarily on racial and ethnic experiences. Interview after interview, I found my respondents talking about their racialized experiences, but they were simultaneously gendered and sexualized. The Asian American men could not talk about racist incidents without the experience also being about challenges regarding their "manhood" and masculinity. Similarly, the Asian American women had experiences unique to their intersecting identities. With issues of gender and sexuality emerging throughout the data collection process, I realized I could no longer ignore them. This is just a brief look, shaped by time and place, into the lives of sixty Asian Americans, and I hope that scholars continue to examine this subject matter to reveal the stories that are waiting to be uncovered.

NOTES

1. Alex Tizon, "Rapists Bet on Victims' Silence—and Lose," *Seattle Times*, May 31, 2001.

2. Tizon, "Rapists Bet."

3. Tizon, "Rapists Bet."

4. Steven Herbert, "Viewership for 'Idol' Finale Highest in 3 Years," *Orange County Register*, June 1, 2011.

5. Patricia Hill Collins, *Black Sexual Politics: African Americans, Gender, and the New Racism* (New York: Routledge, 2005).

6. Collins, *Black Sexual Politics.*

7. Collins, *Black Sexual Politics.*

8. Mia Tuan, *Forever Foreigners or Honorary Whites? The Asian Ethnic Experience* (New Brunswick, NJ: Rutgers University Press, 2003).

9. Sarah Harding, "Your Pheromones Are So Hot: A Study of Sexual Attraction," *Serendip*, Bryn Mawr University,http://serendip.brynmawr.edu/exchange/node/357, accessed May 21, 2011.

10. Kari Grammar, Bernhard Fink, and Nick Neave, "Human Pheromones and Sexual Attraction,"*European Journal of Obstetrics & Gynecology and Reproductive Biology* 118, no. 2 (2005): 135–42.

11. David I. Perret et al., "Symmetry and Human Facial Attractiveness," *Evolution and Human Behavior* 20, no. 5 (1999): 295–307.

12. Barnaby J. Dixson et al., "Eye-Tracking of Men's Preferences for Waist-to-Hip Ratio and Breast Size of Women," *Archives of Sexual Behavior* 40, no. 1 (2011): 43–50.

13. Tufuku Zuberi and Eduardo Bonilla-Silva, *White Logic, White Methods: Racism and Methodology,* (Lanham, MD: Rowman & Littlefield, 2008).

14. Stephen Jay Gould. *The Mismeasure of Man,* rev. and expanded ed. (New York: Norton, 1996).

15. Kenneth Clark and Mamie Clark, "Racial Identification and Preference in Negro Children," in *Readings in Social Psychology,* ed. T. M. Newcomb and E. L. Hartley (New York: Holt, Rinehart & Winston, 1947); Kenneth Clark, *Prejudice and Your Child* (Middletown, CT: Wesleyan University Press, 1988).

16. Kristen Lee, Simon Ho, and Rosalind Chou, "The Myth of the Model University" (unpublished paper, 2011).

17. Hegemonic masculinity—equated here with white, heterosexual middle-class men—refers to those who inhabit the positions of authority in society; it varies across societies and depends on external and internal hegemony. From Anthony Chen, "Lives at the Center of the Periphery, Lives at the Periphery of the Center: Chinese American Masculinities and Bargaining with Hegemony," *Gender and Society* 13, no. 5 (1999): 584–607.

18. Joe R. Feagin, *The White Racial Frame: Centuries of Racial Framing and Counter-Framing* (New York: Routledge, 2009).

19. I use the umbrella term "Asian Americans" to describe my respondents, while acknowledging that the term does not fully embrace the diversity of the population. I use it to describe respondents from East, Southeast, and South Asia. I also have a few respondents from Pacific Islands such as the Philippines.

20. We have lightly edited the interview quotes for grammar, stutter words ("you know"), and clarity. Pseudonyms are given to all respondents to conceal their identity, and some details have been omitted or disguised in the quotes from interviews to increase the anonymity of participants.

21. The interviews were conducted from 2005 to 2010.

22. Sandra Harding, "Rethinking Standpoint Epistemology: What Is 'Strong Objectivity'?" in *Feminist Epistemologies*, ed. Linda Alcoff and Elizabeth Potter (New York: Routledge, 1992).

23. Harding, "Rethinking Standpoint Epistemology."

24. Hélène Cixous, "Laugh of Medusa," in *French Feminism Reader*, ed. Kelly Oliver (New York: Routledge, 2000).

25. Harding, "Rethinking Standpoint Epistemology," 56.

26. Harding, "Rethinking Standpoint Epistemology," 56.

27. Cixous, "Laugh of Medusa."

28. Harding, "Rethinking Standpoint Epistemology," 74.

29. Michael Burawoy, "The Extended Case Method," in *Ethnography Unbound*, edited by M. Burawoy, A. Burton, A. A. Ferguson, K. J. Fox, J. Gamson, N. Gartrell, L. Hurst, C. Kurzman, L. Salzinger, J. Schiffman, & S. Ui, (Berkeley: University of California Press, 1991), 271-287; "The Extended Case Method." *Sociological Theory* (16(1) 1998), 4-33.

30. Michael Burawoy, "The Extended Case Method," in *Ethnography Unbound*, edited by M. Burawoy, A. Burton, A. A. Ferguson, K. J. Fox, J. Gamson, N. Gartrell, L. Hurst, C. Kurzman, L. Salzinger, J. Schiffman, & S. Ui, (Berkeley: University of California Press, 1991), 271-287; "The Extended Case Method." *Sociological Theory* (16(1) 1998), 4-33.

31. The main ideas explaining the use of extended case method are attributed to the work of Jennifer Mueller.

32. Michael Omi and Howard Winant, *Racial Formation in the United States: From the 1960s to the 1980s*, 2nd ed. (New York: Routledge, 1994).

33. Judith Lorber, *Gender Inequality* (New York: Oxford University Press, 2009).

34. Lorber, *Gender Equality*. The terms *homosexuality, heterosexuality, and bisexuality* are used when referring to sexuality. I also use the term *queer* if respondents self-identify in that manner.

35. Michel Foucault, *The History of Sexuality*, vol. 1 (New York: Vintage Press, 1984).

36. Jeffrey Weeks, "The Construction of Homosexuality," in *Queer Theory/ Sociology*, ed. Steven Seidman (Malden, MA: Blackwell, 1996), 41–63.

37. In this and later sections I draw on Joe R. Feagin, *Systemic Racism: A Theory of Oppression* (New York: Routledge, 2006), 1–45 and 290–9, and on Joe R. Feagin and Clairece B. Feagin, *Racial and Ethnic Relations*, 8th ed. (Upper Saddle River, NJ: Prentice Hall, 2008), chapters 10–11.

38. Feagin, *The White Racial Frame*.

39. Rosalind S. Chou and Joe R. Feagin, *The Myth of the Model Minority: Asian Americans Facing Racism*, (Boulder, CO: Paradigm Publishers, 2008).

40. Eduardo Bonilla-Silva, Carla Goar, and David G. Embrick, "When Whites Flock Together: The Social Psychology of White Habitus," *Critical Sociology* 32, nos. 2–3 (2006): 229–53.

41. Eduardo Bonilla-Silva, *Racism without Racists: Color-Blind Racism and the Persistence of Racial Inequality in the United States* (Lanham, MD: Rowman & Littlefield, 2003), 104.

42. Bonilla-Silva, *Racism without Racists*.

43. These terms are theoretical concepts from Eduardo Bonilla-Silva and Patricia Hill Collins that refer to the ever-changing nature of racism and how it has become more covertly hidden in society.

44. Ian F. Haney López, *White by Law: The Legal Construction of Race* (New York: New York University Press, 1996).

45. Much of the emasculation in the media of Asian American men is focused specifically on men of East Asian descent. South Asian men, especially after September 11, 2001, have been constructed more closely to Arab or Middle Eastern men. Southeast Asian men are less prevalent in the media, and when they are present, they are associated with military conflicts in Southeast Asia or constructed similarly to men of color or working-class white uneducated men involved in crime. However, my respondents vary in Asian region of origin, and many of the South Asian, Pacific Islander, and Southeast Asian men share similar experiences with men of East Asian descent. Asian American women also have variations in gendered and racialized stereotyping by geographic region, immigration status, and class. These variations are further explained in subsequent chapters of this book. Please see chapters 4 and 5.

46. Dana Y. Takagi, "Homophobia: Why Bring It Up?" in *The Lesbian and Gay Studies Reader*, ed. Henry Abelove, Michele Aina Barale, and David M. Halperin (New York: Routledge, 1996), 99–102.

47. Bonilla-Silva, *Racism without Racists*.

48. Ronald Takaki, *Strangers from a Different Shore* (Boston: Back Bay, 1998), 217.

49. Takaki, *Strangers from a Different Shore.*

50. Takaki, *Strangers from a Different Shore.*

51. Frank Wu, *Yellow: Race in America Beyond Black and White* (New Haven, CT: Yale University Press, 2003).

52. Feagin, *Systemic Racism.*

53. Yen Le Espiritu, *Asian American Women and Men: Labor, Laws, and Love.* (Lanham, MD: Rowman & Littlefield, 2008).

54. Espiritu, *Asian American Women and Men.*

55. Sheridan Prasso, *The Asian Mystique: Dragon Ladies, Geisha Girls and Our Fantasies of the Exotic Orient* (Cambridge, MA: Public Affairs Books, 2006).

56. R. W. Connell and James W. Messerschmidt, "Hegemonic Masculinity: Rethinking the Concept," *Gender and Society* 19, no. 6 (2005): 829–59; Karen Pyke and Denise Johnson, "Asian American Women and Racialized Femininities: 'Doing' Gender across Cultural Worlds," *Gender and Society* 17 (2003): 33–53; Mimi Schippers, "Recovering the Feminine Other: Masculinity, Femininity, and Gender Hegemony," *Theory and Society* 36, no. 1 (2007): 85–102.

57. Connell and Messerschmidt, "Hegemonic Masculinity"; Pyke and Johnson, "Asian American Women"; Schippers, "Recovering the Feminine Other."

58. Schippers, "Recovering the Feminine Other."

59. Schippers, "Recovering the Feminine Other."

60. Edward W. Said, *Orientalism* (New York: Vintage Press, 1978).

61. Said, *Orientalism.*

62. Vijay Prashad, *The Karma of Brown Folk* (Twin Cities: University of Minnesota Press, 2003).

63. Said, *Orientalism;* Shahnaz Khan, "Reconfiguring the Native Informant: Positionality in the Global Age," in *Signs: Journal of Women in Culture and Society* 30, no. 4 (2005): 2017–37.

64. Ronald Takaki, *Strangers from a Different Shore.*

65. Chou and Feagin, *Myth of the Model Minority.*

66. First-generation Japanese Americans are Issei, second-generation are Nisei, and third-generation are Sansei.

67. Janice Tanaka, *When You're Smiling* (Janice Tanaka Films, 1999); Chou and Feagin, *Myth of the Model Minority.*

68. Angela Y. Davis, *Women, Race, and Class* (New York: Vintage Books, 1983).

69. Davis, *Women, Race, and Class.*

70. Espiritu, *Asian American Women and Men.*

71. Espiritu, *Asian American Women and Men.*

72. Joane Nagel, *Race, Ethnicity, and Sexuality* (New York: Oxford University Press, 2003), 255.

73. Nagel, *Race, Ethnicity, and Sexuality.*

74. Collins, *Black Sexual Politics.*

75. Collins, *Black Sexual Politics,* 11.

76. Collins, *Black Sexual Politics,* 6.

77. Chou and Feagin, *Myth of the Model Minority.*

78. Collins, *Black Sexual Politics,* 7.

79. Collins, *Black Sexual Politics,* 7.

80. Collins, *Black Sexual Politics,* 7.

81. Hung Cam Thai, *For Better or for Worse: Vietnamese International Marriages in the New Global Economy.* (Piscataway, NJ: Rutgers University Press, 2008).

82. Thai, *For Better or for Worse.*

83. Thai, *For Better or for Worse.*

84. Collins, *Black Feminist Thought.*

85. Collins, *Black Feminist Thought.*

86. Collins, *Black Feminist Thought,* 277.

87. Collins, *Black Feminist Thought,* 284.

88. Antonio Gramsci, *Selections from the Prison Notebooks,* trans. and ed. Q. Hoare and G. N. Smith (New York: International Publishers, 1971).

89. Collins, *Black Sexual Politics,* 284.

90. Collins, *Black Sexual Politics,* 284.

91. Collins, *Black Sexual Politics,* 284.

92. Espiritu, *Asian American Women and Men;* Yen Le Espiritu, "All Men are *Not* Created Equal: Asian Men in U.S. History" in *Men's Lives,* 7th ed., ed. Michael Kimmel and Michael Messner (Boston: Allyn & Bacon, 2007), 21–29.

93. Claire Jean Kim, *Bitter Fruit: The Politics of Black-Korean Conflict in New York City* (New Haven, CT: Yale University Press, 2003); Tuan, *Forever Foreigners or Honorary Whites?;* Wu, *Yellow.*

94. Daniel L. Eng, *Racial Castration: Managing Masculinity in Asian America* (Durham, NC: Duke University Press, 2001).

95. Prasso, *The Asian Mystique.*

96. Sucheng Chan, *Asian Americans: An Interpretive History* (Boston: Twayne, 1991), 4.

97. Chan, *Asian Americans,* 20.

98. Gary Y. Okihiro, *Margins and Mainstreams: Asians in American History and Culture* (Seattle: University of Washington Press, 1994).

99. Suecheng Chan, "The Exclusion of Chinese Women," in *Entry Denied: Exclusion and the Chinese Community in America, 1882–1943,* ed. S. Chan (Philadelphia: Temple University Press, 1991), 138.

100. Bruno Lasker, *Filipino Immigration to the United States and to Hawaii* (New York: Arno,1969).

101. Donald Goellnicht, "Tang Ao in America: Male Subject Positions in China Men," in *The New Asian Immigration in Los Angeles and Global Restructuring,* ed. S. G. Lim and A. Ling (Philadelphia: Temple University Press, 1992), 196–226 (specifically pp. 194–95).

102. Feagin, *Systemic Racism.*

103. Espiritu, *Asian American Women and Men,* 25.

104. Peggy Pascoe, *Relations of Rescue: The Search for Female Authority in the American West, 1874–1939,* (New York: Oxford University Press, 1990).

105. Espiritu, *Asian American Women and Men,* 33.

106. Takaki, *Strangers from a Different Shore.*

107. William F. Wu, *The Yellow Peril: Chinese Americans in American Fiction, 1850–1940* (Hamden, CT: Archon, 1982).

108. Espiritu, *Asian American Women and Men,* 40.

109. Evelyn Nakano Glenn, *Issei, Nisei, Warbride: Three Generations of Japanese American Women in Domestic Service* (Philadelphia: Temple University Press, 1986).

110. Espiritu, *Asian American Women and Men,* 41.

111. Espiritu, *Asian American Women and Men,* 41.

112. Espiritu, *Asian American Women and Men,* 50-51.

113. First-generation Japanese Americans are referred to as Issei, second-generation as Nisei, and third-generation as Sansei.

114. Tanaka, *When You're Smiling.*

115. Sylvia J. Yanagisako, "Mixed Metaphors: Native and Anthropological Models of Gender and Kinship Domains," in *Gender and Kinship: Essays toward a Unified Analysis,* ed. J. F. Collier and S. J. Yanagisako (Palo Alto, CA: Stanford University Press, 1987), 92.

116. Chan, *Asian Americans: An Interpretive History,* 121.

117. Espiritu, *Asian American Women and Men.*

118. Espiritu, *Asian American Women and Men.*

119. Espiritu, *Asian American Women and Men.*

120. Espiritu, *Asian American Women and Men.*

121. Feagin, *Systemic Racism.*

122. Espiritu, *Asian American Women and Men,* 104.

123. Kumiko Nemoto, "Intimacy, Desire, and the Construction of Self in Relationships between Asian American Woman and White American Men," *Journal of Asian American Studies* (February 2006): 27– 54.

124. Benson Tong. *Unsubmissive Women: Chinese Prostitutes in Nineteenth-Century San Francisco* (Norman: University of Oklahoma Press, 1994).

125. Espiritu, *Asian American Women and Men*; Eng, *Racial Castration*.

126. Prasso, *Asian Mystique*.

127. Elaine Kim, "'Such Opposite Creatures': Men and Women in Asian American Literature," *Michigan Quarterly Review* 29 (1990): 70.

TWO

The Making of Good Sons and Daughters

Some of my earliest gendered memories involve gendered messages and disciplining. I have very distinct images of my mother telling me that my father really wishes he had a son. Being the youngest of three daughters, I was the supposed "last chance" for a male heir in my family. I never knew for sure if it was something my father really desired or my mother. She just happened to be the one to verbalize it, frequently. In my three-year-old mind, I took this to mean I was already an incredible disappointment as soon as I exited the womb. While unable to articulate my feelings, I knew that "failing" to be born a male-bodied person meant being born female-bodied was inferior. So I made valiant efforts to correct it. Several times in my life, I've had to hear my mother recount a story of a phone call she received from day care. "Mrs. Chou," they told my mother, "Rosalind is a little bit confused. She thinks she's a boy. She walks around telling everyone that she is a boy."

My mother found this amusing. While recounting the story to me, she always chuckled. However, she became more concerned when my style of dress and my hobbies were "tomboyish." Instead of Barbie dolls, I wanted a C.H.I.P.s[1] action set for Christmas. It was fully equipped with a motorcycle helmet, gun belt, and California Highway Patrol badge. I climbed trees instead of making crafts. I jumped off the roof instead of jumping rope. The scrapes and scratches all over my knees became something of deep concern for my mother. She would tell me, "Rosalind, no man will ever want to marry you with those scars." I remember thinking to myself, "I don't want to marry a man anyways."

These were quite clearly early tactics of gender socialization. First, it was clear that boys were valued in my family more than girls. To lack a penis was the final disappointment. Not understanding that I couldn't

29

just become a boy, it seemed quite logical to me to play the part. I did my best to perform masculinity. All my friends were boys, I played sports extensively, I had poor hygiene, and I refused to wear skirts and dresses. I so much wanted to become the son my parents wanted. My performance became so convincing that, for part of my life, family acquaintances and neighbors referred to me as "Charlie (my father's name) Junior." All the nagging and complaining from my mother just pushed me further into rebellion. Every effort she made to force me into "proper" feminine clothing, the more I longed to be as "boyish" as possible.

Gender is socially constructed and is performative.[2] It varies by culture and historical moment, but the distinct categories of "man" and "woman" and "boy" and "girl" function to maintain male dominance over women and marginalized or subordinated men. My attempts to be a boy were based on perceived external pressures, messages conveyed through media images, peers, teachers, and cultural practices where meanings are assigned to gender and to be a boy or man meant that I had access to power and privilege. I sought to mimic what I found to be the most valued of the genders. The mimicry was based on social cues and definitions of what it means to be a boy. However, my female body did not match my performance, which resulted in policing and discipline from my family and day care workers. At a very young age, these behaviors can be seen as playful and as a stage out of which one grows. However, expectations to follow gendered scripts become more pronounced over the life course. As I shared in chapter 1, sexualized, gendered, and racialized expectations became more apparent to my respondents through socialization during their lifespan. Family, peers, and teachers begin to put more pressure on developing children to embody and enact a gender assigned to their anatomical features and move out of a space of androgyny.

For my parents, the importance of disciplining me into a distinct and clear gender category is about maintaining hegemonic masculinity and fitting me into a dichotomous gendered order. A female-bodied person performing masculinity is a disruption, an alternative masculinity and does not fit the constructed gender binary.[3] There were other elements to this early training. First is the transmission of the Taiwanese ideology that values boys and men over girls and women. This is seen in many countries in Asia, but is not necessarily universal. There are a disproportionate number of males in mainland China because of elective abortions and overseas adoptions of Chinese girls. Korea began a major advertising campaign to show that girls are just as good as boys because of similar practices causing gender imbalance.[4] Patriarchy operates in a different manner in the United States, but American girls of all racial and ethnic categories are given messages of gender inferiority with media images that objectify the female body. My experience and the public, direct discussion of the importance of a son were specifically shaped by my parents' socialization in Taiwan. These gendered values were presented to me and greatly influenced my identity and my actions. Similarly, gendered and racialized meanings can shape many aspects of Asian American lives. Gender socialization is mutable over time and contingent on geographic location. However, power and domination consistently play a key role in men's position of power over women.

The second element from my early training is the policing or attempted policing of my body. My mother wanted me to make sure I maintained a scar-free body, not for me to avoid pain and suffering but to increase my ability to attract a husband. I was directed to put my body in specific types of clothing and maintain a certain level of personal hygiene so that I could appeal to the opposite sex. My mother's policing was heteronormative, reifying "compulsory heterosexuality."[5] Similarly, respondents were socialized within their homes to meet specific ethnic and cultural expectations regarding their gender and sexuality.

In this chapter, I take an in-depth look at the gender socialization process for my Asian American respondents within their homes and ethnic or racial communities. Within their homes and communities, they are given both overt and covert messages about their gender, body, and sexuality. Respondents detail ways they were pressured or influenced by their families to meet certain gendered and sexualized expectations while staying true to their ethnic or racial identity.

Using a social constructionist perspective, I acknowledge that the meaning of gender is neither transhistorical nor culturally universal but rather varies from culture to culture and within any one culture over time. Whites, for example, formerly constructed Asian American men as dangerous men—sexual predators[6]—and now they are often constructed as asexual or sexually inept.

I acknowledge that there are numerous masculinities and femininities. This is further complicated by the variety in cultural backgrounds of different Asian Pacific Islander Desi Americans.[7] The common thread shared by these participants is their relationship to *power* and *domination* within the racial hierarchy.

GENDERING IN THE HOME

One key difference between the socialization that my respondents received at home versus outside socialization is that the racialized meanings of inferiority to whiteness were not overtly present. Heteronormative messages and a patriarchal structure would be enforced. Messages are conveyed about how an Indian girl should act or how a good Asian American man or boy is someone who is responsible and educated. The messages of racial inferiority were subtler. These messages came in suggestions for partners or descriptions of some physical attributes as more attractive. Sometimes, there would be suggestions that, in terms of work ethic, Asians performed better than Americans. The things most commonly enforced are heteronormative expectations; queerness was never an expectation. Regulation of sexuality was quite prevalent as well and happened to women and girls, their bodies working under more scrutiny by parents. Additionally, their movements, friend groups, and curfews were more strictly policed than those of brothers or other male relatives. Similarly, housework was usually divided by gender.

Gender can be uniquely personal; gender oppression can happen in our most intimate relationships with our friends, partners, siblings, and parents.[8] When conflict arises racially, typically the oppressive force is outside the family unit, from a larger social group that you are not bedding with. Asian Americans have home lives that can, at times, be insulated from outside forces. Some of my respondents and their family members closely align with an ethnic background, but there are externally imposed labels that place them in a racial category, Asian American. Their ethnic identities may be more salient to my interviewees, especially when isolated from the outside world. These cultures in the home may be influenced by immigration status, nation of origin, tradition, and so forth. These are the first sites of gender socialization. This happens before birth with the preparation of the space for the arrival of a gendered baby; even the way a parent may talk to the baby in the womb sets up a gendered experience before birth.[9]

In the family settings of my respondents, much of the gendered messaging they received was ethnic and home-culture specific. For the men, there was little emphasis on achieving the Western hegemonic masculine ideal, typically associated with white, middle- or upper-class, straight men. The lessons of manhood focused on being a responsible, educated, financially stable, career man who retains some home culture values. Specifically, the Westernized ideas of hegemonic masculinity with the emphasis on a chiseled physique and sexual experience and prowess was of little concern in the socialization process. My respondents felt more pressure from forces outside the home to meet Westernized standards of beauty and socially constructed gender norms.

Gender: Male Preference

For first-generation Asian Americans, it can be difficult to balance the "old world" (home country) and the "new world" (the United States). Similarly, there are powerful ideologies associated with these differing cultures: (1) the home-culture frame and (2) the white racial frame. There are some clear gender sanctions that exist in their home country that can be hard to negotiate due to differences in gender expectations in the United States. Common practices in their home country may shape how they raise their own children. For example, Lily, a Taiwanese American from the East Coast in her sixties, recalls the early gender hierarchy in her family:

> Well, girls couldn't go out and do much. You couldn't go out at night. You couldn't even swim in the river. My brother could swim in the river or creek. We couldn't do that. We weren't allowed to ride a bike. No girls were riding bikes. So I don't even know how to ride a bike. And I don't know how to swim. [My parents] told us everything was dangerous.

The gender inequity in play is not the only area in which disparity exists. The privileges awarded to Lily's brother were greater than being able to swim in a creek or ride a bike. Her brother was valued in all aspects of society. He was worth more than a daughter. Property would be passed along to him, but the daughters would receive nothing. To really highlight the great gender disparity in the home, Lily recalls how her youngest sister was traded away so that the family could have another boy:

> I'm the oldest one; the second was a boy, and the third one was a girl. The fourth one was another girl, so my grandpa talked to someone when my mother was pregnant and he started to look for someone to trade my sister for a boy. My mother was having another girl again and he wanted to trade her with someone else. A neighbor's daughter-in-law was pregnant the same time as my mother, so they had a matchmaker make arrangements for a trade. Because that family already had six or seven boys, we knew this was going to be a boy as well. Three days after my sister was born, they took my mother outside of the house so that she wouldn't be home when the parents of the baby boy came over to make the trade. My mom was crying to get her own child back, but the trade was already planned. So we took care of that boy, but two years later my mother was pregnant again and that was a boy. So, actually we had three girls and two boys in the family. Then after that trade we had three boys and two girls. After the third boy was born, my grandpa was *very happy*.

This was a very clear moment where Lily learned from her family that boys were prized over girls. It was a normalized practice at the time and was not something people questioned as unusual. While her mother was upset about the decision, it was not her decision whether to keep her own child. Her grandfather wielded all the power in deciding to trade her daughter for a boy. When asked about her thoughts on the practice of trading children, Lily replied,

> That's just how things were. We couldn't say anything about it. My sister that was traded was upset about it her whole life. She was traded to a very poor family and they were good to her because she was the only girl. She was lucky like that.

In some respects, her sister received better treatment by being the only girl in the other family. However, she did not receive the benefits of Lily's more affluent family. She did not get to go to a university like Lily and her other sister. While Lily insisted that she tried to raise her daughters differently in the United States, she still had great regret that she never had a son. Additionally, she was protective of her daughters and forbade them to do certain things because they were girls. Lily serves as an example of how her home-culture frame affected how she raised her children in the United States.

Respondents shared that there was often a distinct division of labor in the home when it came to housework. While both parents may have had jobs in the professional realm, traditional roles existed inside the home. Mothers did the reproductive labor: cooking, cleaning, and taking care of children. Daughters were encouraged to participate in and complete these tasks as well. Erin, a second-generation Chinese American in her mid-thirties living in the Southwest, was a recipient of this gender-restrictive parenting. Her parents are from the same generation (baby boomers) as Lily, immigrating to the United States after the civil rights movement. Erin notes that she was given instruction from her mother to be a good hostess and is now well equipped to offer tea and cake to guests. In addition to this domestic training, there were restrictions regarding what she could do.

> There are a lot of things that I wanted to do as a child, and the explanation as to why I could not do them was "because you are a girl." I got that a lot. It really pissed me off. Like why I couldn't go out and play with some people, or do something except with my brother.

Erin's parents drew from their home-culture frame in reproducing the gender hierarchy in the household. Sometimes her brother, who was eight years younger than she, could do things she couldn't do.

> It was kind of ridiculous. I'm older than this person and I can't do the things they get to do. I don't remember anything specific, but I do remember it being drilled into me a lot. The "No, because you're a girl." Like, when I was a little kid, I wanted to play soccer, and there were girls in town who played soccer. It was a girl soccer league even in backwoods [Southern state]. I really wanted to play. I had some friends who played. My mom said, "No. That is a boy thing to do. You can't do that. That's for boys." But I was like, "But there's girls . . ." "No. Absolutely no." So, I never got to do it. I think I held that grudge forever.

Erin was not the only respondent who experienced a gender imbalance with her male siblings. To the parents' credit, the policing of girls' activities was not always motivated by ideas about things girls should and should not do. There were some elements of *protection*. Some respondents' parents restricted the activities of their daughters to protect them from unwanted sexual attention. There was not the same concern about sons being assaulted physically or sexually, which had different consequences for the boys and men, which are discussed at length in chapter 5. These Asian American parents knew that their Asian daughters would be of particular interest to potential predators because of their ethnicity or race. Erin explains why her parents were overprotective:

> There were little things like field trips the school would go on, the optional ones. I fought to go on the ski trip. My cousin, who is a girl, got to go, so my parents thought it was unfair if she got to go and I couldn't. I think that's why they gave in, but they really didn't want me to go. They thought it wouldn't be safe for girls. This is where it starts to merge with sexuality, which I didn't quite understand until later. They said, "It's because you are a girl and because you are Chinese. People think you are different. It's dangerous." And even when I was a kid, I was like, "What the fuck is that? What do you mean, I'm different?" Sure, my skin was different, I looked a little different, but I'm not really different. I'm a girl just like any other girl. When I got older I understood what they meant by that. I think if you're a parent, you get scared. When I was a kid I had no idea. I didn't understand that much.

These concerns tended to be exacerbated by the media. With news reports of predators, her parents, especially her father, were very concerned for her safety. While those proscriptions seemed ridiculous to Erin, there is plenty of evidence that Asian girls and women have been exoticized and fetishized in the United States.[10] Erin saw that concern from her parents. When asked for clarification about her parents' intentions, she explained,

> I think what they meant is that they think that Asian women are exoticized. So men or counselors or whoever . . . I never went to a sleepover. Never in my entire life because they were deathly afraid of what might happen to me. I went to sleepovers at my relatives' house. That's different. They know my parents. That was their biggest excuse: "Well, I don't know their parents, so you can't sleep over there." They just didn't want me to be messed with. That was why. They thought there was that chance because I was Asian . . . because Asian girls are exotic to non-Asian people. They're [Asian women] weird and people want to experience that. That is sort of too weird of a conversation for my parents to have. The most they could say is, "They think you are different." That's the best they could do at explaining that. That's where race, gender, and sexuality come together. And that's not anything I understood until way, way later.

While Erin's parents did not directly spell out that they feared non-Asians would exotify their daughter, research supports their fears. White habitus can accommodate the racial "other" when it lives up to a "particular exotic ideal."[11] Erin's understanding of her parent's protectiveness was accompanied with a greater understanding of sexuality and sexual predators. Erin has only dated whites and has felt exotified, to some extent, in most of those relationships. Men have said directly to her,

"There's something different about you." These statements directly relate to the concerns her parents had when she was younger. This sense of protectiveness was strong in the parents of many respondents, especially with parents who were first-generation Asian Americans. In some cases, they had experiences with colonialism and had seen or experienced acts of war involving sexual assault that their children had not. Immigrating to the United States may not have erased those fears, especially when some of those criminal acts came at the hands of American soldiers.

Charlene, a Taiwanese American in her twenties who grew up in the Southwest, experienced similar disparities with her brother. Even though she graduated from college and works as a teacher, when she comes home to visit her parents, she and her brother are still treated quite differently even though they are just one year apart.

> My brother was allowed to go out with his car and hang out with friends, and I wasn't. And even now when I'm visiting home, I have a curfew. I need to be home by eleven or they'll freak out. And even though I don't have any real consequences for me now that I'm older, I still do it. So we're about the same age except my brother can go out with friends and I can't.

While Charlene, Erin, and Lily all come from East Asian backgrounds, there are great similarities among Asian Indian families. Indira, a second-generation Indian American in her thirties who lives in the Pacific Northwest, was often pushed to achieve and to act like a "good Indian girl." She faced pressures to be a "model minority" that were accompanied by certain gender expectations.

> As I think back, I received messages about how to be a good Indian girl. First and foremost from my mother was how you dress, how you smile, how you greet aunties at an Indian party, how to do the superficial social graces. These social graces mark you as a polite, good-natured Indian girl, and that's important because you're a reflection of your family and the way you behave is a reflection of how your parents raised you. These are things that are important. It occurred to me that I also received messages about what it means to be a good Indian girl from men. My father is kind of special; he doesn't fit what I would call a stereotype of Indian fathers. But it would not be uncommon for a man—an uncle or any elder male in the family—to determine what is appropriate behavior for you. You don't argue, you don't talk back, and it's really your job to set the mood. You set the tone for the environment, and so if you have messed up the tone, it's your fault.

The gendering process was a communal effort in Indira's culture. Not only did she get policed by immediate family members but also by members of the larger Indian community.

In some ways, policing gendered behavior is a method through which immigrants attempt to maintain their cultural ties. While they may be looked upon as archaic and non-Western, in some ways this socializing process also functions to resist the colonizer. To maintain these cultural practices is to maintain agency and one's dignity. Even requests of parents to have their children choose partners from the same racial group are efforts to maintain ties to culture to keep the home-culture frame unharmed or unaltered, and thus combat oppressive components of white racist framing. Indira discusses why her parents had a preference for her to find an Indian male partner.

> I think their thing was to preserve culture. It's not for the bad things. My parents wanted me to be a doctor, and the *skin color* piece was a part of that conversation. My mom wanted me to be in a profession where in spite of skin color, somebody would have to come to you because you save lives. She wanted me to have a profession where even discrimination wouldn't keep me from being able to put food on the table. That has nothing to do with prestige or power. Her thought was everybody is always going to need doctors. In the same way around the Indian male partner, it was, "this is somebody who understands the values of our community the way that you've been raised and is not going the make fun of our cultural background. You'll see why those things are important later; you'll understand later on."

Indira's mother is asserting the contents of two different frames. The supposed "equalizing" effect of becoming a medical doctor draws from the white-crafted "liberty-and-justice frame." This idea is closely tied to the myth of the American Dream; in a fair and just society, a prestigious position such as a doctor should allow some relief from racial oppression.

Indira's mother has to hold on to contradictory beliefs and use multiple frames simultaneously. In order for her to evoke the home-culture frame, she has to acknowledge that the prestige of a doctor may still not prevent whites from "othering" her daughter. However, these "protective" or "strategic" measures by Indira's mother intersected race, gender and sexuality.

> I remember when I went home and finally had the guts to tell my parents that I was not going to medical school. I had no desire to be a doctor, and my mom was very disappointed. One of the first comments out of her mouth was, "Now how are you going find a husband? I want you to go to medical school to find an Indian doctor." It wasn't about me becoming a doctor.

Indira's mother has a vested interest in maintenance of culture while simultaneously trying to *protect* Indira from discrimination. The pressure Indira received from her mother was misconstrued as simple academic pressure, and only later did she realize that her mother wanted the best life possible for Indira, free from racism. As a protective measure, this seemed like the only suitable option for this particular Asian Indian mother. There is an intersection of class and educational expectations, with racial (model minority) and gender (heteronormative marriage) expectations. Indira's mother implies that pursuing a prestigious occupation, like a physician, may be an opportunity to have agency and access power as a racialized other. Fundamentally, to believe that "model minority" efforts will protect Indira, her mother has to hope that meritocracy will provide opportunities to people of color. However, there are still very gender-specific lessons in addition to these racialized strategies.

> Later it occurred to me that at no point in time did my brothers receive these types of messages either around masculinity or manhood or any sort of gender norm. . . . And so systemically I think that becomes a problem because women either fit or reject these norms. We either radically reject them or try our hardest to reconcile ourselves to them because you want to fit into a community. But the men don't have to do this; they have no consciousness or no examination of self this way.

Indira shares another example of the double standard that many of the Asian American women in my sample experienced. While outside of the home or community, girls and women had the freedom to ride bikes and play sports. In the case of Lena, a second-generation Taiwanese American in her forties who grew up in the South, she felt as if her mother had to balance gendered ideas from the "old world" with "American culture." One Christmas Lena was given a set of pencils with the embossed message "Girls can do anything"; but this didn't match the type of restrictive actions her mother placed on her, not allowing her to play outside after dark or go out with friends during the weekend because she was a girl.

The respondents who had vivid memories of gender socialization were predominantly women. Most of the early gendered messages that the male respondents shared were from peers in places such as school, work, and media. Indira points out that the lessons and policing were focused on her in order to regulate her actions. While my male respondents had more freedom and privileges while at home, they had to contend with greater threats of violent policing from boys and men outside of their families. The violent physical threats experienced by my male respondents were tied to Western constructions of masculinity that clashed with the gender socialization within their home-culture frames.

Like Indira, Fareena had a similar experience growing up. She is a second-generation Desi in her twenties, and her family emigrated from Bangladesh.

> In the Bangladeshi community, you definitely get the message of what a proper woman is supposed to do. The ideal girl is supposed to be quiet. She's never to be touched by a man or get *ruined*. There was a period when it seemed women would go into hiding and come out when they were ready to be approached for marriage. Otherwise, they were being *cultivated*. The cultivation is learning to cook, to keep house, and all of that.

Again, there is a certain ritual to create the ideal woman to attract a male partner. It is a *cultivation* process that teaches her skills for keeping a good home and emphasizes chastity before marriage, a cultivation process that boys and men are exempt from. Fareena rebelled a great deal from these expectations and was ostracized by other women in the community for that rebellion:

> Whenever we would go to the Bangladeshi parties, I really hated them because we were the only kids our age. I knew more about sports. I had a pretty high interest in politics. I couldn't go to where all the uncles and dads were and talk about that stuff. I had to be with all the whiney, crying kids and aunties talking about saris.[12] When I would hang around and my dad would let me talk and pay attention, I could tell that other men were *uncomfortable*. I got the message and I left. People addressed it in passive-aggressive ways. My mom would compliment other girls, "So and so's daughter does this. She's so good. She can cook this." On my mom's side, right after high school all they talked about was getting married. They all live in Bangladesh. They're all about being petite, light skinned, light eyes, and all that. I just never got along with them.

Fareena's home-culture frame imparted messages not only about how girls should act but whom they should associate with, the types of interests they should have, and how their bodies should look. These standards of beauty can also be influenced by globalized white ideology. Fareena's family's emphasis on lightness as more attractive has colonial ties as well as historical ties to class elitism in East Asian countries and South Asian countries like India, Pakistan, and Bangladesh. These white standards of beauty have also been incorporated into the lives of Bangladeshi Americans and Fareena's Bangla cousins still living in Bangladesh.

One male respondent had a vivid memory of gender policing in the home that clearly intersected sexuality. While he did not receive overt messages about how to properly behave as a man, he was discouraged from doing anything that was seen as too feminine. Daniel, who is a second-generation Vietnamese American in his twenties who identifies as gay, was discouraged from doing art. His family encouraged him to be involved with sports like football, and when he wanted to watch television programs such as *America's Next Top Model* his father instructed him to "turn that off, that's stupid, only girls watch that." Daniel was one of the few male respondents to get direct gender discipline within the home. His father's gender discipline was a heteronormative response to Daniel's seemingly "feminine" behavior.

The Body Is a Temple, Especially If You're a Woman

After I gave a talk about my first book, *The Myth of the Model Minority,* a group of young East Asian American women began sharing with me the ways in which they related to my discussion of self-esteem and standards of beauty in the media. One woman said, "I remember when I was four years old, my mom looked at me and she said, 'When you get older, we can get you the eyelid surgery.' *I was four.*" The women explained the techniques of using double-sided tape on top of the eyelid that could mimic whites' eyelids. Another woman said, "I was at the hospital when my cousin was born. She did not have the double eyelid. Her mother looked at her, this newborn baby, and said, 'She's going to have the [eyelid] operation.'" The young woman sharing this story could not believe that one of the first things her aunt commented on immediately after the birth of her cousin was how the newborn needed cosmetic surgery to seem "less Asian" looking. Alarmingly, the white standard of beauty is being exported globally. While there is a history of lighter skin preference in China, Japan, and India before European colonization,[13] the inclusion of cosmetic surgical alterations like eyelid surgery has a distinct racial element.

The Asian American body becomes another site of colonization. Brown bodies have been abused and neglected for centuries, and this long history has only cemented a normalized white ideology. When these values of white supremacy become internalized and hegemonic, whites do not have to actively oppress because people of color can do the work themselves. In this instance, Fareena's mother wants to keep tight controls over her body to protect her from potential "invaders." Unfortunately, Fareena had a difficult time balancing the wishes of her parents and the norms at her middle school in the United States.

> I played basketball and was pretty good at it. At a certain point, I got the lecture of, "You should stop wearing shorts and start wearing track pants." Which is insane. We never did that unless it was wintertime. It was basketball. We didn't wear short shorts anyway. We wore the long shorts. I didn't get why, but it was, "Oh, we don't show our legs. That's just too much skin."

When asked if her brother faced the same clothing standards, Fareena replied,

> Of course not. He could be shirtless. A weird thing is my mom would wear tank tops or skirts. And I would say, "But you're wearing a tank top." And she even says this now when I wear something too revealing: "Yeah, but my husband says it's okay. You don't have a husband yet."

In addition to the double standard regarding appropriate clothing, Fareena's mother reinforced patriarchal and heterosexist norms by insisting that Fareena had to have permission from a male partner. The way Fareena presented her body was a point of much contention between her and her mother.

Fareena's mother often emphasized the importance of female chastity. Fareena was expected to exercise modesty at all times so that she would not get a bad reputation. Her mother told her not to shave body hair and to be fully covered, requests that were tied to their home-culture frame but that clashed with what her peers were doing at school. Fareena notes that she disagreed with her mother quite a bit about physical body features:

> A lot of it had to do with me challenging her on issues about my body, how I wanted to present myself, how I wanted to dress and all that. My mom is really weight conscious. She always was, even at eighteen or nineteen. She went through a period where she admits she was anorexic because she was going through so much stress. She's always told me, "Don't become like your aunts. Don't get a big butt. Don't get fat legs." I think I had stretch marks at a very young age, like 10, from playing sports. My muscles just grew. It wasn't even in all the places you're supposed to get stretch marks in. But her thing was, "You have to rub Vaseline on them every day because otherwise you'll be *spoiled*. I didn't have any stretch marks until I was pregnant and you already have them." It was all about not becoming *spoiled*. I was about 110, 115 pounds, really, really skinny. All my ribs would show, but I had wide hips and bigger thighs.

Fareena's mother chose an interesting term when she spoke of Fareena's alleged imperfections as "spoiling" her. Spoiling is often used to described meat that has gone bad or rancid, and the female body is often objectified as nothing more than a "piece of meat" to be consumed by men. Many of my female respondents received messages that they should take great care of physical appearances to attract male partners. The concern voiced by Fareena's mother was largely centered on that, Fareena's ability to attract a male partner. Gender oppression happens at the most intimate level when loved ones and caretakers are constant enforcers of a "sexual contract."[14] The sexual contract facilitates male domination over women; when mothers, sisters, and aunts all participate in maintaining the contract, male domination persists.

To attract a potential partner, the physical body is a location of alteration and adornment. If an Asian American woman does not fit what has been constructed as the ideal woman, she may fall short in getting offers. Indira recalls:

> I never thought of myself as tall, but for my generation of Indian women, the ideal is 5'2", ninety pounds. And you have me at 5'6" and maybe 110, 120 pounds, which I would argue is still very thin. But most Indian men are like 5'8" so I appeared gargantuan next to them. My physical appearance was almost a threat to an Indian male's masculinity.

Hegemonic masculinity relies on the inferiority of femininity to all forms of masculinity. The masculine body must be physically larger than a woman's to maintain the order. Size becomes a central component of emasculation for Asian American men compared to other men in the United States. Further complicating the matter is what appears to be a lack of size differential between Asian American men and women. If Asian American men cannot reap masculine benefit by outsizing their female counterparts, they miss out on an aspect of male privilege. In chapter 5, I address in more depth the way that differences in body features and body size are used by whites to emasculate and "castrate" Asian American men.

SEXUALITY

Michel Foucault critiques the Western discourse on sexuality as scientifically sanitized with the advent of sexology and defined terminology, *scientia sexualis,* in contrast with the idea of sex as art, *ars erotica,* in Eastern cultures.[15] *Ars erotica,* as described by Foucault, constructs Eastern sex as a revered and almost religiously revered, sacred practice passed down from master to novice. But Foucault provides very little evidence of *ars erotica* in regions like East Asia, South Asia, and the Middle East. He seems to fall into the trap of orientalizing the Asian experience. Foucault romanticizes sex and sexual discourse in Asia. He also dismisses rampant sex crimes and the large role that colonialism has played in the sex tourism industry in Asia and the Pacific Islands. While the *Kama Sutra* is a wildly famous text supporting pleasure and eroticism, there are regular practices of sex work by concubines, geisha, and comfort women that counter any simplistic idea of *ars erotica.*

There has been little research critiquing Foucault's interpretation of Eastern sexual discourse.[16] There was certainly no evidence to support his claims in my research. Respondents did not describe such experiences when learning about sex from their families and communities. Instead, there was a code of silence. There are more recent historical factors that could account for a change, such as repressive elements of the Cultural Revolution in China and various religious practices in Asia. But one thing very clear from my interviews is that manhood is far from being based on learning extensive lessons on sensuality and sexual pleasure. Additionally, my respondents do not have romantically formed *ars erotica* descriptions of sex in Asia and in the Asian American community. While there is great diversity in Asia and the Pacific Islands, respondents from many different backgrounds describe a very private and secretive handling of sex in their homes. There was very little emphasis on teaching or physical pleasure, as Foucault asserts. Yuan, a sixty-nine-year-old first-generation

Taiwanese American, discusses his and his parent's perspective on public dress and affection:

> People from Asia are more private. It used to be that some girls couldn't even wear short sleeves or short skirts. It is just a different culture. They don't expose themselves in public. It stays in your private life, and you don't have to show it. If you love somebody you don't say, "I love you, I love you, I love you" all the time. When my parents were here, we took my daughter to school, and she kissed me before she left the car. My mother said, "Your kid's not a cat or dog." They never kissed in public.

Yuan offers no romantic version of physical affection; instead, his parents police him with home-culture framing when he adopts new ways of showing affection. Foucault's *ars erotica* version of sexuality in the East is an Orientalist construction that further exotifies Asian and Pacific Islander peoples. Because there is very little research on the discourse of sexuality in Asia, researchers must be careful not to view the East through "Western eyes" [17] as Foucault may be guilty of doing.

As subsequent generations of Asian Americans develop, the traditions from the home culture can leave certain impressions. Robert, a second-generation Chinese American from the East Coast in his twenties, describes how his parents showed affection to each other:

> [long pause] Yeah, see I'm drawing a blank here. I'm pretty sure I have never really seen my parents kiss each other. Recently I have seen them stay up late together and watch TV, and that's really cute you know, to see that. But, I dunno, looking back I can't really pick out anything too specific. So that shaped my perception of my parents, my perceptions of how they thought about relationships, and how it was better to just not get into them at all. And my dad said this: "Don't get into a relationship until college."

Other respondents shared very similar stories. Phan, a second-generation Vietnamese American in her late thirties, lives in a metropolitan area in the Northeast. She shares, "I first saw my parents holding hands maybe a year ago. And that was after we all moved out." Their parents were not particularly physically affectionate with each other and expected their children to concentrate on things other than romantic relationships until later in life. These expectations influenced the way parents perceived their children as sexual beings. Robert adds:

> I think my parents have this idea that it hasn't crossed my head to "mess around" or have sex, etc. And it might be like a mental crutch. I mean, maybe they think it has something to do with race, or the fact that I'm their biological offspring. That "he's a good kid and he won't think about sex until much later." That actually worked in my benefit, for quite a while, because they trust me.

Robert has some leeway with his parents because they assume he has no current interest in sexual activity. However, this trust is more common for the male respondents. As noted earlier, the female respondents face more policing and supervision of their activities.

There are various forms of sexual oppression throughout Asia with a very strong thread of sanctioning of the female body. As in the United States, there is a double standard regarding sexual activity for men and women. While there is no explicit instruction for sons to be sexually active, daughters receive direct messages of chastity. Charlene's mother warned against losing one's virginity, saying, "Every woman has a fire in them, and once you put that fire out, you can't light it again." Charlene continues:

> My mom would say, "Don't get yourself in trouble." Or don't, in Mandarin, "make a mistake." I guess I saw sex as a mistake. Or that's what I knew that they wanted me to see it as, and so then I saw it as something risqué. Definitely don't engage in, which I did. And made many, many poor choices, because of that. Sexuality was suppressed in our household. Everything was supposed to be about school and your job and getting to that point. And even now my parents sleep in different beds. They have for ten years at least. So, sexuality is really repressed. Although now I've seen my mom give my dad a kiss.

Like other respondents, Charlene's parents were rarely affectionate in front of her. Instead of *ars erotica*, sex was taboo and especially off limits to daughters. Charlene's brother did not get the same messages. Her parents did encourage both of them to concentrate on school before concerning themselves with relationships. However, men's fires are not at risk of being extinguished. The tabooing of sex made it more enticing to Charlene. It was something she wanted to experience as an act of rebellion. Unfortunately, at fourteen, Charlene became involved with an older white classmate who fetishized her.

Fareena also faced strict rules in her house that were attempts by her parents to protect her from sexual predators and to regulate her sexual behavior. She "relied on" her close friends and "intimate" sleepovers with her female classmates. However, her parents banned her from the sleepovers in middle school because men would be in those homes. Fareena shares:

> In seventh or eighth grade, I was told, "you can't sleep over anymore. You can go and stay until 11." My dad asked my mom to tell me. Which, I was thrown off by because my dad and I were really close at that time. He would tell me everything, but apparently this was a woman issue. I didn't get why it was a woman issue at that time. So she said, "You can stay there until late at night, but then I'll come pick you up. You can't stay the night." I didn't know why. I was crying. I threw a fit.

Fareena looked for an explanation from her family and her mother told her, "We're a Muslim family and there are men in the house. Once one of them touches you, you're *ruined*. You could get raped. If boys get raped, it's fine." Fareena clarified that her mother did not mean that it was acceptable for boys to get raped, but that if women are raped, the stigma sticks and they can get pregnant. Fareena's mother was clear with her double standard: girls and women had to remain chaste, and it is a devastating blow if your virginity is lost outside of wedlock.

In Fareena's case, the fear of the men had less to do with her family's religion and more to do with her mother's experience with the Bangladesh Liberation War.[18] The blatant use of rape as a military strategy during the war had a profound effect on Fareena's mother:

> It was the largest war crime in history. [My mother and aunts] were in hiding. They were little kids and they would be in the basement hiding while something else was going on in the next room. You were always told that once you're *ruined*, you're *ruined*.

Fareena continued to detail that after the war, the political leadership had to "reframe" the women who were victims of sexual assault, calling them "heroes" to prevent mass suicides and families killing their daughters. Fareena's mother associated rape with shame and thinks it's "the worst thing that can happen to a woman," so protecting her daughter from that was top priority. This made it difficult to interact with other South Asian Americans. There was a certain "double consciousness" that Fareena had to adopt. In some instances, she learned to adjust her behavior after making a social misstep:

> When I was nineteen I went to a movie theater with my friends. At that time, there weren't a lot of South Asian people in my city. But outside the theater there were two guys talking in Bangla. They looked to be in their mid-twenties, and I was so excited to see other Bangladeshi people, so I started talking to them. I told them my dad's name, to look us up in the Bangladeshi directory. A week later, my dad asked if I had talked to someone at the mall. I said, "Yeah, I met these two dudes who were new to the city." He said, "Other people are saying that they think you're a loose girl and really flirty. And that you tried to get with both of them at the same time." I remember crying because it wasn't anything like that, because of the fact that they would think of me that way. I know what the cultural standards and expectations are, how brown women are supposed to act around brown men. It's different from how we can act around non-brown people, but it's too uncomfortable for me. So I stopped going to Bangladeshi parties after that.

There is a "double consciousness" that Fareena must possess to meet the expectations of her Bangla community and the external white American community. Her religious and Bangla gender expectations are seemingly more strict, protective, even patriarchal compared to those of a non-Asian environment or a Western upbringing. Looking at these participant narratives, the *ars erotica* of Eastern discourse on sexuality seems mythical and completely absent. The discourse they share surrounding sex and sexuality is centered on protectionism and fear of colonization.

If we include the protectionist discourse with "model minority" stereotyping, we see a hybrid strategy in controlling sexuality. There are pressures for new immigrants to succeed, and certain behaviors are encouraged to protect against discrimination.[19] When the emphasis on fitting the "model minority" stereotype is combined with concerns about preserving culture and heteronormative expectations, it becomes a complex set of messages. Indira explains how her mother attempted to train her sexuality.

> When I was pre-puberty the message from my mother was, "Don't talk to boys," period. Like, you have no reason to talk to boys; it's just "Don't talk to boys. This is nonnegotiable." And then post-puberty, obviously, then you begin to understand, "Oh, okay, I get where this is going." I, at least being heterosexual, happen to be attracted to boys but I'm not supposed to talk to boys. But then came my favorite. My mom says, "Cotton and fire should not be in the same space." And men are like cotton and women are fire [laughing]. Silly Asian analogies. So, "Still don't talk to boys. Your job now is to study." That's how things were framed to me. Anything else beyond your studies is a distraction. That was message number one. So then the message changed to, "After college, after your studies are over, we want you to get married. But we don't want you to talk with boys. We don't want you to interact with them." So after you've graduated, all of the sudden you're supposed to be fully equipped to be in a sexual relationship and marriage with somebody because you have all of the skill sets of female communications, which I just find deeply humorous. And now no one seems to see how ridiculous that is. . . . I guess it's as if your gender and your sexuality are separate, and you turn on a switch at the right time. That's kind of how it was relayed to me.

Indira's training from her mother is far from the Foucaultian *ars erotica* master to student. The messages she received were multilayered. There was policing of Indira's behavior that was rooted in values and traditions of her home-culture frame. Her mother thought that education was the most important skill she could acquire. While this lesson is often associated with the "model minority" stereotyping of Asian Americans, it is a conscious strategic move by many Asian immigrants. This strategy pulls from the white-constructed liberty-and-justice frame. Many Asian Americans buy into the belief that the United States is a land of opportunity that is fair and just and where hard work in an academic setting will reap rewards.

Indira's mother is a multiframer in this case. She juggles "home culture" gender values with the desire to use education as an equalizer that will hopefully award Indira opportunities in the future and protect her from discrimination. Yet the de-emphasis on intimate relationships leaves Indira feeling ill equipped as a potential romantic partner. Many respondents envied white friends the freedoms they were allowed in social settings. In later chapters, male respondents cite their Asian upbringing as a disadvantage when it came to relating to and courting potential partners.

CONCLUSION

Gender socialization begins even before birth. Families make plans for their children when first learning the sex of the baby: buying clothing, preparing their living space, choosing gendered names, and so on. Respondents face an ongoing, lifelong process of gendering marked with lessons, expectations, discipline, and a gaze. They are constantly pressured to conform to racialized, gendered, and sexualized expectations.

The gendered and racialized experience for Asian American women and men share similarities but also differences. In their homes, Asian American women face clear heteronormative expectations. There is more policing of their activities so that they may preserve their virginity or be protected from being the exotified "other." There was also more emphasis on the physical bodies and presentation. This is not necessarily a great deal different from the female experience for other races and across the globe.

For the male respondents, the messages were much more vague. They received more freedom and privileges. Unlike Western constructions of masculinity, lessons of manhood were not based on physical and sexual prowess. None of my male respondents received lessons from masters of *ars erotica*. Instead, they received male privilege in the form of freedom.

In the next chapter, respondents discuss external messages from individuals, institutions, and the media beyond the home and their racial/ethnic communities. These messages sometimes concur and sometimes are at odds with the messages they received at home. White racial framing is the central component in these experiences, and Asian Americans struggle to develop anti-oppression frames to combat them.

NOTES

1. A television show popular in the 1970s: *C.H.I.P.s—California Highway Patrol*.
2. Judith Butler, Gender Trouble: Feminism and the Subversion of Identity (New York: Routledge, 1990).
3. Judith Halberstam, "Drag Kings: Masculinity and Performance," in *Female Masculinity* (Durham, NC: Duke University Press, 1998), 231–66.

4. Choe Sang-Hun, "South Koreans Rethink Preference for Sons," *New York Times,* November   28,   2007,   http://www.nytimes.com/2007/11/28/world/asia/28iht-sex.1.8509372.html?_r=1&emc=eta1.

5. Adrienne Rich's classic "Compulsory Heterosexuality and Lesbian Existence," *Signs* 5 (1980): 631–60.

6. Ronald Takaki, *Strangers from a Different Shore* (Boston: Back Bay, 1998), 217.

7. The respondent pool was lacking in representation for Pacific Islander Americans. Desi is defined as a person of Indian, Pakistani, or Bangladeshi birth or descent who lives abroad. Desi-Americans made up 20 percent of my sample.

8. This point is attributed to Wendy Leo Moore.

9. Kara Smith. "Prebirth Gender Talk: A Case Study in Prenatal Socialization," *Women and Language,* 28, no. 1 (2005): 49–53.

10. Sheridan Prasso, *The Asian Mystique: Dragon Ladies, Geisha Girls and Our Fantasies of the Exotic Orient* (Cambridge, MA: Public Affairs Books, 2006).

11. Eduardo Bonilla-Silva, Carla Goar, and David G. Embrick, "When Whites Flock Together: The Social Psychology of White Habitus," *Critical Sociology* 32, nos. 2–3 (2006): 229–53.

12. A "sari" is a strip of unstitched cloth worn by females, ranging from four to nine meters in length, that is draped over the body in various styles popular in India, Bangladesh, Malaysia, Sri Lanka, Burma, Bhutan, and Nepal.

13. Lightness of skin was sometimes associated with wealth. Those with lighter skin did not need to work in harvesting fields.

14. Carole Pateman, *The Sexual Contract* (Cambridge: Polity Press; Palo Alto, CA: Stanford University Press, 1988).

15. Michel Foucault, *The History of Sexuality,* vol. 1 (New York: Vintage Press, 1984).

16. Foucault later backtracked a bit from these assertions.

17. Chandra Talpade Mohanty, "'Under Western Eyes' Revisited: Feminist Solidarity through Anticapitalist Struggles," *Signs: Journal of Women in Culture and Society* 28, no. 2 (2002): 499–535.

18. During the Bangladesh liberation war, the Pakistani government issued a commandment for women to be wrapped from head to toe from age eight and older. Fareena's mother and aunts were forced to be covered in a move to disgrace the women.

19. Rosalind S. Chou and Joe R. Feagin, *The Myth of the Model Minority: Asian Americans Facing Racism* (Boulder, CO: Paradigm Publishers, 2008).

THREE

External Forces — Under Western Eyes

The previous chapter reviewed the role of the home-culture frame in the lives of our respondents. First-generation Asian Americans immigrated to the United States with values and traditions associated with their home country and with a well-formed ethnic identity that sometimes matched and sometimes conflicted with Western constructions of gender and sexuality. First-generation parents and ethnic communities pulled from the home-culture frame when teaching lessons about gender and sexuality to subsequent generations.

But Asian Americans can struggle with a "double consciousness" of sorts, juggling what Feagin might call "multiple frames."[1] In contrast to the home-culture frame discussed in the previous chapter, in this chapter the respondents discuss the messages they received from external forces: in school, in peer groups, and in the media.

HEGEMONIC MASCULINITY

Antonio Gramsci conceptualized cultural hegemony as a rule of society by a social group through imposed "common sense."[2] Hegemony works by normalizing ideologies or everyday beliefs (values, myths, norms, and practices). These normalized ideologies are used as the foundation for complex systems of political, social, and economic domination. Cultural hegemony is not necessarily accomplished through violence, though it could be reinforced by force and coercion or threats of violence. The key to hegemony is how the ideologies of the dominant group become everyday common knowledge to those who are not in the dominant group. Hegemony can be visible, but it is largely invisible as it is naturalized into the culture through practice, language, and media.

Connell and Messerschmidt define hegemonic masculinity as a "pattern of practice (i.e., things done, not just a set of role expectations or an identity) that allowed men's dominance over women to continue."[3] Hegemony is also the "ascendancy [of a social group] achieved through culture, institutions, and persuasion."[4] Sociologists and feminists equate hegemonic masculinity with white, heterosexual, middle-class men or those who inhabit positions of authority in society, which can vary across societies.[5] Hegemonic masculinity is normative and only a small fraction of men may embody or enact it.[6] Hegemonic masculinity is not static; it transitions and changes.[7] Hegemony is both external and internal. External hegemony is men's domination over/of women (valorization of masculinity over femininity). Internal hegemony is men's domination over/of other men (valorization of hegemonic masculinity over other subordinated/marginalized masculinities). Subordinated masculinities are masculinities associated with sexually transgressive men, such as gay or bisexual men. Marginalized masculinities are masculinities associated with men of color or poor or working-class men. These masculinities do not undermine hegemony. In fact, hegemonic masculinity *depends* on the subordination of men who are members of marginalized or subordinate masculine groups and all women. The meaning of masculinity is not constant over the course of any man's life and will change as he grows and matures. Men construct masculinity in accordance with their position and social structures and, therefore, their access to power and resources.[8] To achieve the greatest access to power and resources, there are many tactics used to subordinate women and groups of men.

Other mechanisms of hegemonic masculinity include "cultural consent, discursive centrality, institutionalization, and the marginalization or delegitimation of alternatives."[9] Some mechanisms of hegemony are quite visible (men slapping each other's backs), while other mechanisms "operate by invisibility, removing a dominant form of masculinity from the possibility of censure."[10] Maintenance involves surveillance (of men) and exclusion (of women).[11] At different times, men may benefit from masculine domination because hegemonic masculinity is relational and defined through and against other genders. Even if a man is considered a member of a marginalized or subordinated masculine group, he may receive beneficial actions and behaviors, such as earning a higher salary, being a father, and having easy access to sexual partners.[12]

Similarly, there is a constructed femininity that allows women who closely match the ideal greater access to power and resources. Asian American men and women do not fit the hegemonic masculine or feminine ideal, just as most men and women do not. Additionally, they are unable to access all the privileges accompanying whiteness. There are tremendous pressures, both internal and external, to closely match hegemonic ideals. The following sections of this chapter detail these pressures to meet these ideals.

SCHOOL

School is a central institution in socializing young people and engraining hegemonic ideals.[13] Teachers, staff, and peers become central in shaping individuals in the proper social scripts for race, gender, sexuality, class, and even religion, and they are a major source of gendered policing.[14]

Bullying

One way in which this occurs is through bullying. One form of school bullying is related to masculinity and homophobia.[15] In 2009, eleven-year-old Carl Joseph Walker-Hoover from Massachusetts, committed suicide after being bullied daily for appearing gay despite weekly pleas from his mother to address the problem.[16] In 2008, a fourteen-year-old classmate shot fifteen-year-old Lawrence King of Oxnard, California, because he was openly gay.[17] Some targets of bullying fight back, at times with extreme measures, like school shootings.[18] School shootings in the past two decades have caused great panic, with increased security in these institutions to prevent future tragedies. However, without addressing the bullying that goes on in these schools, based on hegemonic ideals of masculinity, the problems will persist.

Another form of bullying is related more directly to race. Many Asian Americans are attempting to fit the "model minority" stereotype, trying to do their best and excel. But in order to keep from making waves in school, some Asian Americans endure terrible treatment. The most overtly discriminatory cases of school taunting happened to my respondents outside of the West Coast and Hawaii. Respondents who went to school on the West Coast or in Hawaii faced some relief from bullying because of the relatively large Asian American populations in those areas; they were not racially isolated and thus benefitted from visibility and critical mass. However, there were still instances of racial teasing and taunting for respondents growing up in these areas,[19] as exemplified by the UCLA student Alexandra Wallace's 2011 video on YouTube called "Asians in the Library," which went viral.[20] In the video, Wallace complained of "hordes of Asians" at UCLA who didn't have American manners and made a mockery of Asians who speak their native languages."[21] UCLA did not punish Wallace for her actions, as they did not violate any student codes. The lack of action at UCLA was in line with the experiences of our respondents. In their experience, when teachers and administrators were informed of racism, they ineffectively dealt with the problems or not at all.

There has been documentation of widespread racial discrimination against Asian Americans in school.[22] There is a clear difference in how this discrimination is carried out against Asian American boys versus girls. Male respondents reported physical violence and threats as a main method of torment, while the female respondents dealt more with "other-ing" and neglect. Assaults against male participants included being hit with a baseball bat, getting a tooth knocked out walking down the street, and fights every day walking to and from school.[23] The role of violence in the lives of Asian American men and boys is discussed in-depth in chap-ter 5.

Learning the Racial Hierarchy

Irwin Tang, a second-generation Chinese American writer in his thir-ties who asked me to use his real name, has a great deal of experience with racialized violence at school in the Southwest. It has shaped him a great deal, and these experiences have been documented in his book, *How I Became a Black Man and Other Metamorphoses.* Tang likens his experi-ences with racism to the African American experience; African Americans in school were his biggest allies against racist whites. Tang details his life in school:

> [The physical assaults] happened in class, out of class, wherever . . . Especially during those middle years it was very frequent. Like fifth grade to freshman year or something like that in high school. There were a lot of days I didn't want to go to school. I think it really got bad in the fifth grade. It seems like every year there were these kids that were tormenting me for like long periods of time. They would hit me somewhere on the arm, or back, or back of the head and it would hurt—one punch or something like that. Or if it was on the arm, it would be more often but only a couple of times did I just start swing-ing. One time these two kids grabbed me from behind and one had his hands over my eyes, and they just started hitting me.

Irwin's torment lasted for five years, even though he told teachers what was happening to him. It was regarded as child's play. When asked about his teacher's reaction to the treatment he said her response was, "kind of like, boys will be boys." The teachers in his school basically ignored the physical assaults for several years. Finally, Irwin's father gave him some advice. "I remember at one point, maybe it was the fifth grade, my father told me to hit them as hard as I could." A core aspect to masculinity is toughness; to be masculine is to follow the "way of the badass."[24] Part of the gendering process in schools is to encourage "boys to be boys," and part of that identity is to "rough house."[25] By turning a blind eye to the torment Irwin endured, the teachers were reifying mas-culinity and the racial hierarchy. Since Irwin was getting no protection or assistance from his teachers, his father recommended physical retaliation as a last resort. Irwin's experience was racialized in his eyes.

> It was usually boys [who physically harmed me]. White boys. I mean, that's not that unusual considering that most of the population is white [in his Southwestern town]. There's a lot of Asian guys who grew up

having to deal with African American kids messing with them. I really never had that experience. . . . I wasn't a big kid and I wasn't popular in the typical sense. A lot of kids knew me. I had a lot of friends and a lot of enemies. And the only way I could explain the fact that I had a lot of enemies is because I was Asian and I wasn't a big kid. You know like in fifth grade there were these two kids, Derrick and William, and they would come in pairs. Goes to show just how ruled we are by fear. Why would some kid that was bigger than me, much bigger than me, have some partner in crime?

Masculinity is unstable and must be continually reinforced through performances.[26] Derrick and William teamed up for these assaults so there could be a witness to their masculine performance. Oftentimes these "mob" activities occur because of the need to have an audience to provide confirmation of physical domination. White mob violence has been a historical tradition in the United States and used as a disciplining tactic overtly after Reconstruction. Thousands of men of color were lynched during that time period. While they were largely African American, Asians men brought in as laborers were also targeted by whites and white mobs.[27] These violent practices acted as psychological control mechanisms. After the civil rights movement, overtly violent acts of racial terrorism became less socially acceptable. Racial taunting has become clandestine in the "color-blind era." The burden of proof lies with the taunted.

Irwin explains the race of his assailants because of sheer numbers. Whites were the majority in his school, and he acknowledges that his racial taunting was not unique to him. He asserts that other Asian American boys and men experience bullying from other racial groups as well. The construction of Asian American boys as physically weaker than other boys can make them targets on the playground. Undersized boys of all races are often targets in these spaces because male hegemonic dominance emphasizes muscular and large bodies. Hegemonic masculinity and systemic racism create alienated relationships among men, and this can happen along racial lines or even within racial groups.

While Derrick and William's daily taunting was never explicitly racialized, Irwin knew that it was because he was of Asian descent. Today, messages of racial domination are less overt; they become veiled in media, pop culture, and even in microinteractions within "white habitus" and extensions of the white spaces. Hegemony is enacted in our daily interactions with each other, such as male bonding. Male bonding can rely on enacting domination over another person, whether it is in the form of something as seemingly innocuous as jokes or as serious as physical assault.[28]

Ray, a second-generation, twenty-six-year-old Chinese American who grew up in the South, also experienced consistent racial discrimination in school that was, at times, accompanied by physical violence. He rarely retaliated, and if he felt a situation escalate, he would do his best to avoid further conflict, largely because he knew he would be outnumbered.

> I felt like sometimes I would be by myself for some reason and go out to the park where there would be another group of kids. And I know I'm outnumbered, so I would be like, "Whatever, I'm Chinese, I'll just take it, ching chong, whatever. I'm not going to fight you guys."

This survival strategy is a safe choice for Ray, who recognizes that he cannot defend himself against a group of peers. In some ways, the stereotype of Asian passivity is reinforced, but Ray had very few alternatives. In geographic regions with greater populations of Asians, this may be less of an issue. However, even in areas with large numbers of Asians and Asian Americans, anti-Asian stereotypes can still be present. People of color, in this case Asian Americans, can internalize anti-Asian ideology, further complicating how individuals understand their personal identity.

Ray grew up in a geographic region where he clearly understood that he was a racial other. This was clear with the response (or lack thereof) from teachers and administrators to address the bullying he endured. Even if he went to school officials, he was afraid that there would be no relief:

> That stuff happened to me, and I would get pissed off about it sometimes. It was really hard for me to feel like I could tell the teachers to do something about it because, later when I was in high school, I went to a different school. A private school—it was all white. Everyone was everyone else's farm neighbor or whatever. All their parents knew each other, so I never felt comfortable enough to address it with the administration. It just felt like there was a high degree of nepotism there. I didn't feel like I could trust them to understand what I was going through. Thankfully, by the time I was in high school, I did get pissy about it, but I was also more . . . I had more control over it. Like, I'm not going to do anything; I'm not going to punch him or whatever. I'd just walk it off. It also happened a couple times in church, too.

In Ray's southern town, the prevalence of widespread institutional power of whites was apparent to him, even as a child. This omnipresent structural power in various institutions like schools and churches, prevented him from attempting to challenge discrimination. He had to learn techniques to control his anger because administrators did not take him seriously. This lack of trust extended to law enforcement for Ray because his family and other Chinese families were the targets of a government sting of grocery stores that were specifically racially profiled. His family had to battle the federal government for several years.

Earlier in the chapter, Irwin stated that plenty of Asian American kids have dealt with "African American kids messing with them." There is a history of conflict between African Americans and Korean Americans, for example.[29] These conflicts often happen as a residual effect of white supremacy.[30] Additionally, children will adopt the white racial frame and participate in discriminatory behaviors whether they are white or not.[31] However, in a largely non-white environment, Asian Americans can feel true acceptance from their African and Latino American peers. Four of my respondents who had the experience of attending a largely black or black and Latino high school noticed great differences when they had to move to white schools. Erin, a second-generation Chinese American, introduced in the previous chapter, explains:

> When I was a little kid, in kindergarten to fourth grade, I felt like I was *fully myself*. I didn't really restrict how I acted in front of people. The Erin at home, around my family and parents, and the Erin at school was the same Erin. I went to a public school that was primarily black people. I was obviously the minority because I was Asian. There were a handful of white people. I was friends with white people and black people. But really I had more black friends because there were more black people there. But they did group Asians with whites because we were the minority overall. I was pretty free in terms of how I felt around people. But fifth through eighth grade was at a different school. It was a public school that was majority white. Then I encountered this feeling I had never felt before, which I really didn't understand. I was conflicted with it the entire time I was in that school from fifth to eighth grade. It really messed with my head. One thing I realized was that the Erin at home and the Erin at school are completely different people. I became this very quiet, shy person that didn't talk to anybody. I was kind of afraid of other people. But I wasn't like that at all at Smith Elementary [the largely black school]. I didn't understand it. I couldn't really break out of it until I got to high school. I don't think I really fully broke out of it until I got to college or at least late high school, when I was in school with other nerds. All of a sudden, I was relegated to nerd status. Clearly. I was in this group where, "Oh. She's smart, but not social. Not able to talk and communicate with other people." I realized at home I was not like that at all. Among my family, I was loud and boisterous, the person who led crazy little projects and fun games or whatever. So, it was completely different and I think it really bothered me, those times in pre-junior and junior high.

The public Erin contrasted a great deal with the Erin at home. This shift stuck out dramatically in Erin's memory and she spent many years trying to decipher some logical explanations. The only variable she thought made a major difference was the demographical shift racially between the two schools and the type of hostile environment that was part of that shift. School integration after the *Brown v. Board of Education* decision resulted in some damaging effects for African American students who began to attend largely white schools.[32] While allowing access to the same education, it would not abolish issues of racial hostility in the environment from students, teachers, and administration. Erin notes:

The first few days at school I knew I was the new kid, so I knew I would be a little bit more shy. But I felt like I was the new kid the *entire* time. For some reason, I couldn't be myself. If it was like this at the other school, in my elementary school, then I wasn't aware of it. But in fifth grade, there was a clear divide between who the popular kids were and who they were not. There were popular kids and then the pariah kids. Then there was everyone in the middle. I had no concept of that prior to fifth grade. It may have been because at the other school, I was in the cool crowd. But I really don't know. And it wasn't just in the kids' society; it affected the teachers and the administration, too.

This is yet another example of how even at a young age, children can see the power embedded into the structure. Adults who are authority figures and who are supposed to be objective protectors are instead participants in the social stratification of elementary and middle schools. Erin feels the weight of the values of a "white habitus" in this school. Children do participate in maintaining that hierarchy, but they can also help create more egalitarian environments, like the one in Erin's first elementary school. In other settings, children can be surrounded by white racial ideological framing and yet participate in counter-frames like the anti-oppression or liberty-and-justice frames. For example, when Erin went on to a magnet boarding school after eighth grade, the environment was much more comfortable. She felt on equal footing with her peers.

Exclusion and Ostracism

One of Jeremy's earliest memories of going to elementary school was when "some white kids were having a pool party and every kid got an invitation and I didn't. It was from a little girl. I never did anything to her. I was never mean to her. How was it that every kid got invited except myself, this one Arab girl, and a black kid?" Jeremy, a second-generation Bangladeshi American in his twenties from the Southwest, continues to describe middle and high school.

I went to an all-white school for like six weeks just to "try out this neighborhood." We [Jeremy and his sister] had both gone to an all-black school in [my city], and it sounds like a complete stereotype, but in predominantly black schools, the black kids were more welcoming towards Indian folks. The white kids were very cliquish, very stuck up. The white kids that went to my all-black high school were really nice, but when I went to an all-white high school for those couple of weeks, they were kind of mean. It wasn't like they were racist to your face, but it's more like hidden stereotypes and race, you know? I felt like the "invisible man," like the book, when I went to an all-white school, whereas when I went to an all-black school, they welcomed me with more open arms. I know a few kids that go to North Creek, which is an all-white, predominantly affluent high school here, and the Indian kids that have gone there are pretty much just picked on by the white kids. And they kind of struggled with their racial identity. Whereas, me going to an all-black school, I felt right at home. A lot of it had to do with me being an athlete.

While Jeremy attributes his positive experience at the majority black high school to his involvement with sports, Erin was not an athlete but had a similar experience. Jeremy, and many other respondents, felt an element of "invisibility" in these all or largely white spaces. Being involved in activities like athletics had a positive effect on Jeremy's experience at the racially diverse school, but other respondents did not have the same experience and were taunted on their largely or all-white sports teams. Children involved in sports tend to perform better in school than those not involved, but involvement in sports for Jeremy and his sister did not solve their feelings of isolation at the all-white school. They both were involved with basketball and were still outcasts. If they were not involved with sports at the all-white high school, their experience may have been even more difficult. Jeremy continues:

> I felt really out of place. The few friends I did have were East Asian or African American. They were kind of like renegades and misfits in middle school as well because none of the white kids acknowledged us, and you know there wasn't any sports in sixth grade or fifth grade. I had joined the recreational league at age ten and even the white kids on the team barely acknowledged my presence. So, had I not gone to an ethnic school, socially I don't think I'd be the same person now. I work in sales, I work commission only. I work real estate. I don't think I would have the dominant personality for this kind of industry had I not gone to an all-black school. People didn't pick on me physically, because I was big. But I felt really out of place because no one was really open to being friends with me.

The "new racism"[33] or "backstage racism"[34] creates environments that lack overt racism but the presence of racism or racial tension hangs in the air. Jeremy did not fit the mold at his high school not just because of his Bangladeshi heritage but because of his lack of class status as well. The all-white school was a "white habitus": a place with a white racist ideology at the core.

Multiracial environments can possess characteristics of white habitus as well if they have internalized white hegemonic ideology or "white racial framing." This was the case with Jeremy's college. While his university had a large percentage of people of color, the environment was still very much a white space. Geographic areas like the West Coast have greater numbers of Asian Americans, and the primary school experience can be much better. In these regions, there are even more advertisements representing Asians and Asian Americans; however, white habitus still persists.[35]

To deal with the feeling of ostracism in college, Jeremy joined an Indian fraternity. He admits that he is very much an "alpha male" and that his fraternity brothers are similar. There is a shared interest in sports participation and he emphasized several times that athletic ability shielded him from further ostracism. Jeremy asserts, "If you didn't play sports and went to an all-white school, socially you would be pretty awkward, like those [Asian American] spelling bee kids." Jeremy was also advantaged by his physical size. Other respondents like Irwin did not have that advantage. His girlfriend's brother is small in stature and was not nearly as involved with athletics and his school experience was quite different:

> My girlfriend is Bangladeshi and her brother went to an all-white private school. His graduating class was thirty kids and his parents were doctors and really well to do. So they sent her to a public school, but they sent him to this crazy ridiculous all-white private school in [Southern state] which is probably more racist than [the Southwestern state that Jeremy resides]. And, I mean, it's just hardcore, Confederate flag, Mason-Dixon line, Bible belt, you name it—it's the whitest of the white. And, I mean, it's wrong for me to sit here and label his masculinity level or whatnot, but my prospective brother-in-law, he's like 5'2" and super skinny. He didn't play sports. His masculinity level is low to none. And so he was ostracized by the white kids, to the point where this guy, I think he has some serious disorders now. If you go to a mall with him he has trouble asking a security guard where the restroom is. He's thirty years old, and he's really quiet to begin with but never has had a girlfriend. Never even attempted. He has problems talking to a stranger. It's like his personality was *crushed*. Now if he gets to know you and you're friends with him, he's a chatterbox. He's awesome.

Jeremy describes his "prospective brother-in-law" as a marginalized masculine figure. The combination of race, his small size, and an all-white, conservative social space, in Jeremy's eyes, has created an extreme case of a "crushed" man. His class status did not seem to offer him any advantages at his private school. While there is a wide range of responses to oppression, the long-term effects can take a serious toll.[36] Jeremy may be able to talk about his high school and college experiences as almost humorous life experiences, but his brother-in-law's experience was similar to that of other male respondents in the survey.

Sports in School

Jeremy sees athletics as an equalizer, an area in which to demonstrate strength and power as a male. However, athletics are not always free from racism, sexism, or homophobia.[37] In the case of Jeremy Lin, much of the media attention about his rise to stardom related to his racial identity. Scouts overlooked Lin because he did not meet the hegemonic masculine image of professional athletes. And even after Jeremy Lin became visible in the media, he was met with racist stereotyping about his penis size,[38] much like my male respondents.

One respondent, Annie, a second-generation Filipina American in her twenties, was a varsity track athlete at her university. However, she was not always treated well by her coaches. She recalls being targeted by a coach:

> In high school, I did have a coach, and I really feel like he was a little prejudiced toward me because I'm the Asian girl. He would give me so much shit. He would tell me I need to lose weight, he would always call me out, and people knew what he was doing was wrong. You know, he would belittle me and I'm in high school.

In the world of sport, hegemonic forces are ever present. Racism, sexism, and heterosexism are woven into the structures of sport.[39] Annie is not outside of those forces. She said she gained a great deal of self-confidence and strength from participating in sports, and many studies show that this is a positive outcome for women's and girls' participation in athletics.[40] However, variation from the normalized white, middle-class, male, heterosexual athlete can be accompanied with the problems Annie faced as a racialized body.

Gender Policing in School: Prowess for Men and Beauty for Women

Gender policing in school is another way in which hegemonic ideals can be imposed. k.terumi (kt) is a half-Japanese, half-white American in her thirties who grew up in the Northeast and went to high school in Japan. She identifies as a female-bodied gender queer and prefers not to be referred to as a woman. Her family didn't police her gender growing up. She often wore her older brothers' hand-me-down clothes, and her mother was a tomboy growing up. Her family was not concerned with her gender presentation. However, her classmates were:

> I really believe that most of my gender socialization was carried out by my peers. When I was 10 the girls stopped talking to me cause they thought I was a loser. I asked a friend, "Why doesn't anybody want to be my friend?" And my friend was like, "Well, it's because of how you look." And I was like, "Okay, so I'll grow my hair [long] and wear girls' clothes."

The choices for kt boiled down to matching the expected gender presentation for girls or having few friends in school. Shortly after kt altered her gender presentation, she moved to Japan where she found much less emphasis on distinct gender presentation. Many Japanese girls had short hair and they wore the same school uniforms as the boys in school. The different expectations with regard to gender presentation in the United States versus Japan were abundantly clear to kt.

These ideals exist for men as well. Western constructions of hegemonic masculinity define masculine in contrast to all that is feminine, and there is an obsession with "sexual dimorphism." Constructions of the body, specifically for men, emphasize a size difference with women and among men. The most "ideal" male body should be large, hard, and muscular to demonstrate power and prowess.

The emphasis on sexual dimorphism is not as prevalent in other societies or cultures. In some cases, like the precolonial Yoruba culture, gender did not even exist.[41] There was no such emphasis on the difference between those who possessed male or female sexual organs.[42] For Asian Americans, stereotypes exist that there is less size difference in the male and female physical body. Such assumptions also exist in the case with Native Americans and Latinos. This assumed lack of contrast is particularly evident in height, muscle mass, and body hair. Since a key component of hegemonic masculinity is based on highlighting differences between men and women, this becomes a problem area for Asian Americans living amid Western constructions of masculinity. It stigmatizes Asian American men as subordinate or marginalized because they seem to more closely resemble the size of their female counterparts.

Additionally, hegemonic masculinity requires control over women. Especially in the public sphere, the representation of East Asians does not portray East Asian men as strong heads of household. While this may starkly contrast the reality in these homes, the media portrayal is clear. However, South Asian representations vary quite differently. South Asian men are portrayed in the media as dangerous, terrorists, jihadists, and sexist, oppressive male patriarchs. In some respects they are represented as sexually deviant.[43]

These representations of Asian men are forms of sexual regulation. Patricia Hill Collins asserts, "In order to prosper, systems of oppression must regulate sexuality, and they often do so by manufacturing ideologies that render some ideas commonsensical while obscuring others."[44] There are manufactured ideologies about the Asian American body that have become commonsensical to both Asian and non-Asian Americans. In chattel slavery, African American bodies were commodified. Native American, Latino, and Asian American bodies have also been commodified, used for their labor, and discarded. In this era of what Collins calls the "new racism," these bodies are assaulted by ideologies that are projected by the media and individuals.[45] Daniel, a gay-identified second-generation Vietnamese American, was often bombarded with these racialized fictions:

> I remember swimming on the swim team. I swam competitively, [practicing] four hours a day. Obviously, there's always locker room talk, and my experience with that was kind of negative. I think back on it a lot and how it was desexualizing. It made [Asian men] asexual. I mean,

> obviously there were penis jokes and what not. It was just very blunt.
> Like, "You're Asian, you must have a small penis." And [teammates]
> would laugh at that. It wasn't anything witty; it was just stupid com-
> ments like that. And there were obviously the racial comments, accents,
> jokes like that.

In many interviews, when discussion turned to the body, whites and
other non-Asians seemed to be fixated on Asian and Asian American
genitalia. While the centrality of the penis as a symbol of masculine power is not a new phenomenon, this focus has a specific function to maintain
white supremacy. Stereotypes about penis size normalize the size of
whites (just right) and stigmatize the size of blacks (too big) and Asians
(too small). Asian male bodies have been the targets of disparaging sexual stereotypes as long as they have been a threat to whiteness. The sexuality of men of color is seen as dangerous and in need of control.[46] White-
framed images of African, Latino, Arab, and Desi men portray them as
threateningly hypersexual, but East Asian men are seen as asexual or
hyposexual.[47] This hyposexuality is interconnected with historical labor
patterns, but there is also some discourse shift with emergence of the
"model minority" myth. While the stereotypes have changed over time,
the attempted regulation of East Asian male bodies through the belittle-
ment of their penises has *everything* to do with race, specifically maintaining white supremacy. While "white fear of black sexuality is a basic ingredient of white racism," whites' ridicule of the sexuality of Asian men
is another ingredient.[48]

Hegemonic ideologies and white racial framing continue to thrive because "contemporary forms of oppression do not routinely force people
to submit. Instead, they manufacture consent for domination so that we
lose our ability to question and thus collude in our own subordination."[49]
If Asian Americans adopt hegemonic ideologies as truth, the racial status
quo remains unchallenged. Irwin had a very difficult time conceiving of
himself as a masculine being:

> That was freshman year of high school. I think I had a very un-mascu-
> line body. I was real thin, almost like transgendered in some sense
> because my sense of myself was certainly not that I was macho or very
> masculine at all. It didn't help that when I was very young people
> would think that I was a girl because I had kind of poofy hair. I had a
> hard time even conceiving of Asian men—maybe myself—as being a
> man. I still have a hard time calling myself "man."

Irwin internalized hegemonic ideology about his own body. The hegemonic masculine ideal body is also prevalent in the media. The values
and characteristics assigned to the ideal man in the United States is that
of a white, middle-class heterosexual man. That construction relies on
deviations being constructed as inferior. One respondent, Chance, a Filipino American in his 20s wanted "to be, in the back of my mind, I just

wanted to be *normal*. Just being like a white guy, like on T.V." The normalization of whiteness affects how whites and non-whites view their
own bodies.

Gender, race, and sexuality are largely presented as binary categories:
male/female, white/black, heterosexual/homosexual. This binary thinking
shapes our understanding of human difference in oppositional terms.[50]
Racially, this binary provides little room for Asian Americans. Chance
draws from the white constructions of masculinity to try to define and
understand his own identity.

Similarly, women of all races internalize messages of beauty through
media images. As a result of these normalized ideas of beauty, there is an
obsession with losing weight, the popularity of cosmetic surgery, and
problems with eating disorders. There are limited representations of
Asian American women in the media. The images that do exist are over-
exaggerated, lack diversity, and subordinate to the constructions of an
emphasized or arguably hegemonic femininity associated with white
womanhood. This othering can cause internalized conflict and affect self-
image. Fareena struggled with self-esteem when she went to an all-white
school:

> I remember I hated myself in the sixth grade. Hated myself. And that
> was the time I went to an all-white, very rich school. I remember that
> the type of girls that all the boys started liking didn't look like me, you
> know, being a brown woman. Issues of body hair came into play. I
> have body hair that other girls don't have. I have to pluck my eyebrows
> and other girls don't have to. It looks dirty on me. And there is this
> concept of dirt. I had real issues of just wanting to purge, physically
> purge things out of me. You know, my elbows are darker, my knees are
> darker, when I scar I leave a brown mark instead of a pink mark that
> fades. And all that is looked at as dirty or ugly or scarred and not
> simply like a part of life. And I was also curvier than the other girls at
> the time. I started puberty in the fourth grade. By sixth grade, I didn't
> look a lot different from this. And I felt fat. All the other girls were
> skinny. I felt I didn't have muscles the way the other girls did. I was
> really into sports at the time. And I felt puny and couldn't athletically
> compete like them. And there is an attraction with athletic girls. You
> know, the girls' basketball team or track team. There'd be this camarad-
> erie with the boys' basketball team because we had to travel together
> and do things like that. There are a lot of hookups. No one wanted to
> hookup with the lone brown girl.

Fareena's use of words such as "hated," "dirty," and "ugly" highlight the
internalization of racist constructions of beauty. In contrast to whites,
Fareena occupies the inferior half of the white/non-white binary. African
Americans have greater access to magazines, books, television channels,
and movies that convey the message that "Black is beautiful." Certainly,
there are still hierarchical problems with some of these media sources

involving body size, skin color, and objectification of female bodies, but they do offer alternative ideologies for young African American women. Asian American women do not have easy access to these alternatives, and in the options they do have, largely light-skinned women of East Asian descent are displayed. South Asians Americans have fewer resources. Even with some of the anti-hegemonic resistance movements in black-owned media, white standards of beauty pervade.[51]

Not only did Fareena feel the pain of internalizing white standards of beauty, but she also felt the very real consequences in her personal interactions with others. She was left out as a viable option for dating. This is less frequent in geographical regions such as the West Coast or Hawaii. Those regions allow for the development of stronger counter-frames that may redefine beauty in contrast to the white racial frame. However, there were respondents who resided in those regions who still spoke of a hierarchy of physical features that were considered most attractive.

Relationships become politicized by the meanings assigned to racialized bodies. In this case, Fareena's high school experience with dating or hooking up was affected by the "white habitus." Charlotte, a second-generation Chinese American woman in her forties who grew up in the Southwest, struggled with the limited representations of Asian Americans. The prevalence of the "Suzie Wong" stereotype felt degrading, and her body type did not match. While she rejected those images, she still wanted to fit in with other students at school.

> Assimilation was the name of the game. I remember my friend and I talked about it, and all she wanted to have was blonde hair and blue eyes and to be named, I don't know, Chris or something like that. And all I wanted to have was *regular* brown hair and *regular* brown eyes and to be named Janet. And so we would just talk about how all we wanted to do was be like everybody else.

Charlottes defines "regular" as whiteness. The "blonde hair and blue eyes" and "regular brown hair and regular brown eyes" are white physical traits. By specifying "regular" brown hair and eyes, she is differentiating those features from African Americans who have brown hair and eyes as well. By internalizing racist images of the self, Charlotte becomes a conduit for perpetuating racial oppression.[52] Hegemonic whiteness is disseminated through coercion. Internalizing white racist concepts of beauty is a result of that coercion.

Research supports the narrative of our respondents. The preliminary results of a study done at an elite private university found that Asian American survey respondents had more positive views of their body when they more closely matched white features.[53] Respondents who were taller than the "average Asian" or had the "double eyelids" would point these features out as their favorites.

Sex Ed: Imposed Sexuality

Daniel self-identifies as a gay man. He was conscious of his sexuality in high school, but found that staying closeted perpetuated stereotypes of Asian American men. By not outwardly displaying interest in women, he appeared to be an asexual or homosexual Asian American man. Behaviors like "girl watching" are normalized activities in heterosexual masculine performance.[54] Daniel did not want to participate in those performances, but also did not want to further perpetuate stigmatizing Asian American male stereotypes.

> I hated high school, because of racial expectations mixed with trying to hide sexuality. So, it was tough. I did the whole closet thing where you don't talk about it. But if someone brought it up, it turned uncomfortable. And obviously you try to protect those insecurities by trying to defend your straightness or whatnot. And that was really interesting being Asian American, too. It was almost like trying to balance being straight with being asexual. It was really weird. I was like, "I'm not asexual, but I'm not gay either." It's a weird game you play. In terms of my identity as a gay person, it's very interesting because I can play that privilege of not appearing gay because my race is always written on me.

For Daniel, he cannot mask his race. He must negotiate whether he feels like dealing with homophobia in addition to racism. His dilemma demonstrates how racism and heterosexism rely upon each other for meaning.[55] Part of Asian American oppression is the ability for whites to define their sexuality because "sex is raced and race is sexed."[56] Daniel's race is accompanied with numerous assumptions about his sexuality which further complicated his experience in high school.

Phan, a second-generation Vietnamese American in her thirties from the Northeast in an area with a large population of Asian Americans, found herself in a similar conundrum. Remaining a closeted lesbian reinforced the crude sexual stereotypes of Asian women having "tighter vaginas." Phan lacked interest in the men she dated, and that physical disinterest would become evident during intercourse. Phan was not the only female respondent who had been stereotyped in the same way regarding sexual organs. Like African American women and the emphasis on their posteriors as erotic pleasure zones,[57] Asian American women also become just parts instead of a whole. The focus on the racially "othered" bodies is to produce maximum sexual pleasure for the white men that fetishize them.

For South Asian American women, there are also numerous assumptions and controlling images regarding their sexuality, Indira explains.

> We don't get to be who we are. We're perceived, our identities are perceived, and then placed on us. So when East Asian women experience being overly exotified, it becomes like there's the overtone of a

cunning woman who is going to manipulate you with her exotic ways. And I think South Asian women experience that as well. So, for example, in college I'd get, "Hey, do you know about the *Kama Sutra*? I can *Kama Sutra* you." What does that mean? I think that there's these notions of spirituality and sexuality get intertwined in an erotic way that kind of leads to a hypersexualization of South Asian women.

Externalized hypersexuality of South Asian women greatly contrasts with their home culture. The South Asian community often constructs sex, as Fareena put it, as a "punishment" for women. Sex is not something that is supposed to be enjoyed. It is simultaneously sacred and joyless. Only non-Asian men, mostly white men, would use this pick-up line on Indira. The use of the *Kama Sutra* is directly taken from the white racial framing of Indian women. Frames provide shortcuts and help individuals understand a social situation. It is a simplistic step taken by those who are privileged to see the racial world as one-dimensional and stereotypes as real. The framing of Indian women in the white racial frame is that of a woman well versed in the *Kama Sutra* who is dying to serve men. This is a romanticized, eroticized, exoticized, orientalizing, dehumanizing process for Indira. The *Kama Sutra*, since the colonization of India, has been the "white man's sex manual with 'exotic' women." In the mid-1800s, it was common for English men to have Indian mistresses and "in the British imagination and in their daily lives Indian women were sexualized in ways scholars recognize as the typical colonial gaze: Indian women were defined as seductive, sensual, and exotic."[58]

Sometimes these Western pornographic fantasies manifest in the lives of my respondents. Charlene had an even more intimate and what she calls an "abusive" experience with being exotified:

> When I was in my first two years of college, I was still in a "white identification"[59] stage. I was dating a white man and I became really intimate with him and he really sexually exotified me and called me a "China doll" and did all these things in a way that were sexual and really pertained to my ethnicity. And during that time, I didn't realize it was bad, I didn't realize it was wrong, but I knew that I wasn't happy. I was really, really unhappy for that whole two years. I was so angry and I was so sad. There was a lot of crying for no reason. . . . I thought I really loved this person and I just didn't understand what was going on.

Charlene would dress in cheongsams[60] for fantasy role-playing. She participated because she wanted to please him. Her boyfriend's Asian fantasies were constructed from the "discourses of seduction" that define Asian women's sexuality in the West.[61] These images of Asian women have been reproduced for centuries with little alteration.[62] These fantastical constructions play out in real life, like in Charlene's case. Transnationally, these fantasies are played out with the popularity of sex tourism in

Asia and the Pacific Islands. The intersection and interaction between ethnicity and sexuality, or "ethnosexuality," defines and depends on the other for its meaning and power.[63] Racialized and ethnic meanings have been assigned to Asian bodies and are incorporated in how their sexuality is defined. Charlene was more than a girlfriend to her partner; she was an ethnosexualized body connected to these Western fantasies of Asian women.

Glenn is a gay-identified first-generation Malaysian American in his late thirties who went to college in the Midwest. He spent eighteen years in Malaysia before immigrating and noticed many differences in what was considered acceptable masculine behavior. He shared his observations of the contrasting constructions of men in his home country versus the United States.

> In Malaysia there were adult figures in my life that were obviously questionable [in their sexuality]. But some of them got married and had children. And some of them acted as if they're not gay. They were everywhere, and it was okay to act in a *feminine way*. So there is that contrast between what is acceptable [compared to the United States]. In general, a straight Malaysian man is already gentle and quiet to begin with. Plus, when gay men are not coming out but acting and assumed to be straight, [their characteristics as a "straight man"] contribute to the understanding of what it is to be a man in that culture. It's okay to be feminine. It's okay to be gentle, passive, and not aggressive. But in the U.S., people don't want to be identified as being gay, so they try to act in an overly masculine way. Then that becomes a norm.

Glenn's home-culture frame accepts and even embraces men who are gentle and not overly aggressive. In the United States, he quickly learned that those behaviors were associated with weakness and being gay. In college, Glenn had a gay resident assistant (RA) on his floor. He remembers that other students would write derogatory names, such as "fag," on his door or beside his name on floor billboards. This policing made impressions with Glenn that contrasted with his experience in Malaysia.

IT DOESN'T END AT THE SOUND OF THE SCHOOL BELL: COMMUNITY

Outside of school, Asian Americans continue to face racial and gender discipline and controlling images. Being surrounded by your own race in the home can allow for some breaks from the racialized process. But there is no guarantee for people of color that they will be free from racism when they are out in the community. The interlocking social systems of race, gender, and sexuality further complicate how Asian Americans may be responded to in public. In this section, my interviewees share narratives about their experiences outside of the realms of family and school.

Lessons in, or Testing of, Manhood?

Organizations like the Boy Scouts of America are designed to provide a positive, educational environment for youth and young adults. These types of organizations can be major sites of not only lessons on "proper" or normalized gender scripts but also on racial and sexual scripts as well. Historically, the Boy Scouts of America has been a male-only organization with clearly masculine-oriented activities. However, as of 2009, they have opened up the organization to include girls. I begin this section with the Boy Scouts of America because the organization proclaims that it "is one of the nation's largest and most prominent values-based youth development organizations." Taken directly from their literature, "The Boy Scouts of America provides a program for young people that builds character, trains them in the responsibilities of participating citizenship, and develops personal fitness." [64] Ray was an active scout for several years. He was a hardworking scout that moved up to leadership positions within the organization. However, it was at a cost.

> My scoutmaster was this big, confederate history lover. He had these dumb notions about what black people are supposed to be. Even some of the kids in my troop were fucking racist. They didn't like black people. [The troop] was mostly white, middle to poor white. Then there was me. For the most part, I felt like when I was in boy scouts, for six years, I had to put on an *act*. Like being one of those old-timey Chinese characters in one of those old movies. I disagreed with a lot of what they said, but in the end I just did my own thing. A lot of times I would just agree. Like, "Yessuh, master," or "Okay, I totally agree with you. You're number one. I agree with your confederate views of breaking away with the union" and all this other shit. I was outnumbered. I also felt like they didn't understand enough to be objective.

Ray's description of how he had to "perform" in a servile manner with the scouts eerily mimics the earlier roles of a Chinese houseboy. While he references a fictional character in a movie, that character was based on actual Asian male laborers who attended to wealthy whites. There are also many parallels between the Chinese houseboy and African American domestic servants. Here, Ray was a servile, slave-like appendage of the troop. This was a strategy he used to maintain peace in the troop and refrain from challenging racist ideologies, especially since he was outnumbered. There were sexist and heterosexist elements in the troop as well.

> When I was in Boy Scouts, there were always these dumb folks who I have to show "my tested manhood" to. They do this stupid shit. There's no reason for me to whip out my cock and show how manly I am—not that that ever happened, but it would be almost to that point. and I'm like, "This is really stupid. I know I'm a man. I don't have to show you guys." And as far as the hazing went, whenever they tried, I

> just kicked their ass. I'm not going to take that shit. Eventually, when I
> started, the older kids were like, "Yeah, we're not going to mess with
> him." I got respect from that, I guess. They knew, "Oh, we better not
> fuck with him. He doesn't play around."

Ray would resist direct assault on his masculinity with physical force.
However, he did not contend with more generalized racist ideology.
These all-male environments are perfect breeding grounds for hypermasculine performance. Ray is one of few Asian Americans in my research
who would defend himself against taunts and bullying. It is significant to
note that he moves to action when there is a challenge to his masculinity.
In school, as he states earlier in this chapter, Ray felt unable to retaliate
against racist taunts, but he felt more room to take action in the Boy
Scouts. The Boy Scouts of America supposedly help youth because it "is a
key to building a more conscientious, responsible, and productive society."[65] The lessons Ray learned while a member do not quite align with
that mission.

The hegemonic ideals for men in the United States presently put emphasis on size and sexual dimorphism. Physical size *does* matter; one's
height, weight, and penis size all become measures of manhood. However, it is not all about the largest size being the best. Being too large can be
too intimidating and dangerous. Being too small is weak and un-mascu-
line. Black men are constructed as too physical, too threatening, and their
penises too large. On the opposite end of the spectrum, Asian men are
constructed as too small, too passive, with small penises if they have one
at all. Glenn, who identifies as a gay Malaysian American, has run into
this stereotyping from other gay men when he's out at clubs.

> They usually think that you are small and that black guys are the
> biggest. It happened in [my city] only a few weeks ago. I went to [a
> dance club] and was sitting in the front on the sofas. There was this
> drunk guy sitting next to me. He said "Hi," so I said "Hi." Then he
> said, "I heard about you." I said, "What? What did you hear about
> me?" [whispers] "That you have a small penis."

Alcohol in this situation may have made the commenter less discreet
with his racist stereotypes.[66] But such comments appear to be common.
One white woman who is dating a Vietnamese American man shared
with me that non-Asian men consistently ask her why she chose to be
with him since "his penis must be small." She becomes embarrassed by
the fact that they ask her right in front of her Asian American boyfriend.

Online Relief or Reification?

In January 2010, I ran a keyword search for "Asian" on the online
classified site Craigslist for Boston, in the personals section. It resulted in
almost 350 ads. The language used by individuals seeking an Asian part-

ner was quite notable. These words came up repeatedly: clean, submissive, foreign, and smooth. Asian and Asian American men searching for partners often assured folks that their penises were sizeable. In the "male seeking male" section, the Asian American men advertised themselves as good at "servicing" others and they were "faithful bottoms." These ads demonstrate how these constructed racist images are being performed and played out into the real world, becoming internalized, embodied, and enacted. Some of the terms and requests that were present in the ads include "Asian Angel" and seeking someone "smooth and hairless." A married couple sought an Asian woman who "must be shy and soft spoken." Another ad poster claimed, "I am into Asian women who are submissive." More specific examples of the sexually charged, racialized ads follow:

> Title: White Guy in Search of Asian lover
> I had one a few months ago and I must say, nothing beats the soft skin and warm tight pussy of a cute Asian girl. I'm not looking for something real serious, just a little treat every now and then. But I'm really only looking for Asians on here. I have a few white fuck buddies, just need some extra spice. I'm very careful with sex, always safe, get tested regularly, would hope you do too. Looking for authentic Asian, or Asian American is ok too. Even better if you're around my college! So if you're Asian and horny, put "your Asian princess" in the subject line.
> Title: Man Seeking Demure Young Asian Woman
> Professional man, fit, erudite, handsome, successful; seeks young Asian woman with limited sexual experience, and who wants to be introduced to the erotic world, and fully realize her sexual potential. I am gentle, passionate, experienced, attentive, and very well endowed.

Other ads were specifically looking for "foreign" woman, and some men posting were "tired of American women." The younger, the better as one man searched for an Asian "College age girl with daddy issues" and "Foreign exchange student a big plus." Craigslist has become a site where individuals can anonymously pursue their most secret sexual fantasies, but it is also a direct reflection of the social inequality and sexual stereotyping that exists outside of cyberspace.[67]

Most of the Craigslist advertisements were for gay relationships. Many were from older white men looking for Asian men. One was seeking an Asian "House/Slave boy." This "masculine strict daddy" was looking for a "submissive, obedient, smooth Asian or Latino boy" wanting his "slave" to be smaller in stature. There were a number of ads asking for their "fantasies" to be fulfilled. One man wanted a smooth, "naturally non-hairy. One [sic] of my favorite fantasies is that my friend have a naturally non-hairy tummy and not very hairy chest (like Asian/Chinese descended, a plus)." "Smooth" was an adjective used over and again. One asked for a "Smooth boy to be molested." This same poster specifically requested Asian in the title and in the text of the ad again and said,

"Asian is an emphatic plus." In the "male for male" section, many white men were looking to dominate Asian bottoms.

Ads by Asians and Asian Americans sometimes utilized these stereotypes to sell themselves to potential partners. A multiracial Hawaiian/Asian man was looking for a "nice sexy daddy." One Asian poster had a fantasy to be "dominated" and "pimped out" to other men. Asian men were looking for "bigger," "older," and "hairier" men. One even called himself a potential "slave" for someone. When doing a search of the words "white" and "slave" only two ads came up. One was from a white woman looking to be dominated, and another was a white man looking for a woman to dominate him. One Asian man advertised himself as a "little Asian boy" looking to "service masculine cock." His request to service a "masculine cock" would imply that some "cocks" are unmasculine—perhaps his own would fit that category since he infantilizes himself in the ad. Even an Asian lesbian described herself as "a beautiful Asian doll looking to have fun with white or Latin ladies." In the course of my research, I came across four ads from Asian American lesbians that openly said they did not find Asians attractive.

Studies have shown that there is racial discrimination in online dating.[68] Asian American men are the least popular with women. The Craigslist ads are an example of the adoption of racist stereotyping by Asian and non-Asian Americans alike. The advertisements are indicative of age-old racist stereotyping of Asians in the United States. Michael Booth asserts that critics of these types of ads on Craigslist think the format of the anonymous forum "encourages troubled minds."[69] Craigslist allows false racist images and stereotypes that are only present in the mind of "sick individuals" to be publicly displayed. However, Booth's article does not fully capture the widespread systemic issues that are related to institutional discrimination. Certainly, individuals are solely responsible for the content of their ads, but Craigslist posters are pulling thoughts, feelings, and narratives from the white racial frame. Slave and "houseboy" imagery is a not-so-distant historical reality for Asian American men in the United States. Fetishized images of submissive Asian women persist in cyberspace.

MEDIA MATTERS: WIDESPREAD WHITE HEGEMONIC FRAMING

I think in America, in the culture, men have to be muscular, macho, manly, aggressive, tough, and brave. I think there's a pressure for people [men]to act that way no matter what. —Glenn, Malaysian American

Jean Baudrillard argues that in modern society, reality and meaning have been replaced with symbols and signs.[70] Culture and media have created our perceived reality, which has become more real than reality itself.[71]

We have become so reliant on the simulation of reality, or *simulacra*, that we have lost contact with the real world.[72] Contemporary media (TV, film, print, and the Internet) are proliferated, mass-produced copies of the language and ideology used to obscure reality for dominant and politically powerful groups.[73] Respondents look to the media to help explain and make sense of their world. What they often find is that faces like theirs are missing in the media. When images are present in the media, Asian Americans are often in supporting roles, or the portrayals are the same exaggerated racist stereotypes. Greg, a third-generation Japanese American in his 40s who grew up in Hawaii and on the West Coast areas with large Asian populations, observes:

> You don't see anybody in the media who looks like us. The strongest representation would be the exoticized Asian female. The Lucy Liu sex bitch. The images of the demasculinity of the Asian American males. We're still battling the Long Duk Dong from *Sixteen Candles*. Bruce Lee was fabulous, but that just opened up another stereotype, and now everyone's Kung Fu Fighting.

There is a limited representation of Asian Americans in the media.[74] These images are consumed by the viewers, constructing and defining who Asian Americans are supposed to be. Whites and non-whites buy into the idea that these images are real. Noteworthy is that Greg grew up in areas of the country with large populations of Asian Americans. Those regions have the benefit of having community centers and political organizations for many different Asian American groups that could help individuals develop counter frames, but the lack of images in the media is still a signifier of racial inequality to Greg.

In later chapters, we see how these images play out in the lives of my respondents as they try to define themselves and have relationships with others. These media images deliver messages about gender and sexuality as well. Brent, a second-generation Chinese American in his 30s who grew up in the South, observes:

> Women fit some image of Asian in white Western society, the exotic hottie. That sort of thing doesn't exist for Asian men in the Western world; there are no sorts of Asian men sex symbols. Asians in the media, they don't occupy that sort of role. You might as well not even have a *dick* here sometimes.

Brent's comment demonstrates the centralization of the small penis stereotype that plagues Asian and Asian American men. White supremacy begets controlling sexual images of people of color and for Asian American men the stigma persists about a supposed inadequacy of their sexual organs. David Eng contends that it is imperative to take Asian American men's racial formation into account to understand how their sexuality has been constructed. There is a racial castration process that takes place where Asian American men are stripped of all sexual elements. Even in the porn industry, they are searching for their penises.[75] The East Asian American representation is far from complimentary; however, even more alarming is the almost complete lack of representation of Southeast, South Asian and Pacific Islander Americans in the media.

CONCLUSION

My respondents have provided evidence that, outside of individual interactions, white habitus— the "racialized uninterrupted socialization process that conditions and creates whites' racial tastes, perceptions, feelings, and emotions and their views on racial matters"[76]—thrives throughout larger institutions, even when those larger institutions are multiracial. White habitus socializes people of color as well through the powerful nature of hegemonic framing. Whether they are in school, participating in extracurricular activities, at the movies, or in nightclubs they are constantly under the gaze of Western eyes. Male respondents faced more physically violent threats than the female respondents because of the constructions of hegemonic masculinity, and they are constructed as asexual or hyposexual. Asian American women, on the other hand, fulfill an exotic pornographic fantasy. These constructions, while they have an intangible and immeasurable effect on individuals, also have real-life affects on sexual politics. The white racial frame creates parameters on beauty and desirability, determining who the desirable partners are and what kind of characteristics they should possess.

The next two chapters compare and contrast Asian American men and women's ethnosexual experiences. In chapter 4, I discuss the experiences of Asian American women and how their self-image, self-esteem, and identity are shaped by and in opposition to racist imagery. In chapter 5, I focus primarily on Asian American men and how they are positioned in a white hegemonic masculine hierarchy.

NOTES

1. Joe R. Feagin, *The White Racial Frame: Centuries of Racial Framing and Counter-Framing* (New York: Routledge, 2009).

2. Antonio Gramsci, *Selections from the Prison Notebooks,* trans. and ed. Q. Hoare and G. N. Smith (New York: International Publishers, 1971).

3. R. W. Connell and James W. Messerschmidt. "Hegemonic Masculinity: Rethinking the Concept." *Gender and Society* 19, no. 6 (2005): 829–59, esp. 832.

4. Connell and Messerschmidt, "Hegemonic Masculinity," 832.

5. Anthony S. Chen, "Lives at the Center of the Periphery, Lives at the Periphery of the Center: Chinese American Masculinities and Bargaining with Hegemony," *Gender and Society* 13 (1999): 584–607.

6. Connell and Messerschmidt, "Hegemonic Masculinity," 832.

7. Connell and Messerschmidt, "Hegemonic Masculinity," 835.

8. R. W. Connell and James W. Messerschmidt, "Hegemonic Masculinity," in *Gender Inequality*, ed. Judith Lorber (New York: Oxford University Press, 2009).

9. Connell and Messerschmidt, "Hegemonic Masculinity," 839.

10. Connell and Messerschmidt, "Hegemonic Masculinity," 834.

11. Connell and Messerschmidt, "Hegemonic Masculinity," 844.

12. Connell and Messerschmidt, "Hegemonic Masculinity," 840.

13. Barrie Thorne, *Gender Play: Girls and Boys in School* (New Brunswick, NJ: Rutgers University Press, 1993).

14. Thorne, *Gender Play*.

15. Michael Kimmel and Matthew Mahler, "Adolescent Masculinity, Homophobia, and Violence: Random School Shootings," *American Behavioral Scientist* 46, no. 10 (2003): 1439–58.

16. Susan Donaldson Jame, "When Words Can Kill: 'That's So Gay,'" ABC News, July 2, 2009, http://abcnews.go.com/Health/MindMoodNews/story?id=7328091& page=1.

17. Rebecca Cathcart, "Boy's Killing Labeled a Hate Crime, Stuns a Town," *New York Times*, February 23, 2008, http://www.nytimes.com/2008/02/23/us/23oxnard.html.

18. Kimmel and Mahler, "Adolescent Masculinity."

19. For more extensive discussion of this racial discrimination in schools, including those on the West Coast, see Rosalind S. Chou and Joe R. Feagin, *The Myth of the Model Minority: Asian Americans Facing Racism*, (Boulder, CO: Paradigm Publishers, 2008).

20. Allie Grasgreen, "The Mocked Minority," *Inside Higher Ed.Com.*, March 22, 2011.

21. Alexandra Wallace, "Asians in the Library," http://www.youtube.com/watch?v=FNuyDZevKrU, March 2011.

22. Wallace, "Asians in the Library."

23. Wallace, "Asians in the Library."

24. Jackson Katz, "Ways of the Badass," in *Men's Lives*, 7th ed., ed. Michael Kimmel and Michael Messner (Boston: Allyn & Bacon, 2007), 549–74.

25. Jordan Ellen and Angela Cowan, "Warrior Narratives in the Kindergarten Classroom: Renegotiating the Social Contract? " in *Men's Lives*, 7th ed., ed. Michael S. Kimmel and Michael A. Messner (Boston: Allyn & Bacon, 2007), 272–83.

26. Judith Butler, "Imitation and Gender Insubordination," in *Inside/Out: Lesbian Theories, Gay Theories*, ed. Diana Fuss (New York: Routledge, 1991), 13–31.

27. Joe Feagin, *Racist America: Roots, Current Realities, and Future Reparations* (New York: Routledge, 2000).

28. Peter Lyman, "The Fraternal Bond as a Joking Relationship: A Case Study of the Role of Sexist Jokes in Male Group Bonding," in *Men's Lives*, 7th ed., ed. Michael S. Kimmel and Michael A. Messner (Boston: Allyn & Bacon, 2007), 153–62.

29. Claire Jean Kim, "The Racial Triangulation of Asian Americans," *Politics and Society* 27 (March 1999): 105–38; and Claire Jean Kim, *Bitter Fruit: The Politics of Black-Korean Conflict in New York City* (New Haven, CT: Yale University Press, 2003).

30. Kim, *Bitter Fruit*; Chou and Feagin, *Myth of the Model Minority*.

31. Debra Van Ausdale and Joe R. Feagin, *The First R: How Children Learn Race and Racism* (Lanham, MD: Rowman & Littlefield Press, 2001); Chou and Feagin, *Myth of the Model Minority*.

32. Derrick Bell, *Silent Covenants: Brown v. Board of Education and the Unfulfilled Hopes for Racial Reform* (New York: Oxford University Press, 2004).

33. Patricia Hill Collins, *Black Feminist Thought: Knowledge, Consciousness, and the Politics of Empowerment*, 2nd ed. (New York: Routledge, 2000).

34. Leslie Houts Picca and Joe R. Feagin, *Two-Faced Racism: Whites in the Backstage and Frontstage* (New York: Routledge, 2007).

35. Chou and Feagin, *Myth of the Model Minority*.

36. Abraham Kardiner and Lionel Ovesey, *The Mark of Oppression: Explorations in the Personality of the American Negro* (Cleveland: World Publishing, 1962); William H. Grier and Price M. Cobbs, *Black Rage* (New York: Bantam Books, 1968); Joe R. Feagin and

Karyn D. McKinney, *The Many Costs of Racism* (Lanham, MD: Rowman & Littlefield, 2003); Rosalind S. Chou and Joe R. Feagin's *The Myth of the Model Minority*.

37. See Michael Messner, "Boyhood, Organized Sports, and the Construction of Masculinities," in *Sociology: Exploring the Architecture of Everyday Life*, ed. David M. Newman and Jodi A. O'Brien (Newbury Park, CT: Pine Forge Press, 1990); Pat Griffin, "Changing the Game: Homophobia, Sexism, and Lesbians in Sport," in *Contemporary Sociology: An Anthology*, 5th ed., ed. D. Stanley Eitzen (New York: MacMillan Press, 1996).

38. Sportswriter Jason Whitlock tweeted that after a New York Knicks win, "Some lucky lady in NYC is gonna feel a couple inches of pain tonight." From Kelly Dwyer, "Jason Whitlock Apologizes for His Unfunny Jeremy Lin Comment on Twitter," Yahoo! Sports, http://sports.yahoo.com/blogs/nba-ball-dont-lie/jason-whitlock-apolo-gizes-unfunny-jeremy-lin-twitter-145934497.html, accessed March 2012.

39. Dwyer, "Jason Whitlock."

40. Sara Pedersen and Edward Seidman, "Team Sports Achievement and Self-Esteem Development among Urban Adolescent Girls," *Psychology of Women Quarterly* 28, no. 4 (2004): 412–22.

41. Oyeronki Oyewumi, *The Invention of Women: Making an African Sense of Western Gender Discourses* (St. Paul: University of Minnesota Press, 1997).

42. Oyewumi, *Invention of Women*.

43. Jiwani and Dakoury, "Veiling Differences: Mediating Race, Gender, and Nation."

44. Collins, *Black Sexual Politics*, 36.

45. Collins, *Black Sexual Politics*, 36.

46. Collins, *Black Sexual Politics*, 36.

47. Joane Nagel, *Race, Ethnicity, and Sexuality* (New York: Oxford University Press, 2003).

48. Collins, *Black Sexual Politics*.

49. Collins, *Black Sexual Politics*, 50.

50. Collins, *Black Sexual Politics*.

51. Kiri Davis, *A Girl Like Me* (New York: Media Matters, 2005).

52. Collins, *Black Feminist Thought*.

53. Kristen Lee and Simon Ho, "Asian American Sexual Politics" (unpublished manuscript, 2011).

54. Beth A. Quinn. "Sexual Harassment and Masculinity: The Power and Meaning of 'Girl Watching,'" *Gender and Society* 16, no. 3 (2002): 386–402.

55. Collins, *Black Sexual Politics*.

56. Nagel, *Race, Ethnicity, and Sexuality.*

57. Collins, *Black Sexual Politics*.

58. Nagel, *Race, Ethnicity, and Sexuality*, 151.

59. Charlene is referencing the J. Kim article, "The Process of Asian American Identity Development," in *Multicultural Counseling Competencies: Individual and Organizational Development*, ed. Sue et al. (Thousand Oaks, CA: Sage Productions, 1998).

60. The cheongsam is a body-hugging, one-piece Chinese dress for women.

61. Lynn Thiesmeyer, "The West's 'Comfort Women' and the Discourses of Seduction," in *Transnational Asia Pacific: Gender Culture, and the Public Sphere*, ed. Shirley G. Lim, Larry E. Smith, and Wimal Dissanayake (Urbana: University of Illinois Press, 1999).

62. Thiesmeyer, "The West's 'Comfort Women'"; Prasso, *The Asian Mystique*.

63. Nagel, *Race, Ethnicity, and Sexuality*.

64. Taken from the Boys Scouts of America website, http://www.scouting.org/.

65. Boy Scouts website.

66. Houts Picca and Feagin, *Two-Faced Racism*.

67. Michael Booth, "Craigslist Develops a Dark Side," *Denver Post*, January 4, 2007, http://www.denverpost.com/breakingnews/ci_7627735.

68. Cynthia Feliciano, Belinda Robnett, and Golnaz Komaie, "Gendered Racial Exclusion among White Internet Daters," *Social Science Research* 38, no. 1 (2009): 39–54.

69. Booth, "Craigslist Develops a Dark Side."

70. Jean Baudrillard, *Selected Writings,* trans. Jacques Mourrain and ed. Mark Poster (Cambridge: Polity, 1988).

71. Paul Hegarty, *Jean Baudrillard: Live Theory* (London: Continuum, 2004).

72. Hegarty, *Jean Baudrillard.*

73. Hegarty, *Jean Baudrillard.*

74. Jackson Katz, *Tough Guise: Violence, Media and the Crisis in Masculinity* (New York: Challenging Media, 1999).

75. Richard Fung, "Looking For My Penis: The Eroticized Asian in Gay Video Porn," in *A Companion to Asian American Studies,* ed. Kent A. Ono (Malden, MA: Blackwell, 2005), 235–53.

76. Eduardo Bonilla-Silva, *Racism without Racists: Color-Blind Racism and the Persistence of Racial Inequality in the United States* (Lanham, MD: Rowman & Littlefield, 2003), 104.

FOUR

Asian American Women

Self-Image, Self-Esteem, and Identity

"Beauty" is a normative value that is socially constructed.[1] Oppressive hegemonic beauty standards "repress women's freedom, inhibit personal power and self-acceptance, and promote a destructive relationship with the body."[2] These beauty standards are unattainable and are used to punish women physically and psychologically for their failure to achieve and conform to them.[3] All women are subjected to these imposed hegemonic beauty standards, and scholars debate whether women's "body work" (through exercise, make-up, cosmetic surgery, etc.) functions as empowerment or collusion to the oppressive system.[4] However, scholarly work that insists on individual agency (through women's "body work") risks complicity with "neo-liberal emphasis on individual choice, and diverts attention from the political economy of corporate domination."[5] Women's bodies are a location for patriarchal power to be exercised by using disciplining media images to encourage conformity.

For women of color this process becomes more complex. Hegemonic beauty standards are imposed upon all women, but they do not affect women in the same capacity. Women of color, when subjecting their bodies to racialized "body work" (e.g., skin whitening, cosmetic surgery to "whiten" features), are unquestioningly responding to forces of *racial* domination in addition to gender domination. Hegemonic beauty standards affect women of color in the interpersonal domain. In this chapter, my respondents detail their adoption of, responses to, and resistance to the ethnosexualized construction of Asian and Asian American women in the United States.

HEGEMONIC OR EMPHASIZED FEMININITY?

Some scholars agree that femininity is undertheorized in the current literature.[6] There are some definitions of femininity that have been theorized. Pyke and Johnson, Mimi Schippers, and others use the term *hegemonic femininity*. Connell chooses the term *emphasized femininity* to describe what is usually equated with white, heterosexual, middle-class women.[7] *Subordinate(d)* or *pariah femininities* are femininities associated with sexually transgressive women, such as lesbian, bisexual, and nonmonogamous women.[8] *Marginalized femininities* are femininities associated with women of color or poor or working-class women.[9] These scholars assert that other axes of domination must be taken into consideration when theorizing femininity, "such as race, class, sexuality, and age. These other axes mold a hegemonic or emphasized femininity that is venerated and extolled in the dominant culture, and that emphasizes the superiority of some women over others, thereby privileging white upper-class women."[10] Whether using the term "emphasized" or "hegemonic" to describe white femininity, these scholars agree that there is a hierarchy of femininity.

Pyke and Johnson call attention to intersecting identities that complicate the relationship between women. Pyke and Johnson assert:

> white women are constructed as monolithically self-confident, independent, assertive, and successful—characteristics of white hegemonic femininity. That these are the same ruling traits associated with hegemonic masculinity, albeit in a less exaggerated, feminine form, underscores the imitative structure of hegemonic femininity. That is, the supremacy of white femininity over Asian femininity mimics hegemonic masculinity.[11]

Pyke and Johnson are not arguing that hegemonic femininity and masculinity are "equivalent structures. Hegemonic masculinity as superstructure of domination, hegemonic femininity is confined to power relations among women."[12] However, they assert that the two structures are interrelated so that hegemonic femininity serves, upholds, and supports hegemonic masculinity.[13] In essence, a hierarchy of femininity must exist to help in the maintenance of hegemonic masculinity.

There are hegemonic beauty standards. My respondents speak openly about how they are constructed in *contrast* to white women. They internalize messages of inadequacy and inferiority. These messages are reinforced by media and in everyday interactions. In the previous chapter, it was evident that the playground behavior of girls and women to maintain hierarchy operates very differently than for boys and men. Asian American women in my sample did not face the persistent violent physical threats that Asian American men had to endure. However, the emphasis on beauty and the body is a form of symbolic violence.[14] The bodies of Asian American women are under constant scrutiny. I acknowledge that all women's bodies are under constant scrutiny, but white women are awarded psychological and material privileges unavailable to women of color. White women are not the dominant power in political, social, or economic systems, but they do have access to resources unavailable to women of color.

Pyke and Johnson argue, "The construction of a hegemonic femininity not only (re)creates a hierarchy that privileges white women over Asian American women but also makes Asian American women available for white men. In this way, hegemonic femininity serves as a handmaiden to hegemonic masculinity."[15] Indeed, women of color face controlling images when the media places a fantastical pornographic gaze upon them, making them targets of white men; but white women are not exempt from that same gaze. Within the context of male dominant gender roles, femininity is, by definition, a position of subordination in relation to masculinity.[16]

While more research continues to further theorize femininity, it is clear that white women have access to resources and privileges that women of color do not. While constructed by white male desire, the template for the feminine beauty standard is a *white woman*. White men defend white women's honor against men of color who may "corrupt" them. Women of color's bodies are commodified and are available for white male consumption. These hegemonic sexist and gendered ideologies have an effect on Asian American women.

SELF-IMAGE

There have been numerous social science research studies measuring self-image and self-esteem as they relate to social inequality. Most famously, from 1939 to the mid-1950s, psychologists Kenneth and Mamie Clark performed experiments with black children ages six and nine. The Clarks used two dolls, one white and one black, and instructed the children to show which doll they like best or would most like to play with, then which doll is the "nice" doll and which looks "bad," then which doll looks like a white child and which doll looks like a "Negro" child, and finally which doll the children thought looked like them.[17]

The last question was often difficult for the children because, at that point, most black children had picked the black doll as the "bad" one. In past tests, however, many children would refuse to pick either doll and some would start crying and run away. The Clarks gave the test to children in different parts of the country and found that black children who went to segregated schools were more likely to pick the white doll as the nice one. The Clarks served as expert witnesses in several school desegregation cases, including *Briggs v. Elliott*, which was later combined into

Brown v. Board of Education(1954). In 1950, 44 percent of respondents said
the white doll looked like them, and when the children were asked to
color a picture of themselves, most chose a shade of brown markedly
lighter than themselves. In 2005, Kiri Davis repeated the experiment in
Harlem for her film *A Girl Like Me*.[18] She asked twenty-one children the
same questions, and 71 percent responded that the white doll was the
"nice" one. The most powerful image occurs at the end of the video when
a young black girl has answered that the white doll is nice. Davis asks her
to show her the doll that looks like her. The girl hesitates, almost grab-
bing the white doll, but then she begrudgingly moves to the black doll.
Instead of picking it up, she pushes it away. In 2009, after Barack Obama
became president, ABC simulated the test on their show *Good Morning
America*, asking nineteen African American children from Norfolk, Virginia, similar questions but allowed "both" and "neither" as acceptable
responses.[19] They also asked the last question, "Give me the doll that
looks like you," first, which is a stark contrast to the Clark and Davis
studies. Eighty-eight percent of the children said the black doll looked
most like them. ABC added a question, "Which doll is pretty?" The boys
said both, but 47 percent of the black girls said the white doll was the
pretty one.[20]

While the Clark data emphasized the impact of segregation on the
self-image of the children questioned, the contemporary Davis study reveals that racism still affects self-image, regardless of formal legal equality awarded by civil rights legislation. The difficult task is to quantify the
impact racism, sexism, and homophobia has on individuals' psyches. The
Clark and Davis studies, even the 2009 ABC version, provide conclusive
data that racist ideals, messages, and images are still affecting children of
color and thus affecting how they view themselves.

Post–civil rights era racism has largely shifted from blatant and direct
forms to a more elusive and, arguably, more dangerous form. It appears
in what Bonilla-Silva calls a color-blind discourse,[21] appearing less frequently in what Houts Picca and Feagin call the "front stage"[22] and what
Collins calls "the new racism."[23] The media play a central role in the era
of new racism. The media infiltrates our subconscious as a coercive force
in enforcing and maintaining hegemonic ideals. Media scholar Jean Kilbourne argues that

> advertising is the foundation of the mass media. The primary purpose
> of mass media is to sell products. The media does sell products but it
> also sells other things like values, images, concepts of love and sexual-
> ity. . . it also sells ideas of normalcy. Advertising tells us who we are
> and who we should be. . . . . It's part of a cultural climate in which
> women are seen as things, as objects.[24]

The media are a conduit for white hegemonic beauty standards, uphold-
ing hierarchical order. My respondents get these messages directly from

media and from family who have been influenced by hegemonic beauty standards, as Charlene, a second-generation Chinese American introduced in previous chapters, illustrates.

> When I was growing up, I always thought I was fat. I just always thought that I was a chubby kid. And I know I wasn't; I remember getting ready for this middle school dance in the eighth grade, and putting on clothes with my girlfriends, who are all white, and they said, "Oh, Charlene! Charlene's the skinniest one." I was like, "No I'm not. I'm fat." And my mom would always tell me stories about when she was my age she weighed 41 kilograms, which is about 88 pounds. And I was like, "Oh my gosh, I'm a cow. I am huge." And I always saw other Asian American women and girls around me who were just effortlessly skinny. I always thought about weight, always, always thought about it. I thought that because of my mom's stories about how she looked and weighed, I thought that to be Asian American you had to be skinny and petite. And that's what you see. You don't see any larger or even normal body size Asian American women. Like Lucy Liu is tiny. Lisa Ling, I love her, but she's also tiny. Sandra Oh, she's tiny. They're just toothpicks.

Elite, white men largely control media. Images of Asian American women are limited to the same type of women that fulfill the fantastical desires of those white men. These manufactured images influence the desires of men and manifest in real-life relationships. Whites, especially girls and women, also face images of rail-thin models and actresses in the media, and studies have shown a correlation between these media and eating disorders.[25] However, there is greater diversity of white images in the media,[26] offering alternative body types, and whites are at the center of the size acceptance movement.[27]

As mentioned in the previous chapter, Charlene was involved in a relationship with a white man who fetishized her. He fueled her insecurity about her body image, telling her that her "belly got really big" after she ate. This upset Charlene even more, and her struggles with body image reached a dangerous point.

> All of that [struggle with body image] came to fruition in my last semester with college, because in 2007 I went on this crazy bike trip to Alaska. And I was working out, and it was so fun. It gave me endorphins and I was really thin. If I didn't work out, I'd get upset and blow up at people. And I saw a counselor who said, "You need to eat." And I was like, "No." I thought it would change my ability. It does because you don't see any Asian American role models that are different.

Charlene, like many women in the United States, became consumed with reaching an ideal body type that it became almost self-destructive. Besides body size and weight, Charlene has also had issues with her hair. With the limited number of Asians or Asian Americans she would see in the media, they all had straight, sleek hair. Her hair is somewhat wavy and that seemed out of the ordinary to her, even though many Asians have wavy or curly hair. The singular representations in American media do not represent any other kinds of hair. In addition, her mother insisted that she be careful not to get too much sun.

> Mom always wanted me to stay out of the sun. White skin is more beautiful, and [she'd say], "Don't get dark, you need to wear a hat, wear a long sleeve shirt. Don't be in the sun. Because dark is ugly." Well, she always brags about how her mom had really beautiful porcelain white skin. I was like, "Great. Awesome. Thanks, Grandma." And now I don't want to be pasty—I'm healthy. I'm in the sun, and so whatever feels good feels good. My mom felt that need [to be pale]. But I never felt the need to be white. I think I knew that was messed up from the beginning.

There is a history of colorism favoring lighter skin in some Asian countries. There are class elements to this colorism, as those who did not have to work long hours out in the fields were lighter skinned and thus lighter skin denoted greater wealth. In India, there are hierarchies of skin color. While British colonization has also presumably played a role, emphasis on lighter skin does pre-date the British invasion.[28] However, there is a multibillion-dollar skin-whitening industry in Asia that has exploded and accompanied globalized media images. Research has shown that Asians and Asian Americans have adopted white beauty standards.[29]

The preference for lighter skin is not reserved for people of East and South Asian descent. Conflict and colorism throughout the continent of Asia is prevalent. Jessica, a second-generation Vietnamese American in her twenties who grew up in the Southwest, explains:

> You see, Vietnamese people are an interesting kind of Southeast Asian. They are Southeast Asian, but they *think* they are East Asian and they really want to be, they really do. So many of us are really light and want to be Chinese. Because Chinese people are lighter, they have this superiority complex sometimes. And we want to be part of that. It's depressing to be a Vietnamese person sometimes, because the history connected to us is a war-torn people in a developing country—poor rice patties. That's what you think of when you think of Vietnamese. I don't blame the people for having this other kind of, "We are more sophisticated, we have more money, we have this, we have that," and buying into that need. And when you're lighter you can fake that.

Economically and sociopolitically, there is stratification among Asian nations. The different immigration circumstances of Asians in the United States are often overlooked.[30] Many Asians of East and South Asian descent immigrated as part of an "intellectual migration" that began in the 1950s, a "brain drain" of scholars leaving those areas for the United States. The "model minority" stereotype emerged in this era, from this select group of immigrants and second- and third-generation Japanese

Americans after internment during World War II.[31] The immigrants from many Southeast Asian nations, like Laos, Cambodia, Thailand, and Vietnam, were refugees from war and conflict. Refugees had access to fewer resources than the East Asian immigrants. Helena, a second-generation Korean American in her thirties who grew up in the West, recalls an interaction as a young girl with a Vietnamese American girl:

> I would usually play hopscotch by myself, but one day the Vietnamese girl was watching me and so I invited her to play. We started playing after school together. And then one day she finally told me that she was Vietnamese, and it was like this *big secret* that she unloaded, and . . . unfortunately the very next day I had a dentist appointment, right after school. So I told her I couldn't play because I had a dentist appointment, and she got this look on her face. Now I know she just thought I was brushing her off. I went to the dentist, and the day after, I waited out and she was not there; she never came by again. I hope that she doesn't think, "Oh, there was this terrible traumatic incident from my youth, when I told someone I was Vietnamese and she shunned me."

Helena became very quiet at this point in the interview. She spoke of remorse that remained after more than twenty years because she might have further stigmatized the girl she befriended. Helena had articulated earlier in the interview that she had experienced racist incidents growing up that were painful, and to have perhaps accidentally inflicted that feeling on another young Asian American girl was quite uncomfortable.

The singular representation of Asians and Asian Americans in the media is centered on people of East Asian descent. "Model minority" stereotyping is primarily focused on East and now South Asian Americans. Southeast Asian Americans are often left out. Their circumstances for immigration are also different then the Asian Americans associated with "model minority" status.[32] Eduardo Bonilla-Silva theorizes a tri-racial model of racial stratification where Southeast Asian Americans are categorized as "collective blacks."[33] For Asian American women, the umbrella term used for the entire group does not adequately describe the racial stratification that exists with different ethnicities.

The few advertising and media images that exist of Asian American women promote one image of Asian American beauty: that of East Asian descent. Kilbourne asks, "What does advertising tell us about women? Most importantly, it tells women how we look. It tells us that we should spend time and money to look a certain way and if we don't we should feel ashamed and guilty when we fail. Failure is inevitable."[34] Fareena, a Bangladeshi American, recalls,

> I still remember looking at Victoria's Secret models in magazines and thinking, "Their thighs don't touch. I'm fat." The cool thing about my school was the curvier you were, the more it was okay. You would get made fun of if you had a flat butt or you were teeny tiny. My school

had this really alternate idea of what was beautiful. Nobody else needed any confirmation from what was in the media to believe in it, but I was really conflicted between the two. I liked both [ideals]. Every now and then I thought, "I'm going on a diet." I don't know why because now, looking back, I was 110–115 pounds. I'm 140 now, and I'm really comfortable with my weight, which drives my mom nuts. Nuts because my butt is now 40 inches. I'm fine with it because I work a really high-stress job. I'm trying to eat healthy, and I know I have to make slow adjustments. But still it looks cute on me, so I don't have a problem with it.

Fareena had a unique experience compared to other respondents because the counter-frame "Black is Beautiful" was prevalent in her school. African Americans, unlike Asian Americans, have a counter-frame and an established community that help them combat the pressures of hegemonic beauty standards. There are still problems in the African American community that are heteronormative—an emphasis on lighter skin and hair straightening—but the a strong counter-frame exists.

Because of the scarce media images, it's difficult for Asian Americans to create alternative meanings and values about their bodies. While Fareena's understanding of the standard beauty was not necessarily that of a white woman, she still found it difficult to see beauty exemplified as an Asian body. Jessica notes,

> You know what people think is beautiful, and you don't know how to be that. I didn't know how to put on eye shadow right, because they only teach you how to put on eye shadow if you only have a certain shape of eye in a magazine. And if you don't have that eye, how do you put on eye shadow? You look for models in the magazines that have your eyes so you can do it like them, and none of them have your eye. So it's nothing that one person does. But you know how different you are, and it's hard to reconcile it.

There is little diversity in the representations of female beauty in American media. White women are the standard for beauty in the United States, and even many white women fail to meet the ideal. With the emphasis on the beauty of a mythical white femininity in the media, Asian American women, along with most all women, can feel abnormal and unattractive. For women of color, the racialized aspect of beauty politics functions to maintain white supremacy. White women are awarded a psychological wage of whiteness when self-assessing their beauty.

How do Asian American women deal with the controlled sexuality that was detailed in chapter 2? Parents fear their daughters will fall prey to sexual predators, but they also incorporate racialized, gendered, and heterosexualized norms into the policing of their daughters. It can be taxing for Asian American women to battle with both their family expectations and outside pressures. For Fareena, a Bangladeshi American introduced in earlier chapters, she had some experience with some help-ful counter-framing throughout her life. She spent some time at a largely black and Latino high school where standards of beauty were not solely based on whiteness. With her family pulling from a home-culture frame, they often disallowed her to groom in order to protect her sexuality. However, Fareena was able to get some say and independence; when her cousins in Bangladesh were allowed to groom their eyebrows, her moth-er allowed her as well, which proved to be quite liberating. Fareena started buying makeup, but needed a guide. She was able to find Tyra Banks's book, *Tyra's Beauty Inside and Out*[35] at a local bookstore.

> There were pictures of all these different women and showed how to do your make-up for your own face shape. I was like, "Oh, this is like the Bible." Nobody had taught me this! When I came back the next year, I actually looked like a girl! I felt comfortable looking like a girl. I didn't know I wanted to look that way. It was a big thing because I now had different perceptions of myself. As far as the body image goes, I was still conscious about body hair, but I knew what to do with it at this point. I just knew not to tell other girls about it because I didn't know if they had experienced it or not. And most of them didn't. They didn't have thick eyebrows or forearm hair.

Luckily, Fareena was able to find some information to help her feel ac-ceptable with peers, while juggling the wishes of her mother. Other Asian American women may not have access to resources like the Banks book. There is also a fine line between using "body work" as a source of em-powerment and colluding with hegemonic beauty standards. The Banks book is an alternative resource for women of color and has a diverse representation of women, but also reinforces a certain type of beauty to consumers. The beauty industry, in which Tyra Banks participates, ac-tively objectifies women and ranks them by intersecting social identities.

The Craigslist postings mentioned in chapter 3 remind us that the constructions of Asian and Asian American female beauty are based on the history or racial power and dominance in the United States. Women of color are constructed in contrast to white women and are considered subhuman. Kilbourne states:

> Turning a woman into a thing is almost always the first step toward justifying violence against a person. We see this with racism. We see it with homophobia. It is always the same process; we think of the person as less than human and violence is inevitable. Now this is a problem for all women of course, but particularly women of color, who are often literally shown as animals dressed in leopard skins and animal prints and over and over again. The message is, [they are] not fully human.

As exemplified with the doll studies of the Clarks and Davis, the message of being an "other," being different and being physically separated, has a long-term effect on a person's psyche. Their sense of self-worth and self-esteem can suffer.

SELF-ESTEEM

One of the areas in which gendered racism may affect Asian Americans is self-esteem. While bombarded with different messages from family, peers, teachers, and media, fragile self-image can affect self-worth. It is practically impossible for any woman to meet the hegemonic beauty standard. Some white women can get very close, and a large part of the cosmetic surgery industry is fueled by desires to meet this standard. It is absolutely impossible for a woman of color to meet those standards, because it is founded on the concept that whiteness *is* beauty.

Hegemonic beauty standards harm all women, as hegemonic masculinity harms all men and women. During adolescence, a dichotomy develops in how boys and girls talk about and understand their sexuality.[36] Women are supposed to be silent about sex. "Larger society forces of social control in the form of compulsory heterosexuality, the policing of girls' bodies through school codes, and media images play a clear part in forcing this silence and dissociation."[37] For boys and men, their sexual organs are a "sign of male power, assertion, and achievement, a gun to conquer the world."[38] For girls and women, they are taught to "recognize and keep a lid on the sexual desire of boys but not taught to acknowledge their own sexual feelings"[39] and are "emotional, submissive, and pressured "to have a boyfriend."[40]

Race further complicates this developmental process. While girls lack "much say over when and how [they] engage in sexual activity,"[41] girls of color must attempt to create a gendered sexual identity in a dominant cultural context that stereotypes them racially.[42] Marginalized racial groups struggle to meet the hegemonic beauty ideal, and ideals of "good" and "pretty" are internalized, as the dolls studies demonstrate. Iris, a third-generation Chinese American in her twenties who grew up in a Midwestern metropolitan city with a large Asian American population, shares one of her earliest racial memories:

> I remember being on the bus with this dark-skinned girl, her name was Addy, and she said, "Why do your eyes look like that? They're really ugly." I was on the bus, so probably kindergarten, first grade. When I got home, I plopped on my mom's bed and said, what's up with the eyes? Am I ugly? Is it really bad? Mom told me something like you're beautiful anyways, but on a separate occasion she said she used to pray that when I was born I would have double eyelids.

This memory stands out to Iris; she is the racial "other" to her young classmate Addy and her features are constructed as less attractive. Interestingly, Iris' mother tries to assure her that she is still beautiful, but also gives her contradictory messages by saying she wished Iris had been born with double eyelids.

Even at a young age, the white racial frame that normalizes whiteness affects children. Iris's mother was able to pass along some elements of a counter-frame, specifically anti-oppressive framing, which is discussed in chapter 7. However, even Asian Americans who possess strong counter-frames can wish for ways to fit into the mold of whiteness. Iris continues,

> I always felt like I was pretty, but I felt prettier when I had double eyelids. If I would cry a lot for whatever reason, I didn't have double eyelids. I remember getting ready for picture day at school, and I had been crying the day before. And I was like, "oh man, I'm going to be so ugly for this picture." And it was really ugly, yeah.

A study of sixty-five Asian Americans at an elite university found that respondents spoke more positively about their physical features when they seemed "less Asian" and more "white" or "American."[43] Similarly, when Iris was younger, she had ambivalent thoughts about her features. This has changed for her, but many respondents have struggled with self-image and self-esteem associated with their "Asian-ness." Earlier research has shown Asian Americans being ashamed or attempting to hide their race or pass for white.[44] Helena, a second-generation Korean American in her thirties who grew up in the West, discusses her self-esteem:

> I had low self-esteem anyway. My family wasn't really poor, but I lived like a pauper. So I was shunned a little bit because I wasn't wearing the right clothes, I didn't have the right haircut. At least I didn't have a Korean accent; then it would have probably been even worse. I was smarter than everyone too. There were a couple times when I was growing up when girls said stuff like, "You are just too smart, I hate you!" It made an impact over time, when all you hear is the negative instead of the positive. I always felt like the outsider and I was teased for just being Asian. They'd pull their eyes down, and they always thought I was Chinese.

All sixty respondents had memories of being teased and feeling like a racial "other."[45] Helena was one of many respondents who articulated the cumulative effect racism had over time on her self-esteem. Scholars have documented the psychological effects of racism on people of color.[46] Asian Americans, especially girls and women, are disturbingly overrepresented with rates of depression and suicide.[47] As recently as spring of 2011, The National Alliance on Mental Illness released a report that Asian American girls have the highest rates of depressive symptoms of any racial/ethnic or gender group.[48]

Racial health disparity is a reality and a focus of much research. The cumulative effect is difficult to measure because in the "color-blind" era, racism is harder to detect. Daily taunting and neglect are both microaggressions that can have different effects on individuals who possess different coping mechanisms. Ann, a second-generation Vietnamese American in her twenties who grew up in the Northeast, describes her struggles with self-esteem in high school:

> School was really hard. I wasn't comfortable in my own skin and really resented the fact that I was Asian. When the dating phase started kicking in, I never had anyone up until my senior year of high school and all my friends in high school, even in middle school, had boyfriends. Middle school is more like "Let's hold hands" and stuff like that. High school, it got a little more serious and they were dating each other for a long time and I was always third wheel or fifth wheel, never had a date, never had anyone. High school was very *painful*. I just wanted to blend in and not be associated with anyone that is Asian because then that brings out the "I'm different" kind of mentality. Even in college we get pinned as "model minorities." I hid behind my books because I was so ashamed of being an Asian female. Besides my close-knit friends, I didn't feel like anyone really recognized me.

Ann, like other respondents adopted some anti-Asian sentiment and wanted to avoid Asian American identification. Just as the stigma of being LGBTQ can trigger internalized homophobia, racial stigma can produce internalized racism. Ann was largely invisible to her teachers and peers even though she was much more than a good student. She was the co-captain of the volleyball team, which was a very competitive team her senior year. Her white best friend, who was also co-captain, was extremely popular and had the girl-next-door look. Ann shares:

> Well, Proactiv[49] wasn't invented by the time I hit puberty. I had a lot of acne at the time and that didn't help. Also, in high school, I was one of the faster-developing girls but also one of the least noticed. None of the guys I had crushes on ever had a crush on me back. They always had crushes on my other friends. I kept thinking after so many letdowns, it had to be because I was Asian. It didn't make any sense . . . I'm thin, I'm smart, I'm fun; everything was there. Eventually I gave up. It has to just be because I'm Asian.

While Ann did not have any evidence that her race was a factor in her lack of suitors, it seemed like the only logical explanation. Other respondents shared that it was difficult to discern when race played a role when potential romantic partners were interested or lacked interest. The color-blind discourse of the new racism makes it practically impossible for people of color to know when race becomes a factor in their interactions. A recent study at Duke University found that Asian American students were the least likely to "hook up" or be in relationships.[50] Students cite a culture of exclusion and being "invisible," which is similar to the experience of Ann and many other respondents. Even though Ann grew up in a large metropolitan city in the Northeast, she was not shielded from this form of racial microaggressions.

Most respondents did not feel confident confronting any racial teasing or taunting. In intimate relationships, this matter is complicated by affection for that partner and can further complicate the struggle with self-worth. As mentioned previously, Charlene dated a very abusive boyfriend for two years. He fetishized her sexually and was also verbally abusive. In an effort to please him, Charlene would dress in cheongsams[51] to fulfill his sexual fantasies.

> He would just make comments, like, Asian girls are the tightest [in reference to her vagina] or they're the most submissive, know how to serve and cook. I bought [the cheongsams] because I thought it would make him happy, and it did. And I fed into it because I thought that's what he wanted. And he became really abusive. Once he was driving me to the SATs, and I got the directions backwards. He started screaming at me: "How could you look up directions wrong? You're the stupidest fucking bitch I've ever been with, you cunt!" All these really nasty words. And I'm on my way to SATs. Prom, same thing. I got directions and he thought that the exit was sooner than it was and he was like, "We've missed it, we've missed it. You're a fucking dumb shit!" Since he was the first person I slept with and my mom really enforced that you have one chance, I didn't break up with him for two years. And he was always like that, just volatile. I would just cry and feel like crap. I thought I couldn't break up with him because he was the one, because I had slept with him. I had given him my fire.

Part of the reason Charlene continued to endure this mistreatment is because of the gendered meanings assigned to her virginity. Giving her boyfriend her "fire" was a choice she had made, and her mother, as mentioned in chapter 2, emphasized that she must stay with the person who now held it. The moment that Charlene no longer matched the fantasy of a submissive, inferior servant, her boyfriend erupted with his verbal assault. She had challenged the power balance by scoring higher than he did on an exam. She was younger than him, and this disrupted the hierarchy. I do not infer that all Asian American women who date white men have this experience. Interracial relationships will be discussed at length in chapter 6. But Charlene's experience is an appropriate example of how these ethnosexual images can translate to real life.

Charlene's experience was have also been influenced by the double messages she received in the home and community. In many home cultures, a good Asian woman should be sexually pure, a faithful partner, and always giving. But in the outside world, she may be constructed as an exotic, sexually available, kinky freak. Charlene was juggling both messages and working hard to please both constructions of her identity at the expense of her own emotional well-being and happiness. She has done a great deal of work to define herself on her terms.

While East and Southeast Asian women are largely constructed as hypersexualized vixens, South Asian women do not inhabit that same space in the discourse or media. They are exoticized, as with the *Kama Sutra* example from chapter 3; however, there is this absence of sexuality that is also pervasive. Earlier, Indira shared how she was encouraged by her family to focus on school before relationships. The way she has been socialized as an Indian American woman, she would often assume people would not be attracted to her and interested in a relationship.

> Even in our own cultures, we as woman are socialized to serve in our own communities. There's something less appealing about that outside of our communities, so I always thought, "No one's going to be attracted to me, so I'll just do what I want to do." But I still have left my faith in somebody else's hands. If somebody's interested in me and it works, cool. But I never saw myself as attractive. There is a day-in, day-out reality that uniquely exploits women. The Asian woman is seen as somebody who pleases. So I find Asian women to be hypersexualized in terms of how we serve. In pornography, you see the rising increase of hot Asian women; we are the givers of service and the givers of pleasures. We're the canvas, so paint on us.

Women and girls are taught to silence their sexual feelings and desires.[52] This silence keeps them from being able to express their full personhood.[53] When Asian American women discipline their bodies and curb their desires, it is a very logical and understandable way for them to stay physically, socially, and emotionally safe. However, they "lost track of the fact that an inequitable social system renders women's sexual desire a source of danger rather than one of pleasure and power in their lives."[54] Asian American women risk losing out on opportunities that bring joy and agency.[55] White hegemonic ideology is dependent upon the adoption of the ideals by not only agents of oppression, but also the targets.

> In order to perpetuate itself, every type of oppression must corrupt or distort those various sources of power within the culture of the oppressed that can provide energy for change. For women, this has meant the suppression of the erotic as a considered source of power and information within our lives.[56]

When Asian American women adopt distorted images of themselves, it is a by-product of pervasive hegemony, a white racial framing. The racist order is maintained without physical force with the adoption of white beauty as ideal and standard. The racist imagery has a role in shaping the lives of Asian Americans.

A Note on Sexual Violence

There is currently little research on sexual violence in Asian American communities. Resources and services are limited for sexual violence survivors in the United States in general, and even less is available for populations of color. More recent Asian immigrants may also face a language barrier that makes it difficult to get support. Many Asians and Asian Americans have a fear of "rocking the boat."[57] Additionally, newer immigrants and people of color have a history of mistrust of law enforcement. For all these reasons, little information about Asian Americans and sexual violence is currently available.

EXOTIFICATION AND FETISHISM

As mentioned in the introduction of this book, in Spokane, Washington, two white men and a white woman were found to have made elaborate plans to kidnap, rape, sodomize, and torture Japanese women and videotape the whole ordeal. According to police reports, the rapists had a sexual fantasy about and fixation with young Japanese women, who they believed were submissive.[58] In one month in 2000, the predators abducted five Japanese exchange students, ranging in age from 18 to 20. Motivated by their sexual biases about Asian women, all three used both their bodies and objects to repeatedly rape—vaginally, anally, and orally—two of the young women for over seven hours.[59] One of the attackers immediately confessed to searching only for Japanese women to torture and rape; eventually, all pled guilty and were convicted.[60]

However, Spokane is just one example of Asian and Asian American women being targets of sexual assault. In 2005, Tyreese Reed was arrested for assaulting eighteen Asian American women in the Los Angeles area.[61] Michael Lohman, 28, a third-year doctoral student at Princeton, was arrested on March 30 of the same year.[62] He admitted to surreptitiously cutting locks of hair from at least nine Asian women. He also admitted to pouring his urine and semen into the drinks of Asian women more than fifty times in Princeton's graduate student dining hall and other places.[63] Investigators found women's underwear and mittens filled with the hair of Asian women at his apartment, which he shared with his Asian wife. Police believe Lohman stole the mittens from Asian women and then used them to masturbate.[64] In Northern California, there is still a serial rapist on the loose who, for the past fifteen years, has been linked to over a dozen rapes of women, all of East Asian descent and highly educated. Investigators believe that he stalks them for a period of time before he rapes them.[65] In New York, a serial rapist targeting young Asian women in the Union Square subway station is still at large. He raped three women on one day in October 2008.[66] Most recently making the news, a man in San Diego assaulted six women of Asian descent before one of them fought back long enough to eventually lead to his arrest.[67]

While certainly people of non-Asian descent may be attracted to people of Asian descent, it can be difficult to discern when someone has "yellow fever," is a "rice king" or "Asiaphile." White men's affinity for Asian and Asian American women is noted in pop culture. On the popular blog *Stuff White People Like*, "Asian Girls" is number 11 on the list.[68] There is a parenthetical, heteronormative blurb stating that white women are exempt from this object of liking. The blog author explains the entry:

> 95% of white males have at one point in their lives, experienced "yellow fever." Many factors have contributed to this phenomenon, such as guilt from head taxes, internment camps, dropping the nuclear bomb, and the Vietnam War. This exchange works both ways as Asian girls have a tendency to go for white guys. (White girls never go for Asian guys. Bruce Lee and Paul Kariya's dad are the only recorded instances in modern history). Asian girls often do this to get back at their strict traditional fathers. There is also the option of dating black guys, but they know deep down that this would give their non-English speaking grandmother(s) a heart attack.[69]

The blog entry, which has now been published in a book that shares the name of the blog, simultaneously makes a mockery of horrific historical acts of violence, insults Asian and black men, normalizes a fetish for Asian women, and reinforces the "forever foreign" sentiment toward Asian families.

A recent article published in the magazine *Marie Claire* noted that many powerful wealthy white men are marrying younger Asian women, such as Rupert Murdoch, Woody Allen, and Nicholas Cage. This trend has given these Asian brides the title of "new trophy wives."[70] Another stereotyped trend is the nerdy white guy seeking out Asian/Asian American women as partners, as portrayed, for example, in the film *The Social Network*. For many of the female respondents, it can be difficult to distinguish genuine interest from interest resting on fabricated constructions of an othered person. Ann, who had painful memories of high school because she never had a boyfriend, later experienced being pursued by a white man simply because she is Asian American:

> It was senior year and I met someone at [work]. He was white and was my first real boyfriend. He actually said that he was dating a Chinese girl before me but she was in [a bordering state]. So, he said, "Well, if I am interested in [the other woman], I guess Ann is a lot closer. She's just a town away and she's also Asian. I am sure things can work out well with her." It was that type of thing "Oh, all Asians look alike." I felt like that's essentially what he was saying to me [laughter]. I didn't realize it at the time because I wasn't aware of any Asian American identity stuff; so I was just like, "Oh, a guy's interested in me, let's give it a try." But then I went to college and I started realizing how he stereotyped me. If we were on the subway and he would see another interracial couple, he would say, "Hey Ann, look at them; they are

another Asian girl, white guy. It's the Asian Invasion." And I cringed. I know, it's horrible, it's horrible. It's absolutely ridiculous and I realize that now, but at the time I was just still so young and I hadn't learned about everything yet. I knew it didn't sit right, but I didn't understand why.

Like Charlene, Ann quickly started a relationship with a boy who showed interest in her. Because she got little attention from peers in high school, his half-hearted interest was enough. At that point in her life, Ann had yet to develop strong "counter-frames." It took going to college and learning about race, Asian American history, and other forms of oppression for her to re-examine things from the past. While she could "feel" that something was not quite right, it took exposure to anti-oppression frames to be able to articulate the problems with it and thus make different decisions in the future. She is now more wary of dating white men because of this past experience.

Like Charlene and Ann, Iris's first boyfriend was also white. Initially, she had no idea he had a preference for Asian and Asian American women, because she was his first girlfriend. She began to suspect it because he would make statements about another Asian American woman he liked before her, comparing the two. Iris continues to describe this first relationship,

> He was the first one to tell me that Asians are tighter down there [vagina]. Which is obviously false but he had all these really weird conceptual things about his penis and it was really awkward, I Googled[71] it, looked it up, and had to see what was out there. In retrospect, I wish I could have said, "that's not cool" or even think, "why am I with someone like that" because it's kind of *dehumanizing*.

Iris eventually asked her boyfriend directly if he had a preference for Asian women and he admitted it.

In their earliest romantic relationships, these women face ethnosexualized stereotyping. Individuals have preferences for partners, but we must examine how these preferences are influenced by social factors. When women seek men who are wealthy, we must also understand that power and privilege accompanies it. When individuals find certain body types or races attractive, we must deconstruct how these bodies are portrayed stereotypically.

This exotification happens to queer Asian American women as well. Erin, who identifies as a lesbian, hears more benign comments from partners, who note that her skin and hair are different. But sometimes it can be hard to interpret the attention she is getting. She discusses exotification:

> Clearly it happens. Asian women are exoticized in the queer community. So I don't know if someone is attracted to me just because I'm Asian. If you're a straight white male, you never have to wonder if

you're something different. So you wonder if it has anything to do with your personality, the t-shirt I'm wearing, or if it has totally or partly to do with my being Asian. I have no idea. I think it's pretty obvious in the straight world, when a guy wants to talk to me. I'm not totally sure how to approach that or deal with it. It's not the right kind of attention. Like when they ask where you are from as being the opening question. Or stuff about Chinese food. If they're trying to impress you with their Asian knowledge, then they're hitting on you because you're Asian. Or asking questions specifically about being Asian, then they're exoticizing you, while they're hitting on you. If they're talking to you about other things, you don't really know for sure. It could be that that guy is savvy. Or it could be that he really doesn't have that sense of being interested in you just because you are different.

The difficult part of interracial relationships for people of color is how to differentiate genuine interest from attraction based on preconceived notions. There is no real test to accurately determine motives that are not influenced by societal constructions. Then one has to ask, if a relationship seems healthy, is there any harm in initial judgments being based on those factors? These are difficult questions that do not have simple answers.

After giving lectures about the subject of Asian American sexual politics, I have had women come up to me afterward sharing doubts of whether they can ever have white male, and sometimes any non-Asian, partners again. Once they have realized that they were fetishized in the past, it has become almost impossible for them to be clear of any doubt that his interest is free from racial stereotyping. As women of color with increased racial consciousness, they can never be sure.

IDENTITY

There is overwhelming pressure for immigrants and marginalized and subordinated people to fit the norm even if it is impossible for them to match that constructed image, whether with regard to class, race, gender, or sexuality. Scholars have created models to explain assimilation for immigrants and specifically Asian Americans.[72] My Asian American respondents demonstrate that dealing with issues of identity can be a process. Ann shares,

Going through high school, I resented being Asian. I really wanted to be white. I felt like I struggled in high school to be seen by anyone. The whole dating thing was huge and also teachers and expectations and stuff. It was hard for them to see past my skin and to not see the stereotypes and not see their preconceived notions. Going through high school, I was very shy and hesitant to be seen in public with my own parents because it's just we are a sore thumb when we go out to restaurants or shopping in the mall. Eventually, throughout college and just life, I became more empowered by it [her racial identity] because I was finally comfortable with me, comfortable with my background. I was proud of my family history.

Ann struggled with many issues regarding identity and self-esteem. She was invisible to friends, teachers, and other students. While othered racially, it seems like a logical desire to wish to be white, to internalize racism and struggle with self-hatred. Luckily, she was able to have an awakening to social political consciousness.[73] Ann could then develop an anti-oppression frame to counter the white racial frame that left her feeling inadequate.

Jessica is an excellent example of the powerful messages of normalcy being equated with whiteness. There is a comprehensive discussion of racial identity in *The Myth of the Model Minority: Asian Americans Facing Racism*. Coauthor Joe Feagin and I pay specific attention to racial conformity and Asian American struggles with whitening.[74] Jessica illustrated specific examples of feeling different.

> I was always more jealous of white families because that was what I was socialized to appreciate: the grandma who made cookies and the homeroom moms who brought the cupcakes to class and went on the fieldtrips with us. They [whites] talk about Thanksgiving dinner where your grandparents and your aunts and uncles are there, but we never had that. I was always really jealous of that. There's such an order about it. Like they know who they're related to. I remember one year in school we had this family tree assignment. I hated doing family trees because my family's so complicated and I don't know all of my mother's brothers' and sisters' names. She doesn't like to talk about them, especially the ones that passed away. And they didn't pass away because they got in a car accident; they passed away because they were in a war. My dad's family, none of them are here either. He never talks about any of them, and I don't even know their names. I never got to talk to my grandpa on the phone or anything from Vietnam. I never met any of my other grandparents. And it was really hard to get my parents to tell me their names. "Why are you doing this, and why is it in a tree and why does it even matter?" they ask. "It's a long time ago, it doesn't matter." And I'm like, "No, it really does matter. I really need to do this for a grade." Some people can trace back their relatives to famous people and I can't do that. I don't know. So it really sucked.

The involvement in war in Asia and the Pacific Islands has direct, destructive effects on the family, as was the case for Jessica with the U.S. involvement in the Vietnam War. Jessica feels the residual effect of the trauma of her destroyed family. The colonial projects of the United States continue to ripple down the generations for many Southeast Asian Americans and many other Americans as well. Her parents found refuge coming to this country. They felt largely isolated in the U.S. and have made attempts to make white friends, but Jessica is concerned that they are still quite lonely. Her siblings do not have the racial history that she has been lucky enough to gain in college. Similar to Ann, Jessica was also able to form counter-narratives and counter-frames in college. All these historical and political factors influence her life today, but she is now equipped to challenge the white racial frame.

There are identity constructions of the sexualized body. These constructions for women of East Asian descent are at times conflicting, like the "submissive servant" and "the kink." Charlene's identity was confused by the castrating constructions and she tried to live up to both:

> I felt both extremes: should I be really submissive, or should I be really adventurous and freaky and kinky. I think that kind of made me seem a little schizophrenic to people I was with. I was so moldable and just changed myself to whatever I thought someone wanted. I didn't really assert my own needs or desires because I didn't think I should have any.

Some Asian American male respondents commented that they thought Asian and Asian American women had it easier in school and more favorable representations compared to their male counterparts. It is true that white-framed constructions of Asian American women portray them as sexually attractive, but that does not mean they are seen as full human beings. Erin disagrees with the comments made by the male respondents that Asian American girls and women have it easier.

> It's probably actually harder to juggle. The nerdy stereotype about Asian guys applies to Asian girls too—the idea that Asian girls are nice and nerdy. But there's also the exotic whore factor [laughs]. But that doesn't make it easier for Asian girls. It might make you warmer and friendlier, but that's not necessarily easier. It's the wrong kind of attention. You're not seen as a full human being. I think the guys had actually more positive stereotypes in the media when I was growing up than the girls did. The girls were still either seen as like these shy little people that are sort of in the background or whores [laughing].

Erin's laughter was not to make light of sex workers, but was utilized to relieve tension about the drastically extreme constructions of her own Asian female body. While some of the stereotyping of Asian women may seem positive, they are still externally imposed. The representations of Asian women as beautiful, while seemingly complimentary, are not necessarily varied from other sexually exploitative representations of other women. Just because women are displayed as beautiful does not mean they are not seen as commodities or free from racial and gender domination.

The South Asian representation is different. Indira finds that East Asian women are portrayed in much more sexually explicit ways. With the popularity of films like *Bend It Like Beckham* and *Slumdog Millionaire*,

South Asian women are being incorporated in the film industry as leading ladies. However, these films were both directed by British directors, one of whom is a Desi woman.[75] In the American film industry, South Asian American leading ladies are still lacking. Indira discusses her South Asian American identity formation.

> When women [are confronted with these stereotypes] you either radically reject them or you try your hardest to reconcile to that reality, because you want to fit into a community. Men don't have that consciousness or examination of self. Either way, if I reject or embrace them, I have to think about them. The message that I got from movies was that a woman is the one who carries the virtues of a community. And when she pleases herself, she's in fact being unfaithful to those virtues. We then operationalize that, so if I want to date somebody because I'm attracted to them then somehow I'm being unfaithful to this cultural community, to the values that I was raised with. And I very well could be, but I might not be. Maybe a doctor is just a doctor.

The messages Indira has received from both her family and media is that her sexual desire is second to her family and community. Women are denied full access to the power of their own desire by silencing their sexual longings. Our respondents have received messages that there is something wrong with desires and sexual feelings, while simultaneously being constructed as exotic sexually available objects. There are very few available resources for Asian American women to openly discuss their identity, bodies, self-image, and sexual desires.

LEARNING FROM OTHER ASIAN AMERICANS

While there is limited representation of Asians and Asian Americans in the media, Southeast, South, and Pacific Islander Americans are even more scarce. More recently, Asian Americans of East Asian descent have had figures present in mainstream media like Kristi Yamaguchi, Sandra Oh, Margaret Cho, Connie Chung, Michelle Kwan, and Lisa Ling. However, Asian Americans who do not have East Asian roots find themselves having to look elsewhere. Fareena was exposed to other South Asians after high school.

> [My brother] said there were a lot of South Asian people in college. I was fascinated. I went online and looked through all the sororities and fraternities. Let me look at how other brown people my age look. I thought you had to be either absolutely firm Indian or completely white American. Not even some form of Americanization, but just white American. I didn't know other people like me, who grew up facing similar issues of identity, how they groom themselves, what they chose to wear, what they thought was funny. It was the most fascinating thing to me.

A common theme among my respondents who said that they were proud of being Asian American is that they had access to counter-frames. Fareena was able to find communities that had alternative frames to the white racial frame. While large populations of Asian Americans exist on the West Coast and Hawaii, more than 50 percent of Asian Americans live outside of these regions. The feeling of isolation is a real issue for them. Even in areas like California, New York, and Hawaii, Asian Americans can struggle with feelings of isolation and being "othered."[76]

Much of the information Asian Americans garner about their identities is from the media. Any interaction or exposure feels significant and can be a coping mechanism against isolation. Jessica shares:

> I'll be in a parking lot and an SUV will go by with a little Asian woman inside. And I'll notice it—Asian woman in SUV. And if I walk into a restaurant, I'll notice how many Asian American are in there. I always know how many Asian Americans are in each of my classes. But I always see it—you can't help it. If I meet a group of administrators and one of them is Asian American, that's so cool. Teachers? I never had an Asian American teacher. And every time I had a substitute that was Asian American, it was like, "Oh! Look at that!" It just happens, and it's so natural, so natural. I'm fairly certain that it does not happen with my white friends.

Visibility and open dialogue are critically important for Asian Americans to create counter-narratives and to combat the longstanding racist stereotypes that are part of the white racial frame. Jessica uses "natural" to describe her hyperawareness to other Asians as a reaction to isolation and lack of representation. In other parts of the country where there are larger, more visible groups of Asian Americans, it may not be as common. However, even in areas with large Asian American populations, media presence and representation is still lacking.

The Asian American women in this chapter battle gendered, racialized, and heteronormative pressures from their families and external forces. Providing opportunities for them to speak about their experiences and listening and responding to their questions may be an effective way to empower them.

CONCLUSION

The narratives in this chapter show that externally imposed meanings of Asian sexuality are often exploitative and coercive. Asian American women are socialized in a world that defines their sexuality, whether they reside in the United States or elsewhere. As a social being, it takes exceptional strength to define oneself without regard to externally imposed definitions. While other communities of color have already laid the groundwork for counter-narratives, Asian Americans have yet to fully develop a strong collective counter-narrative. Collections like Vickie Nam's *Yello-Oh Girls* are certainly a step in the right direction. In this chapter, my respondents have demonstrated that there are struggles with self-image, self-esteem, and identity formation because of cultural and familial expectations combined with being ethnosexually defined in another capacity in the United States.

In chapter 5, my male respondents share their racialized and gendered experiences. However, as one of my male respondents, Irwin, noted, there are many more voices of support and scholarly research focusing on the experience of Asian American women. In general, there are many gaps to fill and to understand the Asian American male experience, and these men are underrepresented in scholarly research and literary works. One drastically noticeable difference between the experiences between Asian American men and women is the regular threat of violence that the boys and men experience at the hands of other boys and men. While women experience the violence in a different capacity, like the symbolic violence of self-hatred because of hegemonic beauty standards and the threat of sexual violence, the Asian American men experience those threats in addition to the overt threat of physical violence that is central to the construction of masculinity. Ann notes this experience from high school:

> My sophomore year, there was, I realize a guy who was six feet, really heavyset, played football. He picked a fight with one of the Latin American or South American immigrants in the ESL program. He harassed one of them one day, and afterwards a Vietnamese guy told me, "Yeah, Mike's a racist." I got paranoid; we were in the same class together, and I never realized it. We always sat on opposite sides of the classroom, but he never said anything to me and then I realized that's why he never said anything to me. I was like, "Is he gonna do anything to me?" My friend said, "No, no, no. He doesn't harass girls. You're a girl, so you're okay." I'm like, "Ok, but I'm still Asian." It didn't make sense at that time but I was kind of relieved that he would never pick on me because I was a girl. I felt a little threatened but not extremely, where I think my friend felt a little threatened and definitely kept his distance from that guy.

Ann is not free from the psychological threat of violent racism, but in this case her gender seemed to protect her from her classmate's physical violence. In the next chapter, we see that Asian American men are not as sheltered from male posturing. They discuss the role physical violence plays in their intersected gender and racial identity. Their sexualities are often questioned as a means to relegate them to subordinated and marginalized positions in a white hegemonic masculine hierarchy.

NOTES

1. Naomi Wolf, *The Beauty Myth: How Images of Beauty Are Used Against Women* (New York: Harper Collins, 2002).

2. Judy Taylor, "Feminist Consumerism and Fat Activists: Grassroots Activism and the Dove 'Real Beauty' Campaign," in *Feminist Frontiers*, ed. Verta Taylor, Nancy Whittier, and Leila J. Rupp (New York: McGraw-Hill, 2008), 129.

3. Wolf, *The Beauty Myth*.

4. Taylor, "Feminist Consumerism."

5. Taylor, "Feminist Consumerism," 129.

6. R. W. Connell and James W. Messerschmidt, "Hegemonic Masculinity: Rethinking the Concept," *Gender and Society* 19, no. 6 (2005): 829–59; Karen Pyke and Denise Johnson, "Asian American Women and Racialized Femininities: 'Doing' Gender across Cultural Worlds," *Gender and Society* 17, no. 1 (2003): 33–53; Mimi Schippers, "Recovering the Feminine Other: Masculinity, Femininity, and Gender Hegemony," *Theory and Society* 36, no. 1 (2007): 85–102.

7. R. W. Connell, *Gender and Power: Society, the Person, and Sexual Politics* (Palo Alto, CA: Stanford University Press, 1987).

8. Schippers, "Recovering the Feminine Other."

9. Schippers, "Recovering the Feminine Other."

10. Schippers, "Recovering the Feminine Other."

11. Pyke and Johnson, "Asian American Women and Racialized Femininities," 50–51.

12. Pyke and Johnson, "Asian American Women and Racialized Femininities," 50–51.

13. Pyke and Johnson, "Asian American Women and Racialized Femininities," 50–51.

14. Beate Krais, "Gender and Symbolic Violence: Female Oppression in the Light of Pierre Bourdieu's Theory of Social Practice," in *Bourdieu: Critical Perspectives*, ed. Craig J. Calhoun, Edward LiPuma, and Moishe Postone, (Chicago: University of Chicago Press, 1993), 156–76.

15. Karen Pyke and Denise Johnson, "Asian American Women and Racialized Femininities: 'Doing' Gender across Cultural Worlds," *Gender and Society* 17 (2003): 33–53 (esp. p. 51).

16. Connell, *Gender and Power*.

17. Kenneth Clark and Mamie Clark, "Racial Identification and Preference in Negro Children," in *Readings in Social Psychology*, ed. E. Maccoby, T. M. Newcomb, and E. L. Hartley (New York: Holt, Rinehart & Winston, 1947); Kenneth Clark, *Prejudice and Your Child* (Middletown, CT: Wesleyan University Press, 1988).

18. Kiri Davis, *A Girl Like Me* (New York: Media Matters, 2005).

19. From ABC's *Good Morning America*, March 31, 2009.

20. *Good Morning America*, March 31, 2009.

21. Eduardo Bonilla-Silva, *Racism without Racists: Color-Blind Racism and the Persistence of Racial Inequality in the United States* (Lanham, MD: Rowman & Littlefield, 2008).

22. Leslie Houts Picca and Joe R. Feagin. *Two-Faced Racism: Whites in the Backstage and Frontstage* (New York: Routledge, 2007).

23. Patricia Hill Collins, *Black Sexual Politics: African Americans, Gender, and the New Racism* (New York: Routledge, 2005).

24. Jean Kilbourne, *Killing Us Softly 3: Advertising's Image of Women* (videotape) (Northampton, MA: Media Education Foundation, 2000).

25. K. Harrison, "The Body Electric: Thin-Ideal Media and Eating Disorders in Adolescents," *Journal of Communication* 50, no. 3 (September 2000): 119–43.

26. Hernan Vera and Andrew M. Gordon, *Screen Saviors: Hollywood Fictions of Whiteness* (Lanham, MD: Rowman & Littlefield, 2003).

27. L. Bacon et al., "Size Acceptance and Intuitive Eating Improve Health for Obese, Female Chronic Dieters," *Journal of the American Diet Association* 105, no. 6 (June 2005): 929–36.

28. There are religious, regional, and class issues to consider.

29. Rosalind S. Chou and Joe R. Feagin, *The Myth of the Model Minority: Asian Americans Facing Racism* (Boulder, CO: Paradigm, 2008).

30. Chou and Feagin, *Myth of the Model Minority*; Robert T. Teranishi, *Asians in the Ivory Tower: Dilemmas of Racial Inequality in American Higher Education* (New York: Teachers College Press, 2010).

31. Chou and Feagin, *Myth of the Model Minority*.

32. Chou and Feagin, *Myth of the Model Minority*.

33. Eduardo Bonilla Silva, "From Bi-racial to Tri-racial: Towards a New System of Racial Stratification in the USA," *Ethnic and Racial Studies* 27, no. 6 (2004): 931–50.

34. Kilborne, *Killing Us Softly 3*.

35. Tyra Banks, *Tyra's Beauty Inside and Out* (New York: Harper Perennial, 1998).

36. Deborah L. Tolman, *Doing Desire: Adolescent Girls' Struggles for/with Sexuality*, Feminist Frontiers, 8th ed. (New York: McGraw-Hill, 2008).

37. Tolman, *Doing Desire*, 321.

38. Ken Plummer, *Male Sexualities: Handbook of Studies on Men and Masculinities* (Thousand Oaks, CA: Sage, 2005), 179.

39. Tolman, *Doing Desire*.

40. Tolman, *Doing Desire*, 350.

41. Tolman, *Doing Desire*, 348.

42. Tolman, *Doing Desire*.

43. Kristen Lee and Simon Ho, "Asian American Sexual Politics" (unpublished manuscript, 2011).

44. Chou and Feagin, *Myth of the Model Minority*.

45. For more detailed accounts of racial teasing, see Chou and Feagin, *Myth of the Model Minority*.

46. Abraham Kardiner and Lionel Ovesey, *The Mark of Oppression: Explorations in the Personality of the American Negro* (Cleveland: World Publishing, 1962); William H. Grier and Price M. Cobbs, *Black Rage* (New York: Bantam Books, 1968); and Joe R. Feagin and Karyn D. McKinney, *The Many Costs of Racism* (Lanham, MD: Rowman & Littlefield, 2003); Chou and Feagin, *Myth of the Model Minority*.

47. See, for example, C. Browne and A. Broderick, "Asian and Pacific Island Elders: Issues for Social Work Practice and Education," *Social Work* 39 (1994): 252–59; Laura Harder, "Asian Americans Commit Half of Suicides at Cornell," *Cornell Daily Sun*, March 29, 2005; and Janice Tanaka, *When You're Smiling* (Janice Tanaka Films, 1999); Won Moo Hurh, "Adaptation Stages and Mental Health of Korean Male Immigrants in the United States," *International Migration Review* 24 (1990): 456–77; Center for Medicaid Services, *Medicaid Managed Care Enrollment Report: Depression Diagnoses for Adolescent Youth* (New York: Medicaid Statistics Publications, 2002); Chou and Feagin, *Myth of the Model Minority*.

48. Jei Africa and Majose Carrasco, "Asian American and Pacific Islander Mental Health," A Report for The National Alliance on Mental Illness, February 2011, http://www.nami.org/Template.cfm?Section=Multicultural_Support1&Template=/Content-Management/ContentDisplay.cfm&ContentID=115281.

49. An acne medication system.

50. Anita-Yvonne Bryant et al., The Campus Life and Learning Project: A Report on the First Two College Years, Duke University, 2006.

51. A body-hugging one-piece dress for Chinese women.

52. Tolman, *Doing Desire*.

53. Tolman, *Doing Desire*.

54. Tolman, *Doing Desire*.

55. Tolman, *Doing Desire*.

56. Audre Lorde, *Sister Outsider* (Berkeley, CA: The Crossing Press, 1984), 53.

57. Chou and Feagin, *Myth of the Model Minority*.

58. Alex Tizon, "Rapists Bet on Victims' Silence—and Lose," *Seattle Times*, May 31, 2001.

59. Tizon, "Rapists Bet."

60. Tizon, "Rapists Bet."

61. Tracy Zhang, "Koreatown Rapist Caught," *Canyon News*, August 7, 2005.

62. Lisa Wong Macabasco, "Princeton Incident Shows Extreme Case of Asian Fetish," *Asian Week*, April 29, 2005, http://www.asianweek.com/2005/04/29/princeton-incident-shows-extreme-case-ofasian-fetish/.

63. Macabasco, "Princeton Incident."

64. Macabasco, "Princeton Incident."

65. "Police Hunt Serial Rapist in Northern California," Associated Press, November 15, 2006, http://www.msnbc.msn.com/id/15739551/, accessed January 27, 2010.

66. Jaemin Kim, "Asian Women: Rape and Hate Crimes," *Huffington Post*, February 3, 2009, http://www.huffingtonpost.com/jaemin-kim/lets-call-it-what-it_is_b_163698.html.

67. Kristina Davis, "Stay Safe: Serial Rapist Targeting Asian-American Women," *Girls Think Tank*, March 14, 2009, http://girlsthinktank.org/stay-safe-serialrapist-targeting-asian-american-women/.

68. *Stuff White People Like* (blog), http://stuffwhitepeoplelike.com/2008/01/20/11-asiangirls/.

69. *Stuff White People Like*.

70. Ying Chu, "The New Trophy Wives: Asian Women," *Marie Claire*, September 2009.

71. A popular Internet search engine.

72. Milton Gordon, *Assimilation in American Life: The Role of Race, Religion and National Origins* (Oxford: Oxford University Press, 1964); Sue et al., "The Process of Asian American Identity Development," in *Multicultural Counseling Competencies: Individual and Organizational Development* (Thousand Oaks, CA: Sage, 1998).

73. The third stage in the Asian American identity development model.

74. Chou and Feagin, *Myth of the Model Minority*.

75. *Bend It Like Beckham* was directed by Gurinder Chadha; *Slumdog Millionaire* was directed by Danny Boyle.

76. Chou and Feagin, *Myth of the Model Minority*.

FIVE

Asian American Masculinity

I hate him [William Hung], and I hate the system that put him there. He's a joke, and everyone is laughing at him. People who are ignorant think Asian guys are all like him. I hope he's made a lot of money because his ten minutes of fame are up. I hope he got laid a lot too, but I doubt it. I saw him in an interview where he said he's a virgin and is waiting for marriage. They have to get the biggest Asian geek and put the spotlight on him. *American Idol* is America's #1 show! Everything about him just perpetuates and reinforces Asian stereotypes. In fact, it makes it ten times worse. But people think it's funny. —Controversial SAM[1]

After finishing the first draft of this chapter, I realized I had to go back to the beginning. After a long, thirteen-hour day of writing, I was overcome with emotion. I felt so proud and appreciative that my male respondents found a place to finally talk about fear, violence, and self-esteem. I undertook this project for them because I kept hearing the same stories again and again during my early graduate school research. Too many times they felt that their only public voice and face was that of the William Hungs[2] and Long Duk Dongs[3] of the world. There are Asian American men walking around every day, disregarded, tormented, spurned by love interests, and seen as half-men with no platform on which to speak.

Even at the end of our interview, Irwin, a second-generation Taiwanese American in his thirties introduced in an earlier chapter, was still in disbelief that I wanted to do research and write about Asian American men. He is frustrated with the lack of attention to Asian American men, especially straight Asian American men, because the little research that exists is largely focused on women and gay Asian American men. Irwin notes, "There needs to be a huge correction. It just mirrors our society, sadly. The one group that is lost when we're not talking about writing history is Asian American heterosexual men." While research is still lack-

103

ing for Asian American gay and bisexual men, Irwin's observation is also disappointingly true. In a search for scholarly social science articles about Asian American men, I was only able to find forty-nine articles dating back as far as 1977.[4]

THE INVISIBLE MEN

There is a desperate need to openly talk about Asian American men and their relationship to white racism and hegemonic masculinity. There are so few resources and platforms. In the spring of 2011, I gave a talk at the University of Oregon and was thrilled to find such a large group of Asian American men at the Asian Pacific American Student Union meeting. It was an environment that encouraged discussion and development of counter-frames, but this is not common. Without communities like this, Asian American men can be an invisible population. As Indira notes,

> My mom used to always say that everything that goes in will come out in some way. I used to hold my temper. I used to hold everything in and would never talk about things. And as I got older, she would say, "It will come out. It will come out as an illness. It will come out as cancer. If it doesn't come out now in tears or yelling or screaming, it's going to come out in some way later on, but you never escape what you hold." Asian men who are bullied are socialized to not express emotion. If you're continually bullied and you think it's your strength that you're holding it in, really it's breaking you down. In effect, you're a container. At some point, the container overflows and what happens when any individual breaks is beyond imagination. For somebody who is at the edge, it could be a response in violence.

One example of a response in violence occurred in April 2007, when Cho Seung Hui killed thirty-two people and wounded twenty-five on the Virginia Tech campus before taking his own life. It was the single most deadly shooting by a single gunman in U.S. history. Cho was quiet as a child and adult. Classmates say he was bullied, and women had very little interest in him.[5] Cho's experience as an Asian immigrant to the United States is not unique. Many of my male respondents have similar experiences, especially in all-white spaces. Cho Seung Hui was bullied by his fellow high school classmates.[6] His peers mocked his speech even though in elementary school he was "noted for being good at mathematics and English, and teachers pointed to him as an example for other students."[7] Interestingly, a friend from elementary school said that Cho was "recognized by friends as a boy of knowledge . . . a good dresser who was popular with the girls."[8] However, things changed a great deal for Cho in middle school. Another classmate noted, "there were just some people who were really cruel to him, and they would push him down and laugh at him. He didn't speak English really well, and they would really make fun of him."[9]

Cho's story is not very different from those shared in earlier chapters when respondents recall changes in self-esteem when attending all-white schools, whether they were recent immigrants to or born in the United States. Cho spoke very little after being mocked openly in the classroom in high school. He held in his anger and frustration, which grew into a "cancer" that led him to plan an attack. Reporter Sarah Baxter writes, "High on his list [of targets] were his classmates from Westfield High School, who jeered at him to 'go back to China' without bothering to check his nationality. . . . Then there were the college girls who reported him to the police for stalking and got him carted off to a mental hospital after he sent them shy love messages full of yearning."[10] What Baxter misses is that the sting of insults from classmates is not about getting the country of origin correct. It would not be less harmful for them to have said, "Go back to South Korea!" The racial mistreatment he received is the common treatment of Asian Americans as "foreigners" who should "go back" to some far-off Eastern place. Even fourth- or fifth-generation Asian Americans face similar insults. Research has shown that tragedies often occur at the hands of men because of a combination of sexual frustration and gender issues,[11] and Asian American men face a unique combination of "racial castration."

While all men of color face racist, gender-specific constructions, there is something clearly unique about the construction of Asian American men that makes emasculating public humiliation seem safer to the assailants. East Asian–looking men are constructed as physically weak and nonthreatening in the white racial frame. Perhaps had Cho been a six-foot-tall African American man, the teasing in school may have not been so public or without fear of retribution. Cho was diagnosed before moving to the United States with psychological disorders, so there are a number of factors at play. But years of racist taunts when he was already psychologically unstable may have pushed him over the edge. Psychosis, if untreated, can be further stressed by discrimination based on race, gender, and sexuality.

An interesting factor in the tragedy at Virginia Tech is Cho's race and the stereotypes and assumptions that accompany Asian American masculinity may have had a role in his ability to "slip through the cracks," moving almost undetected as a violent threat. He was writing graphic stories and poetry in one of his creative writing courses, and his professor sought professional help for him. Cho was asked to leave the class and got a psychological evaluation: it determined he was not a threat to anyone. Having been reported to the police by female classmates and to the dean by a professor, Cho still seemed like an unlikely killer. For fifteen years in the United States, Cho was largely treated as an impotent foreigner.

Elements of hegemonic masculinity are wed to nationality.[12] This complicates things for Asian Americans because of their "perpetual foreignness." Specifically, it complicates things for Asian American men. If hegemonic masculinity is wed to nationality, then their foreignness further marginalizes or subordinates Asian American men. One of my respondents, Irwin, predicted a decade before Cho's attack that an Asian American man would go on a violent rampage. Irwin speaks from his own personal experiences, since he was bullied for a number of years in middle and high school. While Irwin experienced physical threats and harm, he notes the unspoken acts of racism he endured daily from his white classmates as an "other" or "outsider" were extremely powerful:

> I think what's more powerful [than physical threats and harm] are things that aren't even said. If everyone responds to you the same way for like 25 years of your life . . . this is why I think Asian men and African American men are probably the most psychologically fucked-up people in America because there is a sort of response that we get all the time just for what we look like. Not something that we do or say. In some ways, it is that sort of lack of interest, you know, sexually for one thing. And then fear and loathing from men. For whatever reason, you'd rather not have [the Asian American man] around. You pick up on this subconsciously or consciously sometimes. It's more obvious for African American males. I mean, starting from the age of 13 probably, they're gonna start to pick up fear from other people in certain circumstances. You can imagine what effect that has on a person over the course of a lifetime.

Cho Seung Hui experienced fifteen years of repetitive responses of disdain and disinterest. Scholars have argued that people living in a racist, white supremacist society are psychologically damaged by the effects of racist oppression. This damage can cause people of color to act abnormally in certain situations.[13] The men I interviewed openly speak of repetitive poor treatment they received from others, largely whites. They are invisible men and it is difficult to measure what the long-term effects may ultimately be. One respondent, Helena, a second-generation Korean American introduced in the previous chapter, spoke of her father:

> My mother had other Korean friends through the church. My father was completely isolated because he wasn't into the religious thing. Which I found out about later, actually, after he died. I never knew how alone he was, which made me feel really bad. It was kind of weird; my father was so stoic and he never talked to the kids, so I didn't really even know my father even though he lived with us the entire time.

Social constructions of manhood do not provide many outlets for men and boys to talk about emotions in a meaningful way outside of violent actions. This is not unique to Asian and Asian American men, but they are uniquely racially isolated and "castrated." In this chapter, my male respondents reveal how their self-esteem, self-image, and identity have formed as a result of and in response to their racialized experiences. Additionally, my respondents discuss their experiences with physical and psychological violence as both survivors and perpetrators.

SELF-IMAGE AND SELF-ESTEEM

To be considered the perfect male in the United States is to suppress all female tendencies and dispositions.[14] However, Asian and Asian American men are feminized in representations of hegemonic white Western masculinity. Men construct masculinities according to their position in social structure and access to power and resources.[15] Asian and Asian American men have faced obstacles in accessing power and resources, not only in the United States but also within the global empire. Thus, their masculinity is constructed according to their position in this social structure. By being constructed as more feminine in the Western discourse, Asian and Asian American men can never achieve perfect male status. This can have a profound effect on the self-image and self-esteem of Asian American men and boys. Like the Clark and Davis doll studies mentioned in the previous chapter, living in a society that makes it clear, both overtly and covertly, that you are inferior can affect perceptions of self.

Indira, commenting on Asian American male self-esteem, says, "I think self-esteem is tied to the gender piece of identity for men, and so when you don't have your self-esteem and then that intersects with racism that happens, there's no outlet." To express emotion and discuss being racialized and being subordinated or marginalized in a gendered sense only further stigmatizes boys and men. Irwin illustrates how external messages about his gendered race affected his self-image; he had a difficult time identifying with masculine constructions.

> I've either emasculated myself or given myself a different identity as an adult male. I've thought of myself as something other than what you think of when you think of the word "man," "guy," a "male," a "dude," whatever, but not a man. Obviously I think it has something to do with my environment. When I say that, I mean that I took what was around me and believed it. I internalized all of that.

Irwin's environment was very much a white habitus. In that setting, the definition of manhood is based on white hegemonic masculinity. The intersection of race and gender for Asian American men, like Irwin, can be so stigmatizing that they may internalize the stereotypes about themselves. The effects of racist oppression psychologically damage people living within it.[16] Irwin questioned his own manhood, and this took a toll:[17]

I definitely felt like I had to prove stuff growing up. Through college, through graduate school. You know all my graduate school. [I had to] prove my masculinity, prove my heterosexuality. For some Asian guys it has to do with their mannerisms and such. Traditionally, Asian men are not necessarily going to carry themselves the same ways as white men. A lot of Asian guys don't feel like they have to prove anything. Some of the external traits like the hairless face probably contribute to that. Experiences in repetitive images and repetitive narrative types can be very powerful. They create negative feelings about one's self and, on the flip side, positive feelings about one's self when you see Asian American heroes in your narratives or in your histories or images, pictures. Simple as that.

Irwin describes being able to be both negatively and positively influenced by representations of Asian Americans. Whites benefit from consistent positive portrayals in the media. They consistently see images of white heroes and saviors in movies.[18] There are numerous examples of whites as successful professionals, government officials, CEOs, and lead characters in books, movies, and television programs. People of color see these images much less often. So when there is an Asian American that challenges stereotypes, it can be significantly meaningful, as in the emergence of Jeremy Lin in the NBA.

Irwin observes the contrasting aspects of Asian and white masculinity. Simple body movement and mannerisms have different meanings in different cultures. There are performative aspects to these masculinities. The way a person physically carries himself is not biological; it is taught, practiced, and performed over and over again. There are biologically associated characteristics of Asian and white men, for example the amount of facial hair, but the value and meaning of these characteristics are socially constructed and used to maintain dominance. In chapter 3, Glenn, a first-generation Malaysian American, discussed the very different constructions of men in his home country. Men were allowed to be affectionate with each other, and it was common for them to be gentle and seemingly "effeminate" without their sexuality being questioned.

Both Irwin and Glenn present contrasting constructions of Asian and white masculinity. Their constructions of Asian men emphasize smaller bodies and a gentle, less competitive demeanor. Glenn makes an insightful connection between acting aggressively and competitively and sexuality. Real men are constructed as tough and combative in the United States.[19] These U.S. constructions of masculinity are spreading across the globe. They have become global and are affecting Asian nations.

This long assault has taken its toll on Asian Americans. Asian and Asian American men, in particular, have been dealt a number of blows, ideological, physical, and to their patriarchal domains. Irwin shares an example:

I went to Atlanta to speak at a conference. Some of the facilitators and I went to the Martin Luther King museum. There were three of us, Asian American men, standing there watching this video about segregation, and it occurred to us that we have a difficult time just physically standing up straight, looking people in the eye, and physically manifesting this sense of pride, dignity, or equality. It's taken me thirty years to feel like I can do that on a regular basis. But one of these guys was third- or fourth-generation Asian American. One of his parents was Chinese American, one was Japanese American. And he said, "You know, I've always been praised for my posture. People look at me and see me as different somehow because of the way I stand up and the way I hold myself." And the way he would stand is very straightforward. No sense of shame, being less than, or hiding something; he didn't have diverted eyes or anything like that. And I was like, "Yeah, that's the first thing I noticed about you. Man, you need to be on television." I couldn't quite put my finger on why I was thinking that but then I realized that this guy is lacking insecurity, lacking shame of being what he is, lacking fear. He didn't have that hunched-overness that I had for a long time.

Irwin went through a long process to gain confidence and overcome his fear. His fear of white men "messing with him," is something that is explored in greater detail later in this chapter. Irwin regarded his poor posture as a norm for Asian American men, something that he shared with other men and demonstrated the unconscious effect racism can have on how people carry themselves. There is growing evidence that racism is a factor in health disparity, but it can be difficult for researchers to tease out clear connections between mind, body, and spirit. One of my colleagues, after hearing Irwin's discussion of posture, wondered if there might be any long-term physical back problems due to this. There may be racism-health connections that researchers have not begun to consider. It's known that children who have been physically abused will tend to shrink when adults approach.[20] It could be that Asian American men who have had lengthy exposure to racialized bullying could also unconsciously develop a physical response to that treatment. Earlier, Irwin stated that Asian and Asian American men have different mannerisms and body movement based on "tradition"; however, here he speaks specifically of bodily responses to racism.

IDENTITY

My respondents all spoke about forming their identities, and some struggled more than others with this process. As demonstrated in chapters 2 and 3, there is a combination of factors in identity formation. There are familial, cultural, and external expectations of personhood that collide with internal thoughts and desires. A person may struggle with whether they develop a characteristic because they are "wired" that way or if they have been shaped by society. Brent, a third-generation Chinese American in his thirties who grew up in the South, explains:

> In terms of being physical, or that whole Bruce Lee thing, on one level I'm really interested in the martial arts and I haven't had a chance to do it. Sometimes the idea would come to my head: Why am I into this? Because people have been blasting that Asians are supposed to be good at this sort of thing, or is it because I really like to do it?

Brent cannot differentiate whether his interest in martial arts is something he genuinely likes or if the racial associations of Asians as martial artists have pushed him in that direction. When I teach gender to undergraduates, I often use dolls and Barbie as an example of the power of socialization and gendered norms. Female-bodied infants are not wired with a genetic code to love the color pink and to play with dolls. The color and activity have been assigned a gender. Boys who wear pink or play with dolls are at risk of gender disciplining. Similarly, martial arts are first a gendered activity in Asia. Second, it has been specifically racialized as a form of physical combat. We then see it reinforced repeatedly in the media with limited representations of Asian men as martial artists. With very few representations, it would make sense that Brent associates with martial arts if he embraces some aspects of his "Asianness."

Ray, a third-generation Chinese American in his twenties who grew up in the South, also found very few images and role models in the media. He had to independently construct a masculine identity that was antihegemonic.

> When I was growing up, there was no model character that I could go along with. Some traits are more important. A lot of them I got from watching cartoons and reading comics. Things about being smart. Smart means being clever, understanding losing. Losing's not a total loss if you understand why you lost. And don't be a douche bag. You don't need to kick some guy around all the time. Those were things I felt like, "I'll just take these things and be myself. I'm not happy with any of these models that I've seen." I don't feel like an Asian American kid needs to grow up watching one group; they just need to be themselves. They don't need to follow one or the other, but just understand that there are a lot of things out there. They shouldn't be totally white. I don't know how to describe that in any tangible way. I knew I didn't want to be totally white.

Ray's experience with racist whites kept him from emulating whiteness. He has been put off by an aunt and cousin who worked hard to "whiten" themselves. Ray gained self-confidence and strength from his experiences with racism. While they were painful experiences, Ray sees them as character-building exercises. In forming identity, my male interviewees are responding to gendered and racialized scripts. They struggle to be model minority-esque, emulate whiteness or other men of color, or try to create an original identity.

The Asian American "Model Minority Man" — The King of Geekdom

For a long time, Ray has fought against white hegemonic constructions of masculinity. He rejects notions that a "real man" has to be physically dominant. Ray worked to redefine himself and find self-valuation that counters hegemonic masculine constructions:

> For me, a real man doesn't have to always physically show how powerful he is. Power isn't anything. For me, a real man is a person who has to restrain themselves more rather than showing themselves off. I developed that a real long time ago.

Ray prides himself as being the "king of geekdom and dorkdom." He is very self-confident and comfortable in his masculinity and sexuality. While Ray is comfortable with his identity, he still becomes angry when a racist incident happens. Just a month before he was interviewed, two white men walking behind him and his family threw out racist epithets. His cousin's wife, who is white, confronted the two men. They laughed at her, turned a corner, and screamed "White Power!" Ray shared that he was bothered by this event and became angry because he was unable to protect himself and his family from the two men. But ignoring the racists further emasculated Ray and his cousin.

Samir, a second-generation Asian Indian American in his twenties who grew up in the Southwest, jokes that Asian Indian Americans actually fit the stereotype. Samir is very athletic and was heavily involved with a Desi fraternity in college. While studying medicine, he works to define his own masculinity even with the stereotypes.

> Most Indian kids are like the spelling bee kids, to be honest with you. We're the smart brainiac guys who solve all the problems. We're the guys who make our family and our parents happy because that's how our culture is. In terms of masculinity level, I don't think we're labeled as very masculine.

John, a second-generation Chinese American in his late thirties who grew up in the South, said that he identified with being a geek before identifying as an Asian American. He hung out mainly with advanced students, largely Asian American, in high school, college, and now at work. He is in the computer software industry and lives in a "culture of computer geekdom." He separates geekdom from race, while some respondents argue that they are interchangeable. Many things become "raced," "gendered," and "sexualized:" clothing, food, furniture, hobbies, and sports. It is arguable that "geekdom" is male, straight, white, and Asian.

This construction of geekdom has historical roots in "model minority" stereotyping. The pursuit of academic excellence was and is a defense strategy against racism.[21] In some ways, respondents used the geek route because they did not want to imitate or pursue hegemonic masculinity, while other respondents would choose to either emulate whiteness or, as respondents described, "gangster." The geek is a safe alternative for those who do not choose to perform hypermasculinity. They feel comfortable being smart and do not choose to get in physical altercations. Their coping mechanism in dealing with racism is to assume that the assailant is just "ignorant."

The nerd type is antithetical to the mainstream notion of authentic black male identity but accepted as an accurate representation of an Asian American man. Black buddy films portray the black buddy as asexual, but still underlining that is the assumption that he is heterosexual. There are a growing number of Asian buddy movies.[22] "Traditional, orientalist, racial prejudice is still alive and well. It is probably no coincidence that the self-effacing, sexually nonthreatening Jackie Chan has made the most successful and sustained crossover into mainstream American cinema."[23] When African American men are portrayed as gay in movies, they are overwhelmingly shown as effeminate "sissies" or "Snap! Queens."[24] There's great variance in the representations of heterosexual black men versus gay black men because black masculinity is constructed as intensely hypermasculine and so black gay men, "cannot be black."[25] Thus, we see the exaggerated hypersexuality versus the exaggerated effeminate gay man. For Asian American males, there is not as much contrast in the constructions of the gay Asian man and the straight Asian man. The Asian gay man is not as antithetical to the construction of the Asian man because he is constructed as hypomasculine.

White Hegemonic Masculinity or "Bad Boy" Posturing?

While there were very few Asian Americans at my high school, one particular classmate stuck out. His father was a successful doctor who had emigrated from China, and his mother was white. Whenever a peer would ask him about his racial makeup, he would fervently say, "I'm white." If questioned again, because physically he looked multiracial, he would get very angry and shout that he was "not Chinese" but rather white. I realized that there was something unsettling about this but didn't yet realize that there was something he detested about his Asian heritage. When I went to college, I met another Asian American man who had Chinese parents and called himself "The Caucasian Asian." Every time I saw him hanging outside of the dorm, he was engaged in these male performances of hypermasculinity. He was loud, walking with an exaggerated swagger, and constantly yelling out that he was the "Caucasian Asian." Perhaps I was judgmental because he did not fit my constructions of an Asian American man. However, in both cases, I saw these two men overtly and publicly reject their Asianness.

David Eng asserts that "whiteness is a social construct which acts to covertly draw the boundaries of normative heterosexuality and to exclude the non-white subjects such as the Asian male from masculinity's associated roles of power."[26] Asian American men may attempt to emulate whiteness hoping to access masculine power. This is a coping strategy for some Asian American men and women.[27] However, as Eng suggests, there is a long history of exclusion of the Asian man from power and normative masculinity.[28] One respondent, Brent, has some animosity toward a cousin who has abandoned the family. Brent is angry at his cousin and feels like his cousin is ashamed of his Asianness:

> He's a dick, mostly because he doesn't have any dealings with his family, with us. After a certain point, he just didn't want to have anything to do with us. I think it's that Chinese part [he dislikes]. He went to [a large state university] and he's a doctor now, but from high school on he got this idea that he would be a rich kid even though his parents aren't rich. He started to dress like the preppy white kids and trying to get in their circles. Eventually, he just split off from us, even though we would see each other every Sunday dinner at my grandma's house. It was kind of sad, but he started dating a rich white girl and started to live this rich Southern lifestyle. His wife, or his girlfriend at the time, was whining to me about how he refused for a very long time to bring her over to meet us and when he finally did he and his girlfriend didn't even stay at his mom and dad's house. They went and stayed at a hotel. I don't know if he's just ashamed of where he's from or who he is or what.

Brent's cousin's abandonment of the family hurts Brent a great deal. He continues:

> When our families get together and we're all having a great time, his parents say, "Gosh, I really wish my son was here. Everyone looks so happy." I've never walked away from him. He walked away from us. I almost have zero sympathy for him now. If someone slapped money down and said, "Brent, here's your $5,000. Have you and your cousin fight in the cage." I'm like give me that money. I feel so insulted that he doesn't want to be part of us because, one, we're not white, and, two, we were kind of poor. He only shows up at Grandma's funeral or as some token person in my brother's marriage. That's the story with him. I think he probably has great desires to be a white man.

Like the two examples of Asian American men I knew in high school and college, Brent's cousin is attempting to abandon his Asian heritage.[29] He is specifically emulating whiteness as he attempts to rise in class status. Brent's cousin is not alone; many Asian Americans choose to downplay their Asianness for various reasons.[30] Sometimes it's to protect themselves from further racial stigma or stereotyping; sometimes they may have internalized white racial framing.[31] Much of the "whitening," however, is a strategy to avoid racism.

Another strategy some Asian American men use to combat gendered racism is to build a larger physique. Jackson Katz noted in *Tough Guise* that representations of the male body in movies, television, and action figures have continued to grow larger while women's bodies and dolls have gotten smaller.[32] These changes in body size have become so exaggerated that a G.I. Joe action figure's bicep has reached a proportion impossible for any human being to reach.[33] Glenn describes an Asian American friend who he believes is a model of Asian American masculinity.

> I have a friend, born in Singapore and raised in the U.S., who is a personal trainer. He exhibits what I call the ideal Asian American type. He's very masculine. He's very built. He acts in a very American way. If you paint him white, he is completely American. Not saying that Asian Americans are not Americans. I think there is a misunderstanding that Asian Americans are not Americans because they're not *American*. Americans are supposed to be white. At the same time, I think black is also understood to be a part of the American model. Now Latino men are moving into the mainstream. But Asian men are lagging behind. They are not there yet. He represents what I would say a lot of heterosexual Asian American men would like to become. He's big, huge. He really trains to develop the physique that is competitive with other "Americans"—white, Latino, black. Bruce Lee had a great body, but he's lean, very lean. He's not really muscular. He's lean and tall. I would say the body types are a little different. Asian men are lean and toned, not muscular. Lean and toned aren't what is most desirable.

Glenn's friend is a representation of an Asian American male conforming to whiteness. What Glenn describes is a person working hard to shape and form a body associated with non-Asian men. Glenn is arguing that to become truly American, Asian Americans must not act Asian, something he does not clearly describe. Glenn puts a great deal of emphasis on constructions of whiteness and Asianness. Race and gender are sociohistorically constructed. There is no real biological basis to acting white or male; there is only performance and perceptions of those performances. Glenn's friend attempts to access whiteness by doing "body work," using the gym rather than plastic surgery to shape his body in what is perceived as white and male.

The Asian American Bad Boy?

White hegemonic masculinity relies on the subordination of women and other forms of masculinity. Appearing weak, effeminate, or gay marginalizes a man in this hegemonic structure. Asian American men, as opposed to non-Asian American men, are burdened with these stereotypes. If they whiten, they hope to reap the benefits of white masculinity. Another strategy for Asian American men is affirming their masculinity through "bad boy" posturing.[34] This posturing is identified with working-class white men or men of color.[35] However, performing this bad boy act is not without consequence. Krais contends that "fears of appearing effeminate, hence homosexual—that is, of not being a "real man"—are common among men, and demonstrating "real" male behavior seems to put great strain on them."[36] Men of color are extremely vilified compared to white men who are also posturing themselves as deviant.

Bad-boy posturing for Asian American men is most visible in the discourse of an Asian gangster who is of East or Southeast Asian descent. Chance, a second-generation Filipino American in his twenties who grew up in the Southwest, recalls the Asian bad boys at his high school:

> They drove Hondas and Acuras, had spiked hair. They always had these black jackets. It was kind of the Asian jacket. Before Myspace[37] and even before Zynga[38] there was Asianave.com[39] and all the Asians would be on it. They would also have all these caricatures, the hair. It's all there—gangster Asians, guns, and the cars and stuff.

Chance says he was not particularly interested in Asianave.com, though he did try to have the Asian spiked hair but was unable to get his curly hair to stand up. Chance was not the only respondent to notice the trend of some Asian American men trying to portray themselves as tough or violent, as Brent illustrates.

> It seems like a lot of younger Asian males are getting into this hip-hop thing, trying to blend into that culture. It's okay to be Asian and in your face and try to take part in that street, hip-hop sort look, even though you might live in the suburbs. Sometimes I'll be in [major city with a large population of Asians] with my cousin and some of his friends are like, "When Asians get up in the club, someone's going to get shot!" And you would never hear anything like that before! Wow. Not a good thing, but you're just like, "What?" I think the whole hip-hop street thing has become an alternative for Asian men. It's an alternative to either being straight-up Asian in your culture or being white. It's trying to be a part of a group or to create some sort of identity. Maybe being Asian isn't enough, or it's just not as accepted a form of status.

Brent provides examples of Asian Americans having very rigid boundaries of identity. There is this foreign, "model minority" construction where Asians are not the cool kids. The normal popular kids are white, and embracing hip-hop and violence is reserved for other people of color and is largely classed. Bonilla-Silva has formulated a tri-racial model where a few Asian Americans are categorized as whites, and largely East and Asian Indian Americans are "honorary whites."[40] Southeast Asian Americans are deemed "collective blacks" due to class stratification, method of immigration, and, in part, skin color. However, if a gender component were added to Bonilla-Silva's model, these classifications would be insufficient. Asian American men, especially those with East

Asian roots, would be in the lowest tier of the intersected order. In accepting that they will rarely achieve the status of white men, there is a
move to emulate men of color.

There have been movies portraying Asian and Asian American men
in this role. Recent films such as *The Fast and the Furious: Tokyo Drift,*
Better Luck Tomorrow, and *Gran Torino* portray East and Southeast Asian
Americans as hypermasculine criminals. The criminality is not a new
portrayal of Asians in Hollywood, but the close resemblance of hypermasculinity to Latinos and African Americans has increased as rap and
hip-hop have become mainstream. As Brent observed, "going hip-hop" is
an alternative to what is constructed as inaccessible white and low-status
Asian masculinity. Brent attended a prestigious math and science boarding school where his Asian American male roommate was "straight
gangster." His roommate would be very disrespectful to dining hall staff
and would be loud and obnoxious in the dining room, threatening to
harm people and being disruptive. These masculine displays, however,
were just gendered public performances. While he would occasionally
test his strength against Brent, he most often was very different when
there was no audience.

> It was funny that he would be so in your face, but not when we were in
> our room or with our friends in the dorm. But occasionally he would
> really want to fight me. It was just like, dude, we're roommates, and he
> would get on my nerves wanting to know if I was going to hit him
> back. Somehow we would just kind of fight. I mean, I don't want to just
> be bragging but he would never beat me up; it's just not possible for
> him. He was the type the guy who lifted weights and was very body
> conscious, that sort of guy.

There are benefits to bad-boy posturing. Appearing more physically
threatening may work to deter others from bothering you. Also, Katz
asserts that women validate and support bad-boy posturing by being
attracted to men who act tough.[41] Asian American men are already considered unappealing by white hegemonic beauty standards, so they may
gain some attention from women with this bad boy image. It is also a
survival mechanism to "survive in whatever peer culture they happen to
be in. But putting on the tough guise comes with a cost in terms of
damage to their psyches and their ability to be decent human beings."[42]

In one case, Robert, a second-generation Chinese American in his
twenties who grew up on the East Coast, was able to gain some respect
by fitting into a tough-guy role. Robert was able to fit into the Asian
stereotype of martial artist, so the role was easy for outsiders to believe as
authentic. Earlier examples from respondents noted the strangeness of
Asian American men who tried to be too "gangster." Robert shares,

> Because I do martial arts, I am fitted to the "Kung-Fu Master" stereo-
> type, which is not exactly good but I'd say it's *less bad* than the nerdy

Asian male who can't get women. I think it is somewhat part of my identity, especially when I'm getting to know more people. My friends will introduce me like "Hey, here's Robert, he does martial arts and could totally beat your ass up."

Robert identifies that all racial stereotyping of Asian and Asian American men is damaging, but that this particular stereotyped awarded him some masculine status. In his view, to be seen as the dangerous, highly skilled martial artist is better than being a socially and sexually inept "nerdy Asian male." He continues,

I actually felt that, masculinity-wise, I was respected. When I was with black guys, they would talk to me as if I was experienced in like the "hook-up culture." They said, "you must get a lot of women because you can do like crazy shit and fly in the air, right?" And I kind of went along with what they said, because I didn't want to feel more alienated.

For Robert, he was able to get a respite from alienation and stigma. His African American male peers assumed that his abilities would garner popularity with women. In contrast, Hollywood martial arts movies rarely portray Asian martial arts masters as womanizers or sexual at all. For example, in the 2000 film *Romeo Must Die*, the original ending was supposed to be a kiss shared between Jet Li and actress Aaliyah, but the producers changed the ending because it did not "test well" with audiences.[43] Martial artists turned actors, like Bruce Lee and Jackie Chan, rarely get the girl. In contrast, white action heroes like James Bond have a sexual drive incorporated into their characters—even in parodies like Austin Powers. But Robert, even if briefly, was able to be seen as a "ladies man" by his male peers.

VIOLENCE

If you're a boy, it's pretty clear there's a lot of pressure on you to conform, to put up the act to be just one of the guys. Obviously, they learn this in many different places, from their families, their community. But one of the most important places they learn it is the powerful and pervasive media system that provides a steady stream of images that define manhood as connected with power, dominance and control. This is true across all racial and ethnic groups, but it's even more pronounced for men of color because there is so little diversity of images of them to begin with in the media culture. For example, Latino men are almost always presented as boxers, criminals, or tough guys in the barrio. Asian American men are disproportionately portrayed as martial artists or violent criminals. But, transcending race, what the media do is help to construct violent masculinity as a cultural norm. In other words, violence isn't so much a deviation as it is an accepted part of masculinity. —Jackson Katz, *Tough Guise*

Jackson Katz asserts that violent masculinity has become an accepted cultural norm. It has been normalized on playgrounds for boys to uphold a white hegemonic masculine hierarchy with little consequence from teachers.[44] In action movies, men of color are repeatedly shown as agents of violence. However, in the "model minority" stereotyping of the emasculated Asian American man, Asian American men are the recipients of physical, emotional, and symbolic violence at the hands of other men. Patricia Hill Collins notes that black men face violence at the hands of black men most frequently.[45]

However, Asian men in the United States and across the globe face violence largely at the hands of non-Asian men, especially white men. The violence and emasculation that Asian American men and boys face has an effect on their self-esteem and also masks the violence within the Asian American community—the self-hatred, internalized oppression, domestic violence, and disdain for their own community members.

Targets of Physical Violence

> An awful lot of boys and men are inflicting an incredible level of pain and suffering on themselves and others. —Jackson Katz, *Tough Guise*

Hegemonic masculinity is based on highlighting differences between men and women. For Asian American men, this becomes a problem because there are less obvious contrasts between Asian American men and women in terms of size, muscle mass, body hair, and even perceived intelligence. This further stigmatizes Asian American men as subordinate or marginalized because they may appear to more closely resemble the gender of which they are oppositely constructed. Additionally, hegemonic masculinity requires control over women. Especially in the public sphere, the representation of East Asians does not portray East Asian men as dominant or strong heads of household. While this may starkly contrast reality in these homes, the media portrayal is clear.[46] These elements influence the level of violence and bullying that Asian American men and boys face.

Six of my male respondents experienced violent hate crimes at the hands of white men.[47] Henry, a first-generation Chinese American in his seventies living on the West Coast, has been beaten and harassed by whites for over fifty years. Bari, a first-generation Asian Indian American in his thirties living in the Southwest, was hit with a baseball bat by a white assailant and called a "fucking foreigner" while biking home from his college campus. A white man jumped out of a car at a stoplight to hurl racial epithets and punch Conrad, a second-generation Chinese American in his thirties living in the Southwest, knocking out a tooth while he was walking with a group of friends. After September 11, 2001, Ahmed, a first-generation Pakistani-American living in the Southwest, received threatening phone calls and e-mails, and white drivers on the highway forced Paul, a second-generation Asian Indian American in his thirties living in the Southwest, off the road. Henry verbally protests the physical assaults that continue to this day, and Guang, a second-generation Chinese American in his twenties living in a major metropolitan city in the Northeast, consistently uses force because he does not want people to "assume [he's] just a passive Asian" because "they'll take advantage of that."

Among my respondents, the targets of violent racism have all been men. This is a notable difference that Brent mentioned in his interview. He and his male cousins received physical threats, while his female cousin and another Asian American girl in his school were able to avoid that level of conflict. Indira also notes that she receives different treatment than her brother, viewing her treatment from a historical perspective.

> The terrorist stereotype is not going to affect me as much as it's going to affect my brother. The type of violence that he would likely experience is way different than what I would experience. Every foreign war the U.S. has been engaged in for the last century was with a country that has an Asian face—whether that's a brown Asian face or a Middle Eastern face, which out of compassion I tend to include in an Asian capacity. Our men are the unfortunate beneficiaries of the impact of those stereotypes. I don't want to sound clichéd, but on 9/11 it happened to be South Asian men. Post-Vietnam war, the face was different. Post-World War II, the face was different; the treatment again was just as violent. I can't even imagine how to have a conversation around masculinity with Asian men. On the one hand, on the grand scale, Asian men really don't get to be "masculine" because they're not seen as manly, whatever that's supposed to be. And yet I don't think that they experience the true notions of what masculinity means, and the byproduct of that is that masculinity shows up in not the best ways internal to community.

Since the revolutionary war, white working-class men have joined or been drafted into the military to enforce policies often made without their input, but Asian American men occupy a different space.[48] These wars have been wars against Asian faces. These wars legitimate violence against Asian peoples. School shootings are not seen as a white problem. The Virginia Tech shooting was racialized. Terrorists are black and brown people, but when we analyze these events of violence a missing dimension is the preceding violence against people from these countries. More clearly, the continual wars the United States wages against people in Asia, Africa, and the Middle East seem to be absent from the conscious forefront of most Americans. There is little blame assigned the United States for an assault on these people across the globe. However, in the United States, when people who seem to be citizens of or have ancestry in these regions, it becomes inexplicable why they would want to attack Americans. There is a short or selective white, patriotic memory, or *collec-*

tive forgetting,[49] that sees only brown and black faces as violent. We do not see whiteness as the greatest source of violence across the globe.

Living in Fear

The immigration experience can be terrifying. While many Americans worry about brown and black faces invading, corrupting, and planning to attack or take over the United States, we miss just how difficult the immigrant experience can be. Paul explains:

> My father told me one of the most scariest moments in his life was moving to the U.S. to go to school because his English was just horrible and he had a super thick accent. He is still very self-conscious, like he won't order pizza over the phone. Somebody else has to order, like one of the little kids. My sister was seven; she had to order it over the phone because he was always afraid of people just making fun of him.

Paul continues:

> My dad got robbed at a grocery store one time. Got held up at gun-point. That stuff's got to really fuck with your head. Because he came over here to make money to give back to his family back home. You fly all the way over here and you go through all this shit, and you almost get killed in the place that's supposed to be the place where you're supposed to make it. So there's my little immigrant dad, 5'5" just sitting with his big mustache, waiting to go to Kroger to sack groceries. I can't imagine how awful it is. Especially getting loans. Getting everything. And they never talk about it with me. I have to really prod them to find out; the only reason I found out he got robbed was his friend told me. They have this new house and they're outside planting and you always wonder, how lame are your parents because they don't ever want to go out? They're so happy sitting at home. And I think it's because of what they have gone through. They remember 1971, just struggling to make rent. And now we have this big house and I can sit here. And nobody is going to fuck with me. I can sit here and plant whatever I want, and nobody is going to yell at me and I'm safe. My dad has been wanting a new house since he moved here in 1970. They've been struggling for so long.

Many immigrant men with families have the added burden of navigating a new, racist society in addition to all the responsibilities of taking care of their families in the United States and, in some cases, their family members living in Asia. Paul tried to imagine moving to China and trying to navigate through daily life. He has a great deal of empathy and appreciation for the sacrifices his parents made coming to the United States. There is intense pressure on those heads of household.

The male breadwinner model is said to be in decline.[50] Studies show that professional work settings still require the performance of a masculine breadwinner mentality to be successful.[51] The decline in the model has different impacts on men and women because women often have networks centered on home.[52] This provides a much greater threat to identity for men than their women counterparts.[53] Men suffer differently from job loss. Indira notes a recent trend with Desi families:

> I have seen at least three or four [news articles] where the head of the household of an Indian family, the father, has shot the entire family including grandparents and children, wife, everybody. Just a family suicide and then shot himself. There is no definition of masculinity for our men, and it does not allow for output of emotion and seeking of health to be seen as a good thing, so it comes out in some level of harm. I would argue there's no parallel. Most of my friends were Vietnamese American growing up, and it wasn't uncommon to hear that their fathers often didn't talk about anything to them. The stress of a father who was disengaged and shot down because of their experience of immigrating to the United States—you know what it must have been like leaving everything, losing family.

Indira provided me with links to three articles of Desi American men who, after facing financial trouble, murdered their families and then committed suicide.[54] Men's work makes up a bigger part of their identity; therefore it is more difficult for them to build an identity based on home life while they are without a job, meaning they tend to feel more socially excluded.[55] The economic downturn is adding stress to the lives of most citizens in the United States; however, with these tragic incidents Indira finds a connection with masculinity and race.

Asian American men are not the only ones living in fear of physical harm. Asian American boys in and outside of school have that fear as well. Brent shares, "I know that in high school, the idea of a fight was always looming out there. It depends on how far this personality will take the verbal assault." The respondents reported very little intervention from school staff regarding these physical threats. Bullying has become normalized as an acceptable behavior to expect from boys. Jackson Katz argues that

> one of the major consequences of all [the violence in the media] is there's a growing connection made in our society between being a man and being violent. In fact, some of the most serious problems in contemporary American society, especially those connected with violence, can be looked at essentially problems in contemporary masculinity.

These contemporary problems with masculinity take various forms. While there is overt physical violence, there is also symbolic violence. Emasculation can occur in ways other than physical bullying; it can also take place with exclusion and symbolic "racial castration."

Symbolic Castration

What is stereotyped as "natural" black heterosexuality is actually rooted in the white construction of the hypersexual African American man.[56] Whites do not stereotype Asian American men as naturally hypersexual; instead they are stereotyped as hypo- or asexual. Hyposexuality is defined as having an abnormal sexual drive. So these representations of Asian American men as hyposexual in the media perpetuate the stereotyping of abnormal sexuality. Even in gay porn, Asian bodies are symbolically castrated where camera angles never show their penises and they are consistently portrayed as bottoms.[57] One male respondent, Zac, a second-generation Chinese American in his thirties who lives in a metropolitan city in the Northeast with a large Asian population, encouraged me to visit the website www.bitterasianmen.com.[58] He explains, "I found this site while surfing one day. And it's about these two highly educated med school students that are bitter because they lost their girlfriends to white guys." On the website, there is a section titled "Rant" where the website creators have articles published like, "White Girls Don't Want Us," "Asian Girls Don't Want Us," "Western Society Hates Us," and "Nature Hates Us." Interestingly, the article "Nature Hates Us" details the penis sizes of various racial groups.

The authors of the now defunct website are perpetuating stereotypes that race is connected to innate biological differences that have social value and significance. The authors use their site for social commentary that "God" or "nature" has punished Asian American men by giving them smaller penises, shorter stature, and hairless bodies. They use these physical disadvantages to explain why Asian American men are unable to court and satisfy women. The value placed on the size of male genitalia, body hair, and height is a socially constructed value. This concept of ideal body type is racialized and gendered, based on hegemonic masculine ideals. Again, in Western thought, the mind and body are dichotomous. This discourse has been used to reinforce white male power and privilege.

Asian American men have not always been symbolically castrated. Formerly, they were grouped with other men of color accused of being sexual predators with a predilection for white women and girls. However, the discourse shifted with the rise of the "model minority" stereotype. Whites were no longer able to infer Asian American racial inferiority because of their apparent success in education and the professional realm, so the script had to change. Judith Butler argues that masculinity is extremely fragile and must always be reproduced in performance,[59] but the gender script is different for Asian American men than for other men of color. Whereas African and Latino American men are attributed a hypermasculine status, Asian American men start with an assumed deficiency. The media perpetuates these images, portraying Asian American men as sexless and undesirable. These images take root in reality as Asian American men bitterly cope with being ignored by non-Asian women and watch Asian American women partnered with white men. The shift in Asian American masculinity demonstrates the transformative nature of systems of oppression. Political strides for African American men postslavery led to oppressive segregation laws. The advances for African Americans were met with resistance from whites in other forms.[60] African American men continued to be disempowered by Black Codes, Jim Crow laws, and the prison industrial complex.

Asian American success as "model minorities" has also been met with white resistance. The sexual stereotypes have been more widely dispersed through media sources, as Irwin explains.

> Well, speaking about the sexual insecurities of white men. [White men have] got to come up with something for each group in order to keep them away from white women. So, for black men it is that they are dangerous or violent, blah blah blah. And then for Asian men it's supposed to be opposite. But at the same time there's this dangerous thing that is propagated through the stereotypes of gangsters and evil villains and things like this. So you look at these contradicting stereotypes. You've got these evil bad guys who have to be powerful in order to make a good villain for the white hero, and at the same time you have these weak nerds who are sexless or asexual.

Stereotypes about people of color do not have to be logical. The contradictory depictions of Asian American men show the centrality of maintaining the image of "virtuous whites" in the white racial frame.[61] This has an effect on the Asian American male psyche. As Brent mentioned in chapter 3, the media portrayals of Asian American men are so emasculating that he asserted, "you might as well not even have a dick sometimes." The "small penis" stereotype was always in the back of Robert's mind. He explains,

> I always had thought that one of the reasons why I wasn't so comfortable with talking with women was a confidence issue. The stereotypes about sexual organs plays into that a little bit, or a lot now that I think of it. So while it was never like a "oh, I can't talk to women because my penis is small" kind of thing, it was there in the back of my head; it was always there.

Robert was relieved when a girlfriend told him that his "penis was big in relation to her previous experiences." This helped him with his confidence: "What I think I related that to was height, because penis size is more proportional to height than it is to race, and I thought that I had gotten a 'get out of jail free' card or something, like I thought I had been '*spared*.'" Robert's language reveals the psychological burden of the racial stereotyping of Asian American men; he is relieved to not match that particularly emasculating stereotype.

The racial castration of Asian American men operates differently for Daniel, a second-generation Vietnamese American introduced earlier. In some ways, the stereotype worked to his advantage, allowing him to mask his sexuality. While other classmates would talk about sexual attraction to members of the opposite sex, Daniel could abstain from conversations without letting on to his friends that he is gay.

> I never had to pretend [to be sexually interested in women]. It's different for Asians; you're supposed to be asexual, not interested in sex I think appearing to be asexual is almost like a defense mechanism when it comes to appearing homosexual. I think that was something I picked up, just trying to appear asexual so people wouldn't question [my sexuality]. The Asian stereotype overrides the homosexuality stereotype of being submissive because Asians are submissive, so you have to be a bottom. And that goes into the gender stereotype of Asian males are submissive, they're mindless and they do what they're told. They're intelligent, but they're machines. It's very tough to explain, but I can definitely feel it.

There is a racialized power incorporated in sexuality. Queer Asian American men are in a very precarious position; they are likely to perpetuate stereotypes about Asian American men while trying to protect their queer identities. Within the queer community, there is a hierarchy of power. During the colonial period in Hong Kong, Asian men were largely bottoms for British men. After the colony was abolished, there was a shift in bottom and top politics.[62]

The way that black masculinity is constructed, African American men can only define their masculinity with prowess and conquering "booty."[63] For Asian American men, the "booty-conquering" player seems like the exception. There is a push in systems of gender and race to fit a script. Oppressed people are internally driven to meet those expectations in some fashion. Even in gay male pornography, Asian American men are symbolically castrated.[64] The pornography is used to graphically affirm white men's sexual domination and power over others.[65]

Psychological Costs

Jackson Katz asserts that "there are millions of male trauma survivors walking around today, men who were bullied in adolescence."[66] There is a great societal cost to the normalization of male violence. Much of the focus of gender studies thus far has been on women and feminist theory. More recently, there has been great growth in the study of masculinities and the long-term harm of male-on-male violence. The effect of violence on Asian American men has not been thoroughly researched. As one respondent, Indira, poignantly states, "American history has isolated the Asian man to not be able to speak, and that can only result in deep harm."

Irwin was deeply affected from the ethnosexualized treatment he received growing up. He was living in fear for many years.

> I would sit on the edge of a seat. I didn't want to take too much space up. Part of it was I didn't feel like I deserved to take up space, and part of it was fear of someone hitting me. I looked down a lot because I didn't want to confront people in the sense that a lot of people didn't like me for what I was. I didn't want to have to deal with that. Walking across a college campus, I had a hard time looking people in the eye, especially men, without glaring at them. That was the way I dealt with it, like "don't fuck with me." Either that or keep my head down low, I don't want anyone to bother me. So yeah, that's typical of any male who's had to deal with physical confrontations in his life.

Irwin fought back once in middle school, and it slowed the bullying for a time. But such long-term exposure to physical abuse had definite residual effects. Irwin went through a difficult time from middle through graduate school.

> When I was around 11, I really became very hateful and wanted to commit my own violence against these other kids. One day I was really, really angry and I drew these pictures of these two kids dying or being killed in some different fashion. After that I was a really strong believer in non-violence. Like, Gandhi was my idol. I actually read about this stuff. So at that point there must have been some kind of a split personality developing where one part of me wanted to actually taste the blood of people, of certain people, whoever was my enemy at that time. And the other person who abhorred violence and wanted to stop it in this world and studied politics and history to see what the best way of doing that would be. And I was empathetic to people who were victims of this and studied counseling—I have a degree in counseling, and I was a big political activist. A left-wing political activist protesting the war and certain American foreign policies. But on the other side, I was this really angry person.

Irwin's inner turmoil worsened. He went from being angry at the whites that inflicted the pain to hating men in his community.

> I went into this downward spiral. My anxiety was jacked up to enormous levels and I had these unbelievable mood swings. I started having this very twisted understanding of Asian masculinity, Asian men, and hatred [of] Asian men as people who I wish I didn't have to be associated with. I followed the Hitler complex. And it was very, very weird. I had obsessive thoughts about my girlfriend, about myself, about news; I guess these feelings got projected onto construed people that I thought were *inferior, Asian men*. I wished that they would *all die*. Disappear or something like that and it was very, very strange. It took me a long time to get over. I was prescribed Lithium for a while and I didn't like it. It's a combination of all those things. Certainly it was

worsened by the insecurities and such that are complicated by being an Asian American male born in America and having grown up here.

Whites perpetuate and maintain white supremacy by colonizing people of color, teaching them to repress rage, and never making whites the target of any anger they feel about racism.[67] Irwin never acted on his anger, though it consumed him. Instead, he took it out on himself and other men that looked like him. By internalizing the rage and stress from racism, people of color are at risk of negatively affecting their health.[68] While some will handle the stress of racism in a healthier manner, it can still be a burden.

Ray, who has done much work over the years building a strong sense of self, still carries some of the weight of racism. While he's forgiven much of the childhood racism he experienced, he has a harder time dealing with discrimination from white adults.

> Sometimes, I do feel really jaded about [dealing with racism growing up], but at the same time that jadedness has helped me become better at shrugging stuff off; I feel like I couldn't have gotten all these [good] traits without having gone through that kind of dumb shit. Other times, I'm just angry. Especially now, at my age, and in college. We're 18 and up—why are you still doing this shit? I shouldn't have to be the one to explain it to you why this is wrong. You are old enough. You are an adult. At the same time, you're ignorant of it and I'm mad, but I shouldn't be, because you are ignorant of it. But I have to be mad at something. I get really mad at a lot of things and I don't know why. I can't focus on anything. I don't feel like it's right for me to focus on being mad at these people for being stupid. That's why I feel jaded.

Where white rage is condoned by the state, there is no place for the rage of people of color.[69] Ray does not have a platform or voice to be angry at ignorant whites. He has to perform mental gymnastics to forgive "innocent," "ignorant," whites. Ray is engaging this image of "virtuous whites"[70] while simultaneously blaming himself for being the bad guy for having an emotional reaction to racism.

In addition to repression of rage, many respondents had direct instruction from family members to avoid conflict and to keep from rocking the boat.[71] Brent retains some regret for not having fought back against racism when he was younger.

> My mom and dad would always emphasize, "Look, don't get into fights with these people." "They're bigger than you and they're all white," or "They're bigger than you and they're all black." That just didn't sit right with me. The idea that there's no way in hell I would ever be able to win a fistfight with anyone—that comes from Mom and Dad. Of course that didn't feel good. I would go to dumbass Tai Kwon Do class, and they'd be like "Yeah, that's good! Oh, but don't really get into a fight because you'd get your ass whipped." And I felt like, "That

makes no damn sense. So what if I got my ass whipped a little bit? It's not going to be that bad." I never did get in a fight. It never happened.

While attempting to protect their son, Brent's parents gave him the impression that he was not strong enough to defend himself. His parents, in essence, emasculated him while trying to keep him from harm. Such conflicting messages demonstrate the difficulty in multiframing. On the one hand, Brent's parents want him to learn to defend himself, a strategy from an anti-oppression counter-frame. But then they insist that he is too weak to fight against non-Asians, which is a stereotype from the white racial frame. Multiframing can cause this type of internal conflict. Finding coping strategies to combat white racial framing is not always as simple as learning to fight physically. There is a great need to develop psychological strength as well.

Asian American Men as Perpetrators, a Nuanced Example

The stereotyping of Asian American men as symbolically castrated, weak, and passive can mask the violence and gender inequality that can exist in the Asian American communities. Irwin was open and honest throughout his interview and was even able to give a nuanced example of when Asian American men, like him, can try and take advantage of male privilege. He notes:

> I mean, as an Asian man, people tend to think that I'm a decent person or I'm not gonna commit a crime against them or I'm not going to rape a woman or at the very least, I don't have the strength to rape a woman or something like that. And so in a lot of ways, I can use that either consciously or subconsciously to my advantage.

Irwin uses these assumptions about his character and strength to get closer to women. He is perceived as nonthreatening. However, when he changes the way he presents himself, he will suddenly be perceived as a threat.

> It's pretty subdued most of the time; you just get a sense that people aren't comfortable. Maybe I'm at a place where they don't expect to see Asians. There's this stereotype of, "You gotta watch out for these Asian gangsters because they're more violent and ruthless than the other gangsters." I've heard that from both whites and blacks. So there's that fear too, the fear of physical safety. And that springs from not knowing us. Maybe one stereotype feeds off the other. If you can't conceive of the humanity of this sort of inscrutable nerd or weak person, then there's no place where that person can accept the sort of complex humanity of all Asians period. If all you're working with is two or three different stereotypes, then you can't understand anyone. It's "there's a bunch of Asian gangsters" or "there's a bunch of Asian nerds" — they're all extremified. I think there are all sorts of reasons why white Americans fear other people. I would expect it to be guilt. Well, they

have this sort of vague understanding of history. Like we really treated those people bad so now they're gonna want to get us back.

There is such extreme polarity in the perceptions and representations of Asian American men. They are asexual/homosexual, socially inept nerds, or degenerate gangsters, perceived to be mimicking the image of other men of color. In some cases the Asian gangster is seen as more ruthless and cunning because of their perceived greater intelligence. However, there is no middle ground, only extreme images. These are all imposed stereotypes; it's not an option to be just a "regular guy" if you are not white.

With years of racist taunting and physical abuse, Irwin had a great deal of anger inside of him. Irwin dealt with anger by getting into "gangster" stuff. He wrote a rap song warning that "one of these days, one of these Asian guys is going to retaliate." Irwin speaks in reference to Cho Seung Hui and the Virginia Tech shooting.

> I said that ten years before [the Virginia Tech shooting] happened. I could see it in little ways. There was a friend of mine, more like an acquaintance, who was kind of this angry Asian man. He was in the military. And he told me that him and some guys would go out where they thought somebody would mess with them, like a country club, country music club, anywhere where there's a lot of more right-wing white people. They would essentially be goading [them into violence]. And when someone did respond to them, they would take the guy out and beat the shit out of him. That was their way of retaliating.

Irwin did not condone the actions of his military acquaintance. However, because of the cruel racist treatment he endured while growing up, he was able to empathize with him and Cho Seung Hui. The Virginia Tech shooting, while he predicted it a decade prior, was still quite rattling.

> I had a hard time sleeping for a long time. I was sad, I identified with this guy, just like I had identified with this Vietnamese kid at [the local university] who shot and killed one or two white guys for messing with him. It was obvious to me. American stereotypes of Asian people—East Asian people—are very distorted. We tend to tone it down around people, but the reality is we're as fiery and ill-tempered as any other group of people. A lot of Asian men out there, especially people my age, need or seek subconsciously this revenge. They either find it in some way or grow older and it's not such an important part of their psyche. But I think there are a lot of Asian men who do still have it in their heads that this revenge has never been realized. It's like they're deformed; gestalt psychology says people need to finish their unfinished business, and if they don't it stays with them.

Irwin has been able to find outlets for his anger through his writing and teaching. It is still a challenge for him to feel fully equal to other men, but he is constantly making strides. This nuanced example exemplifies the psychological effects of white racism. Irwin has felt the effects of white habitus through feelings of inferiority. But he also pushes back against the racist notion that Asian men are incapable of violence or rage.

Asian American men are simultaneously silent and silenced. There is no social reward or encouragement for them to discuss their racial teasing or taunting. Jackson Katz, antiviolence scholar and activist, warns that these masculine performances can be costly and create cultures of violence. Hopefully, Asian American men and boys will have access to counter-frames and will create counter-narratives to the racist framing that is in place.

SPORTS AS A COPING MECHANISM

Numerous studies suggest that sports build self-esteem.[72] Sport is also central in the construction of masculinities.[73] However, sports have a hierarchical structure based on the ability to excel in performance.[74] There is also growing emphasis in sport on competitive physique. The media reflect this emphasis in sports marketing. The size of body builders, athletes, and action heroes continues to exponentially grow.[75] For Asian Americans who participated in sports, they may have been able to reap some benefits by excelling in a very masculine identified arena. Jeremy notes,

> I think really it boils down to what you were involved in when you were younger. If you were involved in sports and bonded in team activities, you were more likely to keep these friends later on. We were involved in sports at a young age. Our parents didn't always just stress education, so we're well-rounded individuals. I feel like if you didn't do that, you would have a harder time adjusting.

Jeremy credits his involvement in sports for helping him be outgoing. However, there were differences in his experiences on all-white sports teams and teams with more people of color. The all-white environments did not provide long-lasting friendships with teammates.

While Brent was not really allowed to participate in sports, he still saw it as a valuable tool to build self-esteem and protect individuals from racism.

> Inclusion into social clubs like sports helps protect against bullying because sports are the sort of things those kids are into. Once you become a part of that group, you probably get teased less or at least teased in an inclusive way. You can make fun of someone in your group, but once someone outside of your group makes fun of that person, the entire group will stand with this person that got made fun of.

Brent sees the teasing culture of sports as a way to be included. Certainly, the fraternal bond can be a joking relationship.[76] However, that male joking relationship is a controlled use of aggression that maintains a hierarchical order.[77] Jason, a Chinese American, was a baseball player in high school. They consistently made fun of his Chinese surname because it sounded like slang for "penis."[78] For years on the high school team, they defaced his uniform, hat, equipment, and school notebooks with drawings of the phallus. He knew it was "just a joke," but it often turned into repetitive jokes about his penis being inadequate. He eventually had to physically confront his teammates because they would not stop even when he urged them.

Specific sports can be racialized, perpetuating racist and sexist stereotypes to maintain white hegemonic masculine supremacy. When African Americans excel at sport, the white racist response is to dehumanize them. They are described as animals, and white athletes are intelligent.[79] Oftentimes, Asian American men are seen as too small or weak, which positions them lower in a masculine hierarchy. However, when an Asian American male athlete exceeds expectations, this can be a significant boost to Asian American boys and men starved of strong examples that look like them. Irwin became swept up with Manny Pacquiao fever when the Filipino boxer upset the welterweight champion Oscar De La Hoya. Irwin explains the significance of the win:

> The last three days I've had a bit of Manny Pacquiao fever. I didn't pay to watch this fight in part because I figured that Pacquiao was gonna lose, just like everyone thought. I wanted to go watch it because this Asian badass is gonna fight and, so when I found out that he won I was searching on the web for videos and I was able to find this grainy bootleg version of the fight. I watched clips of his old fights and I was up until 5 o'clock in the morning. Then the next night, I stayed up again until like 4 or 5 o'clock in the morning just watching these old fights and reading about him. In a lot of ways it was good. I don't know how else to put it. There was some kind of neurochemical response. Some psychological subconscious, unconscious thing going on that made me feel good by watching all of that. I mean on a very conscious level I was being inspired by this guy who worked so hard and who trained so hard and made himself into this basically stone statue. Basically no one had any doubts [that De La Hoya would win] until the weigh-in. At the weigh-in Pacquiao was standing there flexing his entire torso, and people were like, "Holy guacamole, what is this guy doing? You know this guy is made out of stone or something." Pretty consciously I felt inspired by all the hard work he put in to get it and also, I think on a very subconscious level you buy into this genetic thing. That's what race is all about; I think on a subconscious level I bought into this idea that somewhere inside me is Manny Pacquiao's essence. Somewhere in my subconscious, after eight hours of highlights and reading articles, I got it. I got what white boys got through 18 years of getting to watch the

Lone Ranger and Superman and everything else where the heroes are white and they're good looking and they're good people and they get the woman. And I was usually on the opposite end of that. Because the hero usually has some sort of goofball cook or some enemy who is Asian.

Finally, in his mid-thirties, Irwin found a real-life Asian-bodied male figure who was in the media spotlight. It happened serendipitously, but it finally happened. While there will not be dramatic structural changes to improve race relations and abolish hegemonic masculinity, Manny Pacquiao provided a psychological boost that had been absent in Irwin's life. Similarly, NBA player Jeremy Lin's visibility is providing an alternative image of Asian American men in professional sports. These two athletes can be a source of pride for Asian Americans, especially men, because the societal privileges of masculinity and manhood are largely withheld from them. Indira notes that in her company's diversity training, Asian American men in the seminar had difficulty identifying with the concept of "male privilege."

I've heard heterosexual Asian American men say, "it's even hard for me to understand male privilege. In a lot of ways I experience the same level heterosexism [that LGBT people do]." But if a heterosexual Asian American man experiences what they believe to be the same gender treatment as an LGBT-identified white man, you know there's a conversation there. Most Asian American men feel like, "How can I own something that I don't even really feel like I have? I don't even get to feel like a man most of the time."

Asian American boys and men need to see alternative portrayals in the media. My hope is not that the definition of hegemonic masculinity grows to include Asian American men. I urge that broader and wider positive representations of races, genders, and sexualities be created. Jackson Katz urges that we must "change the institutions, the monopoly of media systems run by rich white men." [80] If changes can be made at the institutional level, then future Irwins may not have to wait thirty or more years to find a person who inspires them instead of images that belittle them and feed self-disgust.

CONCLUSION

In domestic violence literature, there are a number of tactics used by abusers to maintain control over others: dominance, humiliation, isolation, threats, intimidation, denial, and blame. [81] Collectively, the Asian American men in this chapter described the use of all these tactics by other boys and men to maintain the racialized, masculine hierarchy. In essence, the socialization process of white habitus for Asian American men can be likened to an abusive relationship. Asian American men are bombarded with messages degrading their manliness and challenging their sexuality. Heterosexual Asian American men must constantly prove their "straightness" and contend with disinterest from women. Gay Asian American men are assumed to be passive bottoms and still have to prove their manhood in queer spaces.

Throughout the past century, Asian faces have been the enemy in numerous military conflicts and colonial projects that further emasculate Asian and Asian American men. Men in Asia deal with the occupation of their countries, exploitation of their labor, and theft of their resources. In the United States, Asian American men deal with the daily challenges of invisibility in the media, harassment on the playground, struggles with identity, and, at times, difficulty in personal relationships. This all stems from persistent white racist framing. The white racial frame is centuries old and is imbedded in social institutions, interpersonal interactions, and played in a loop in the largely white-owned media. Emasculating racist imagery and interactions can add up over time. There is no outlet for their rage. Literature on helping victims of abuse warns, "Remember, abusers are very good at controlling and manipulating their victims. People who have been emotionally abused or battered are depressed, drained, scared, ashamed, and confused."[82] While some respondents have had lasting effects from their experiences with racism, others resisted the framing enough to redefine what "manhood" meant or mimicked alternate forms of masculinity of other men of color.

In the next chapter, my respondents discuss love and relationships. After extensive discussion of the uniquely shaped gender and sexualized experiences of Asian American men, the sexual politics of Asian Americans will be examined at length. The respondents' narratives will demonstrate how Asian Americans relate to other men and women, how this affects sexual politics, and how this process affects how they choose partners.

NOTES

1. Controversial SAM is one of two main writers on the website I AM S.A.M., described as a "website about Asian Anger, Dating, Sex and Culture . . . from a Single Asian Male's perspective." http://www.singleasianmale.com.

2. William Hung is an American singer who gained fame in early 2004 as a result of his off-key audition performance of Ricky Martin's hit song "She Bangs" on the third season of the television series *American Idol*.

3. Long Duk Dong is a fictional character from the 1984 John Hughes film *Sixteen Candles*. Long Duk Dong is a bizarre Asian foreign exchange student brought in by a white family. He is portrayed as an oddball, socially inept, sexually repressed Asian male.

4. I performed the search on January 29, 2010, using Google Scholar. I chose "Asian American Men" for the keyword title search. Eighty-six articles were found,

and thirty-seven of those articles were either for gay and bi-sexual Asian American men or redundant articles or reviews.

5. Alex Johnson, Petra Cahil, and Bill Dedman of MSNBC.com; Pete Williams, Jim Popkin, and Steve Handelsman of NBC News; and the Associated Press contributed to this report, 2007. "High school classmates say gunman was bullied: Police say package sent to NBC News between shootings is of little use," msnbc.com,http://www.msnbc. msn.com/id/18169776/, accessed January 24, 2010.

6. msnbc.com,http://www.msnbc.msn.com/id/18169776/.

7. "Classmates laughed at him when he spoke." *The New Paper*, April 21, 2007, http://newpaper.asia1.com.sg/error/0,6313,6,00.html, accessed January 26, 2008.

8. Lee Hyeon-gu, "Childhood Friend Recalls a Different Side of Cho," *Joong Ang Ilbo [Korean Joong Ang Daily]*, April 20, 2007.

9. M. Apuzzo and S. Cohen, "Va. Tech Gunman Seen as Textbook Killer," Associated Press, April 19, 2007, http://www.pantagraph.com/news/article_4969a4cb-4da7-5f6b-9e27-a78e3b414625.html, accessed January 26, 2010.

10. Sarah Baxter, "American Psycho: Cho Seung-Hui and the Crisis of Young Men in a Feminised Society,"April 22, 2007, http://www.freerepublic.com/focus/f-news/1821481/posts, accessed January 24, 2010.

11. Baxter, "American Psycho."

12. Joane Nagel, *Race, Ethnicity, and Sexuality* (New York: Oxford University Press, 2003).

13. See William H. Grier and Price M. Cobbs, *Black Rage* (Eugene, OR: Wipf and Stock, 2000).

14. Beate Krais, "Gender and Symbolic Violence: Female Oppression in the Light of Pierre Bourdieu's Theory of Social Practice," in *Bourdieu: Critical Perspectives*, ed. Craig J. Calhoun, Edward LiPuma, and Moishe Postone (Chicago: University of Chicago Press, 1993), 156–76.

15. Michael A. Messerschmidt, "Varieties of 'Real Men,'" in *Men's Lives*, 7th ed., ed. Michael S. Kimmel and Michael A. Messner (Boston: Allyn & Bacon, 2007), 3.

16. See Grier and Cobbs, *Black Rage*; Abraham Kardiner and Lionel Ovesey, *The Mark of Oppression: Explorations in the Personality of the American Negro* (Cleveland, OH: World Publishing Company, 1962); Thomas LaVeist, *Minority Populations and Health: An Introduction to Health Disparities in the United States* (San Francisco: Jossey-Bass, 2005); Joe R. Feagin and Karyn D. McKinney, *The Many Costs of Racism* (Lanham, MD: Rowman & Littlefield, 2003); Verna Keith and Cedric Herring, "Skin Tone and Stratification in the Black Community," *American Journal of Sociology* 97 (1991): 760.

17. Grier and Cobbs, *Black Rage*; Kardiner and Ovesey, *Mark of Oppression*; LaVeist, *Minority Populations*; Feagin and McKinney, *Many Costs of Racism*; Keith and Herring, "Skin Tone."

18. Hernan Vera and Andrew M. Gordon, *Screen Saviors: Hollywood Fictions of Whiteness* (Lanham, MD: Rowman & Littlefield Publishers, 2003).

19. Jackson Katz, *Tough Guise: Violence, Media and the Crisis in Masculinity* (video) Challenging Media, 1999).

20. Taken from a fact sheet on child abuse, *Recognizing Child Abuse: What Parents Should Know* (Prevent Child Abuse America, 2003).

21. See Janice Tanaka, *When You're Smiling* (Janice Tanaka Films, 1999); Rosalind S. Chou and Joe R. Feagin, *The Myth of the Model Minority: Asian Americans Facing Racism* (Boulder, CO: Paradigm, 2008).

22. For example, *Rush Hour I, II, and III*; *Shanghai Knights* and *Shanghai Noon*.

23. Allen Walzem, "Asian Masculinity and Contemporary Hollywood Film," presentation at the Annual Asian Cultural Studies Association Conference (ACSA), http://ir.lib.stut.edu.tw/bitstream/987654321/10332/1/asian_masc.[1].pdf, 2007.

24. Marlon T. Riggs, "Black Macho Revisited: Reflections of a Snap! Queen," *Black American Literature Forum* (Black Film Issue) 25, no. 2 (1991): 389–94.

25. Riggs, "Black Macho Revisited."

26. David L. Eng, "Heterosexuality in the Face of Whiteness: Divided Belief in *M. Butterfly*," in *Q & A: Queer in Asian America,* ed. David L. Eng and Alice Y. Hom (New York: Temple University Press, 2000), 335–65.

27. Chou and Feagin, *Myth of the Model Minority.*

28. David L. Eng, *Racial Castration: Managing Masculinity in Asian America* (Durham, NC: Duke University Press, 2001).

29. For extensive discussion of Asian Americans who choose to whiten, see Chou and Feagin, *Myth of the Model Minority.*

30. Chou and Feagin, *Myth of the Model Minority.*

31. Chou and Feagin, *Myth of the Model Minority.*

32. Katz, *Tough Guise.*

33. Katz, *Tough Guise.*

34. Katz, *Tough Guise.*

35. Katz, *Tough Guise.*

36. Krais, "Gender and Symbolic Violence."

37. A social networking website.

38. A social networking website focused on connecting people through online games.

39. A social networking website focused on the Asian American community.

40. Eduardo Bonilla-Silva, *Racism without Racists: Color-Blind Racism and the Persistence of Racial Inequality in the United States* (Lanham, MD: Rowman & Littlefield, 2003).

41. Katz, *Tough Guise.*

42. Katz, *Tough Guise.*

43. Jose Antonio Vargas, "'Slanted Screen' Rues the Absence of Asians." *Washington Post,* May 25, 2007.

44. Ellen Jordan and Angela Cowan, "Warrior Narratives in the Kindergarten Classroom: Renegotiating the Social Contract? " in *Men's Lives,* 7th ed., ed. Michael S. Kimmel and Michael A. Messner (Boston: Allyn & Bacon, 2007), 272–83.

45. Patricia Hill Collins, *Black Sexual Politics: African Americans, Gender, and the New Racism* (New York: Routledge, 2005).

46. Media representations of South Asian men are quite limited. They are often portrayed as "foreign" or gas station store attendants with thick accents.

47. For detailed accounts of these racist incidents, see Chou and Feagin, *Myth of the Model Minority.*

48. Collins, *Black Sexual Politics,*190.

49. Joe R. Feagin, *The White Racial Frame: Centuries of Racial Framing and Counter-Framing* (New York: Routledge, 2009).

50. J. Lewis, "The Decline of the Male Breadwinner Model: Implications for Work and Care," *Social Politics* 8, no. 2 (2001): 152–69.

51. Elizabeth Kelan, "Gender, Risk, and Employment Insecurity: The Masculine Breadwinner Subtext," *Human Relations* 61, no. 9 (2008): 1171–1202.

52. H. Russell, "Friends in Low Places: Gender, Unemployment and Sociability," *Work, Employment & Society* 6, no. 13 (1999): 205–24.

53. Kelan, "Gender, Risk, and Employment Insecurity."

54. http://www.oregonlive.com/washingtoncounty/index.ssf/2009/11/three_bodies_found_in_home_in.html;http://www.medindia.net/news/Broke-Indian-American-kills-all-of-his-family-before-committing-suicide-42682-1.htm;http://www.riazhaq.com/2009/04/murder-suicide-in-slicon-valleys-indian.html.

55. Russell, "Friends in Low Places."

56. Collins, *Black Sexual Politics.*

57. Richard Fung, "Looking For My Penis: The Eroticized Asian in Gay Video Porn," in *A Companion to Asian American Studies,* ed. by Kent A. Ono (Malden, MA: Blackwell, 2005), 235–53.

58. The website was shut down in the spring of 2009; however, you can find articles about the site at http://www.saigonnezumi.com/2007/05/10/bitter-asian-men/.

59. Judith Butler, *Gender Trouble: Feminism and the Subversion of Identity* (New York: Routledge, 1990).

60. Collins, *Black Sexual Politics*.

61. Feagin, *The White Racial Frame*.

62. Nagel, *Race, Ethnicity, and Sexuality*.

63. Collins, *Black Sexual Politics*.

64. Fung, "Looking For My Penis."

65. Fung, "Looking For My Penis."

66. Katz, *Tough Guise*.

67. bell hooks, *Killing Rage: Ending Racism* (New York: Holt, 1995).

68. See Kardiner and Ovesey, *Mark of Oppression*; Grier and Cobbs, *Black Rage*; and Joe R. Feagin and Karyn D. McKinney, *The Many Costs of Racism* (Lanham, MD: Rowman & Littlefield, 2003).

69. hooks, *Killing Rage*.

70. Feagin, *The White Racial Frame*.

71. For an in-depth discussion of the fear of "rocking the boat," see Chou and Feagin, *Myth of the Model Minority*, chapter 5.

72. Sara Pedersen and Edward Seidman, "Team Sports Achievement and Self-Esteem Development among Urban Adolescent Girls," *Psychology of Women Quarterly* 28, no. 4 (2004): 412–22.

73. Michael Messner, "Boyhood, Organized Sports, and the Construction of Masculinities," in *Sociology: Exploring the Architecture of Everyday Life*, ed. David M. Newman and Jodi A. O'Brien (Thousand Oaks, CA: Pine Forge Press, 1995).

74. Messner, "Boyhood."

75. Jackson Katz, *Tough Guise*.

76. Peter Lyman, "The Fraternal Bond as a Joking Relationship: A Case Study of the Role of Sexist Jokes in Male Group Bonding," in *Men's Lives*, 7th ed., ed. Michael S. Kimmel and Michael A. Messner (Boston: Allyn & Bacon, 2007).

77. Lyman, "Fraternal Bond."

78. For a detailed account about the racial harassment Jason endured, see Chou and Feagin, *Myth of the Model Minority*, 66.

79. T. Bruce, "Marking the Boundaries of the 'Normal' in Televised Sports: The Play-by-Play of Race," *Media, Culture, and Society* 26, no. 6 (2004): 861–79; D. Buffington and T. Fraley, "Skill in Black and White: Negotiating Images of Race in a Sporting Context," *Journal of Communication Inquiry* 32, no. 3 (2008): 292–310.

80. Jackson Katz, *Tough Guise*.

81. Melinda Smith and Jeanne Segal, "Domestic Violence and Abuse: Signs of Abuse and Abusive Relationships," http://www.helpguide.org/mental/domestic_violence_abuse_types_signs_causes_effects.htm, December 2011.

82. Smith and Segal, "Domestic Violence."

SIX

Asian American Sexual Politics

Love and Relationships

While I was teaching a senior research seminar on intersectionality at Duke University in the spring of 2011 a student, an Asian American woman, announced to the class that she was tired of the singular representations of Asian American women in the media. I had recently had them watch the Sut Jhally documentary *Dreamworlds III: Desire, Sex, and Power in Music Video*,[1] and she lamented, "I used to watch those music videos and wish that there were women that looked like me. Now I've changed my mind. I am tired of being portrayed like Brenda Song in The Social Network, giving fellatio in a bathroom stall!" In addition to her anger about the portrayal in the popular fictionalized life of Facebook cofounder Mark Zuckerberg, who happens to be in a long-term relationship with an Asian American woman he met in college, she declared that regardless of whether a relationship is intra or interracial, there are negotiations she has to make, and ultimately she bemoaned "it's all political."

In just a few short statements, this student was able to articulate the conundrum for people of color in the media and the deep complexities involved with relationships that are seemingly outside of politics. The lack of faces in the media of people of color creates a desire for more representation and envy for the diverse white faces. However, with the power of the media held largely in the hands of whites, or even when people of color are part of the industry, a white habitus shapes any portrayals, making any diversity in the roles look more like racial caricatures. Asian American women continue to play the exotic sex toy role and Asian American men are largely absent or presented as socially inept buffoons. The student also noted that her choice of partner is politicized on either side of the coin. If an Asian American woman chooses an Asian partner, sometimes that choice is made out of convenience, familial pressure or preference, veiled statements as if it is better to "protect the children" or "avoid cultural differences." The white racial frame shapes how we view others and ourselves. Thus, it plays a role in the choices we make in our intimate relationships.

INTERRACIAL MARRIAGE BY THE NUMBERS

Oppression impacts gender and family identity, as does resistance.[2] Throughout the history of the United States, race laws and practices have had a direct affect on the gendering and family formation of people of color. Antimiscegenation laws were institutionally oppressive measures that racially shaped families for centuries. After *Loving v. Virginia,*[3] there was a steady increase in interracial marriage in the United States. However, there is a gender imbalance that is very apparent for Asian Americans. Almost 20 percent of married Asian American women and just over 7 percent of married Asian American men have a non-Asian spouse, 17.1 percent of married Asian American women are married to a white spouse, and 3.5% of married Asian men have a spouse classified as "other".

There is a notable disparity in the rates of exogamy by Asian males and females. Only 25 percent of Asian/white marriages involve an Asian male and white female, and the remaining 75 percent is Asian female with white male. White hegemony has a direct affect on this imbalance. Collins notes, "Love may appear to come from nowhere, but it is profoundly affected by the political, economic, and social conditions of the new racism."[4] My respondent Lee, a first-generation Thai American in her forties who lives in the mid-Atlantic region, immigrated to the United States after working in a sweatshop in her home country.[5] She was so happy about finding a white American husband and having a half-white child. She openly admitted that white Americans were valued very highly to Thai people over other Americans and that her half-white child would be treated as special if she returned. There are historical roots to Lee's preference for hegemonic white Western masculinity.[6]

There was a spike in white male/Asian female marriages during and following the U.S.'s involvement with wars in Asia (WWII, Korea, and Vietnam). The military industrial complex largely created the sex tourism industry in Southeast Asia.[7] During the Vietnam War, the U.S. military set up sexual rest and relaxation destinations in Southeast Asia for allied soldiers with financial assistance from the World Bank.[8] These sexual ports were created to maintain morale, so that American soldiers could maintain masculinity with the availability of prostitutes.[9]

The number of Asian American interracial marriages fell from 42 to 33 percent from 1990 to 2000.[10] Researchers argue that the growth in the immigrant population for Latinos and Asian Americans is a major factor in the downward trend.[11] On the other hand, there is an increase in intraracial marriages, where Asian Americans are marrying other Asian Americans from different ethnic groups or ancestries. Another factor in interracial marriages that is not explicitly linked in the research is the role of racism and racial prejudice.

Asian American women are the most likely of all races to marry outside of their race, and they make up 75 percent of the Asian American intermarriages. This introduces another cause of declining interracial marriages. There has been a significant decrease in Asian war brides as the U.S. military focuses their fighting forces in other locations around the globe. Collins points out that the rules about crossing the color line are very clear in the African American community. While it might be less clear than before the civil rights movement, these rules differ for the Asian American community. Though Asian Americans acknowledge the color line and unspoken rules for selecting mates, there is a long history of high rates of interracial marriages, especially between Asian women and white men. Interestingly, there have been a great deal of war brides from Asian countries, but despite the United States being at war in Somalia and the Middle East, we have not seen the same ratio of war brides from those countries. This speaks to the exotification of Asian female bodies and their appeal to whites over African and Middle Eastern female bodies.

PARENTAL EXPECTATIONS: RACE AND CLASS DO MATTER

Many of my second-generation respondents were given explicit messages about whom they were expected to date and eventually marry. Heterosexuality was a basic assumption by parents across the board. There were also preferences by race, ethnic group, class, education level, and career. However, there were cases in which, regardless of other factors, race became the ultimate determinant in parental approval or disapproval.

Brent, a third-generation Chinese American introduced earlier, is married to a white woman named Ashley. He recalls his parents' racial preferences for dating and eventually for his spouse:

> As far as I can remember from discussions about dating, they really, really wanted you to date a Chinese girl, and white girls would be okay. There's no way in hell you would ever date a black girl. If it were up to my mom and dad, I would never have dated her [his wife] until I had my job now. They were trying to force that need to date a good Chinese girl and get married. When I told them I was dating this really good girl and she's white, they seemed to be okay with things after they had retired and gone out to [city in the Southwest]. I guess it

chilled out a little bit. But since they didn't know her personality or what she was like, they were still like, "I don't know. You should just be thinking about your college thing." I would get some hints that they weren't happy. I also got the impression that if she were Chinese they would be cooler about it. But when they finally met her, she won them over.

It was common among second-generation respondents to receive explicit anti-black messages from their parents. Many of their parents had very few interactions with African Americans and largely constructed their preferences from anti-black imagery in the media.[12] However, Brent's family actually operated a store in a lower-income black neighborhood, and he recounted that working and living there strengthened many of their negative racial views. This outcome becomes understandable when his parents, like most Americans, lack knowledge of systemic racism and how it has structured the geography of inequality, sequestering African Americans in areas of concentrated poverty with few resources and opportunities.

Even with all the positive portrayals in the media of whites, why would Brent's parents prefer a Chinese American for their son to date? Repeatedly, respondents indicated that their parents wanted to retain their "culture." This reliance on the home-culture frame is common among newer immigrants. In Brent's case, his family lived in an especially hostile racial environment with a history of anti-black discrimination, which extended to other people of color as they settled in the area. Even though they were third-generation Asian Americans, his family, which in addition to his nuclear family included cousins, uncles, aunts, and grandparents, had experienced overt discrimination. Brent's family and extended family had negative racist experiences with whites in his Southern town. So their trust level of whites was low. Even after Brent had been dating this white woman for some time, his family hoped he would change his mind, and before he and Ashley officially tied the knot, his parents continued to try and set him up with Asian women. Brent felt disrespected by his family and said that they did not fully accept his relationship with his partner. Eventually, Brent's parents accepted and embraced Ashley as their daughter-in-law, unlike Brent's cousin, who married a white woman and abandoned the family. Brent has remained incredibly loyal to his parents and extended family and is still very proud of his Chinese roots.

Erin, a third-generation Chinese American from the South, describes an aunt who married a white man as "practically white." Her aunt is wealthy and lives in a suburb, and throughout Erin's life her parents have vocalized that they want her to have the same kind of life as her aunt. They were comfortable with her marrying a white or Asian man, and they began to set Erin up on dates with Chinese boys when she was in high school. Her father did not want her to even ride in a car with black male friends because he didn't want people to think she was dating them. She would go on these dates to entertain her parents' wishes, but she recounted that there were "no sparks." Class and race were important for her parents. Erin explains, "They wanted me to marry a Chinese guy who was also a professional, a doctor, an engineer." This attempted matchmaking continued into her late twenties, and she was forced to come out to them so that it would stop. Erin is now married to a white woman, which her parents have not fully accepted.

Researchers recently surveyed Asian American college students at an elite university and found that 68 percent of respondents spoke about family preference for same-race partner selection.[13] Brent and Erin are not alone: 72 percent (43 respondents) of the sample said that their family preferred same-race partner selection and had a racial hierarchy of preference if they did not choose Asian. Whites, when not preferred over Asian partners, were the second most preferred partners in every case. Charlene's parents, who are first-generation Taiwanese Americans in their sixties living in the Southwest, also want her to marry someone of the same race and ethnicity:

> They want me to find someone Taiwanese who knows a lot about the culture and who can speak Mandarin. They started in middle school, especially when I started getting boyfriends. In high school, [I dated a white guy] and they were worried then. He was my serious boyfriend. They still want me to marry this ideal East Asian man. When I told my mom I was dating a black guy, she flipped out. She just shut down, slammed the knife on the table and just said, "It's not that I'm racist, but you shouldn't think about anything long term with those people." My mom and I are very close, so I could see the struggle in her face; she really didn't like that I was dating a black guy, yet she also wanted me to be able to talk to her about that. The relationship wasn't serious, so I told her, "oh it's nothing serious." But I thought, "oh no." I knew that she wants me to end up with somebody Taiwanese.

Charlene's parents have had very little experience or contact with African Americans, but anti-black stereotyping has been at the core of white racial framing since the late seventeenth century.[14] African American men have been stereotyped as dangerous sexual predators and these images have become globalized in the media.[15] White racial framing creates alienating relationships and can keep racial minority groups from building coalitions for racial justice. Her father has been the target of anti-Asian discrimination throughout his entire life, getting passed up for several promotions even when overqualified. Yet both her parents would not approve of a black partner. While her mother was not pleased with a white boyfriend, she had a much more fearful response when Charlene dated an African American man as opposed to her subtle confusion when she dated an abusive white man.

This emotional response is connected to the racialized images of African American men as dangerous predators. These images have been constructed and reproduced for over four hundred years.[16] Alex, a third-generation Korean American in his forties living on the West Coast, was perplexed by his Korean grandparents because they "never really liked" African Americans even though they had never had any interactions with them. These white-created racist images are broadcast globally through pervasive media systems where new immigrants to the United States, like Alex's parents, arrive with racial biases, which can often be left un-challenged or worsened by anti-black framing here. Ann, a second-gener-ation Vietnamese American from the Northeast, shares a similar experi-ence:

> I swear to god, if I ever dated a black man and brought him home, I would be *disowned* by my father. Regardless of whether he went to an Ivy League college, is a doctor, a lawyer or whatever—he could be the most gentle person, the greatest person on the face of this earth, and my father would disown me because he does not believe in it; he thinks that every black person is on welfare and no good.

This is a case where race and manufactured racist notions trump class, educational attainment, and career prestige. Ann's father's view of African Americans sounds like it has been taken straight out of the white racial frame. The strength of anti-black stereotypes and images are so strong that an Ivy League–educated African American man could not impress her father in any way.

These parental dating and marrying guidelines exclude African Americans outright. And Asian American parents can discourage dating other people of color, even Asian Americans themselves. If Asians were not the preferred partners for parents, whites were either seen as more desirable or more acceptable than other people of color for all respon-dents that spoke of family racial preference. Whites are the preference for both of Ann's parents:

> Even if I went for a Cambodian guy, I think my dad would think the same way; he doesn't think highly of the Cambodians either. My dad has that idea of a "dirty Mexican" and kind of stereotypic and racist ideals against the blacks and the Latinos. Whites of course, of course are better than any Asian person I could ever be with. My mom thinks so too. She thinks, "go for a white guy, your life would be so much easier, it would be great. [laughter] Don't go for an Asian man, they're thick-headed, they're stubborn, they're hotheaded, they'll just never treat you well, as well as a white man would."

Asian American parents do not always encourage their children to marry other Asian Americans. Because of the diversity of nationalities repre-sented by the umbrella term Asian American, there are sociopolitical histories that may cause rifts between members of certain Asian

American ethnic groups. While the home-culture frame is counter to the white racial frame, it can be in conflict with the anti-oppression counter-frames. The various sociopolitical histories among Asian cultures can prevent the formation of multiethnic and multiracial alliances.

Additionally, globalized white racial framing can lead some Asians and Asian Americans to believe that they are inferior to whites. White hegemonic ideology makes it common knowledge that white masculinity reigns over all others. The home-culture frame that counters the white racial frame may sometimes overlap with it in terms of anti-black or anti-Latino stereotypes. The response can also vary by the gender of the parent. Some Asian American mothers who have lived in traditional patriarchal homes may discourage their daughters from marrying men of their own ethnic group. While parents may want to protect their children or give their children the best opportunities by voicing their racial or ethnic preferences, it can also be an added burden to the partner selection process.

ASIAN AMERICAN WOMEN ON RELATIONSHIPS

Not all of my participants dealt with parents who voiced strict dating and marriage preferences. Latika, a second-generation Asian Indian American in her late twenties from the Northeast, is "really lucky because my parents never told me they expected me to marry an Indian boy. They never, ever tried to arrange my marriage. They haven't set any expectations on me." Latika says that she would prefer to marry another Asian Indian American, but is open to any potential partner. There are varying degrees to which individuals believe they have the freedom to choose partners outside of external pressure. However, power and domination can play a role in shaping what we find attractive or who we deem partner worthy.

Asiaphiles and "Yellow Fever"

A person may insist that they prefer blondes or brunettes. Another person may prefer tall partners to those who are short. When is physical attraction actually physical? When do social forces influence it? Untangling the innate from the externally influenced is a seemingly impossible task. What is the difference between an attraction and a fetish? A white man who prefers dating Asian women began a website in 1998 called Sell-Outs and Asiaphiles, trying to differentiate his "preference" from a fetish. [17] The website no longer exists and the links all lead to "Asian-white.com," a site that directs you to other links for dating and pornographic sites of Asian women. The web author provides definitions of "philia" (attraction to characteristics) and "fetish" (attraction to objects) to justify his preference of Asian women in contrast to other white men who are just attracted to them as objects.[18] However, "selective attraction to 'Asian characteristics' and a desire for Asian women as objects are closely related and cannot be disguised or brushed over by romantic dressing" because the problem is "ignoring the part of societal and historical context that determine person-to person interaction *as well as* racial domination."[19] Not every white man who dates an Asian or Asian American woman is exercising racial domination. But, as my students insisted, "every relationship is politicized," and it can be useful for Asian American women to analyze their personal interactions when involved in these relationships. There may be patterns of practice that indicate some form of racialized objectification and exercises in racial domination.

Violet, a half-Chinese and half-Mexican American from the West Coast, is very happy with her white boyfriend. She claims that he is "more Asian" than she is. His last girlfriend, whom he dated for a number of years, is Japanese. He enjoys rolling sushi and many aspects of the "Asian culture." Violet never mentioned feeling fetishized by her boyfriend and has not had some of the negative experiences those other participants, like Charlene, Ann, and Iris. For those three, their experiences with white men have left impressions.

As mentioned in chapter 3, Ann had a white boyfriend who dated her because she was closer to his home than his Asian American ex-girlfriend, who had moved away for college. There were two significant racist incidents that happened to Ann and her boyfriend when they were out in public, on the subway and at an amusement park, where the interracial couple overtly disgusted whites.[20] In each case, her boyfriend invalidated Ann's feelings:

> I really think now that he has an Asian fetish because every girlfriend since me has been Asian. Looking back I realize that being in an interracial couple is really hard and not necessarily the greatest thing to do. For me now, if I'm with someone who is not Asian, he has to really "get it." You have to really understand your privilege or that we are what we are. It's just that with [the first boyfriend], he just didn't want to recognize there was anything wrong. He shaped my relationship with white men ever since, in that I am very hesitant when I go out with them now.

While not completely closed to the idea of dating another white man, Ann requires a future non-Asian partner to have some critical views of race. However, the same cannot be said for Charlene. Her experience with her abusive white boyfriend has possibly shut the door for any other white men in the future. Initially, Charlene was not seeking out a white partner. In middle school, Charlene wanted to date East Asian American guys, but there were very few of them in her school. She also fears that she appeared too "aggressive" or "loud" for them, so she ended up with the abusive white boyfriend. Charlene shares:

> I really have become completely unattracted to white males. [Pause and uncomfortable laughter] I just don't find myself attracted to them because every time I see one or find myself partially attracted, I think about that experience and how painful that would be. When people accuse me of being reversed racist it irritates me because I have been through this traumatizing personal experience; why would I ever want myself to do it again? I find myself a lot more attracted to Asian American men and men of color. It's especially attractive when they involve themselves in their own community, their own ethnic community.

Soon after Charlene broke up with her abusive boyfriend, he got engaged to an Italian woman. While worried for her ex-boyfriend's fiancé, Charlene hopes, "May no Asian American girl suffer at his hands again." For these women, the experiences with men afflicted with "yellow fever" has helped them develop anti-oppression counter-frames. At the time, they were not necessarily able to articulate the role that race played in the relationship, but they recognized some things felt wrong about their boyfriends' attraction. These women were exotified fantasies that are repeatedly recreated in mainstream media and pornography.

Dating and Relationships: Black, White, Latino/a, or Asian?

One dramatic difference between the Asian American women in my sample, compared to the men, is that they spoke of very few obstacles or barriers in finding partners who were racially diverse. Some of these women felt as if race was an obstacle when finding dates in high school, but as they went on to college and beyond, they had a diverse choice in partners. At the same time, some women adopted the white racial frame and stereotyped Asian American men as asexual or hyposexual.

Olivia, a second-generation Chinese American in her thirties who grew up in the Midwest, has "no attraction" to Asian men. She was not alone; two other women openly shared similar sentiments. Recent research of Asian American college students at an elite Southern university found similar results, where one respondent, Janice, claims,

> Asian men tend to be very androgynous in their features. I can't date a guy that's prettier than me, and Asian boys tend to be prettier than me. I don't know but for some reason I don't see them as handsome; I see them as pretty and when a boy is prettier than me it's kind of like a blow to your ego. So I find them attractive but I don't think I'd ever want to date any of them. [21]

This Asian American woman perpetuates the stereotypes of Asian American men as effeminate. Her use of "handsome" differentiates beauty by gender, where handsome is seen as a masculine form of attractiveness that Asian and Asian American men do not possess. Janice is making a conscious decision not to date any Asian or Asian American man. This was not an uncommon finding and can be a great point of tension between Asian American men and women. Janice does not seem to critically examine her partner choice or exclusivity, but in other cases, some respondents were much more self-reflexive.

Indira, a third-generation Asian Indian American living on the West Coast, did not date in high school. Indira is a self-proclaimed "rule follower." Her mother did not allow her to date in high school and Indira had no problems with that. As discussed in chapter 3, because of her darker skin, tall height, and outspokenness, Indira did not fit into the Asian Indian feminine box which her community proscribed. She did not receive much training in the social etiquette of courtship and dating. When she reached college, she often had trouble identifying when men were interested in her. Her inability to see men's interest was related to her self-worth. She assumed that no one would be interested in her because of her height, skin, and personality. However, one man was able to initially break through:

> One of the most meaningful relationships and one that shaped my life quite strongly was somebody who is white and Christian and one of my best friends in college. It totally hit me by surprise. He said, "can you not see that I'm attracted to you?" I'm like, "what are you talking about? You're not even on my list [of potential partners]." That relationship was really meaningful to me because it was the one relationship that made me realize, "Wait, I'm really worth something and I can ask for what I want."

While that relationship was pivotal in Indira's life, looking back she realizes that she passed up on a number of Asian Indian men who were interested in her. She is curious about why it took a white man for her to finally realize her self-worth. Indira explains:

> There was a piece of me that invalidated Indian men and held white men to a better standard. I think several Indian men expressed some level of attraction, but I didn't consider who they were, didn't validate their feelings. But I didn't have that same level of insecurity for a non-Indian man. And I wonder why I did that. It's a moment of, "Why do I have this list? Why have I never found Indian men attractive? And why is it that the first time I'm choosing to take risks and being outwardly social in a single capacity with a male, it would be a white male?"

White racist ideologies run so deep that someone as self-aware as Indira still has unanswered questions about her avoidance of Asian Indian men in the past. Even when someone has a critical perspective of social systems, there is an unconscious script running in the mind connected to the white racial frame. Most of us do not critically examine our relationships.

We find someone that we get along with and are attracted to and don't always ask "what shapes my attraction?" Indira did not become fully immersed in critical scholarship until graduate school, which allows her now to reflect back analytically.

Other participants, like Annie, have put little thought into why they prefer certain partners. Annie is attracted to white women, and when I asked her what she liked about them, she answered:

> I don't know. I guess I like the athletes, and you know I'm not attracted to African Americans. And you don't see many Asian athletes. So maybe it's related to that, because there are tons of Caucasian athletes out there and they are "All American."

Feagin argues that the centuries-old anti-black stereotyping of African Americans excludes them from full citizenship and consideration as "real Americans."[22] African Americans have been constructed as barbaric and animalistic.[23] Asian Americans are perpetual or "forever" foreigners.[24] In my earlier research, I found that many Asian Americans equate "American" with "white."[25] Annie had put little thought into why her "type" is white women. She contradicts herself when saying she prefers athletes. As a college athlete, Annie participates in a specific sport where African American women make up 23.7 percent of the athlete population.[26] A sizeable proportion of her teammates are African American women. Her tone was matter-of-fact when she said, "I'm not attracted to African Americans," as if it was an understandable given. Annie uses stereotypes from the white racial frame by painting non-whites as un-American, with her description of white athletes as "All American." Her attraction to white women athletes seems "natural" as opposed to shaped by sociopolitical ideology.

Fareena has been able to date men from many different races. As a Bangladeshi American in the Southwest, she did not have an opportunity to date other Bangladeshi or South Asian Americans while she was in high school. When she went to college, however, she began to meet South Asian American men. Fareena's parents allowed her some leeway when she was in high school when it came to dating. She was allowed to talk to boys on the phone and go on group dates with friends, so she had some practice with the social graces of dating. However, the South Asian American men she met in college were not as practiced in the art of dating. The experience was not as easy as she thought it would be:

> They didn't really know how to date; they would say the most awkward things. There was this one guy who hated himself. And he was a really good-looking guy. He was probably a little lighter than me, and he kept saying how every other person in his family was so much more light skinned that they could even pass for Italian. That was the big thing— Indians who looked Italian. He was the darkest of his family. He said he used to be fat. He lost a lot of weight right before he came to

college. He was so caught up in himself, and his ideal was a white girl. He said, "I can only date white girls. I can't date brown girls because that's disrespectful to her." I was like, "If you're dark and you think dark is ugly, what do you think of me?" And he'd say, "But you're cute for a dark girl." I had never been called dark in my life. I know I am but I've never been caught up in it. We're both brown. He told me his ideal girl would be a little blonde actress. Tara Reid. That's his ideal girl. I look nothing like her! I never would. I couldn't even have plastic surgery and look like her! Nor would I want to.

Collins argues that the "new racism relies more heavily on the manipulation of ideas within the mass media."[27] Due to globalization and transnationalism there is a growth of these hegemonic ideologies throughout the diaspora, and brown communities and individuals are buying into white hegemonic beauty standards. Fareena's date has internalized these white standards. There is also a clash with traditional culture. There is an assumption that South Asian American men can only date South Asian American women if they intend to marry them. Recreational dating is not acceptable in the community. Fareena's attempt to date South Asian American men was complicated by the controlled sexuality of brown women:

> There was a lot of that, that if I date a brown girl and don't intend to marry her, that is really disrespectful. My mom told me, "They get this idea that white girls are the one they play around with, mess around with and have sex with. Then they settle down with a brown girl." Brown girls are not supposed to have sex. The idea is that, if you are trying to have sex with a brown girl, you are forcing her into it. Because brown girls don't like sex. And you don't want to disrespect her; you don't want to ruin her unless you plan to marry her. But if the brown girl wants to have sex, have sex with her.

The controlled sexuality of brown women stems from patriarchal tradition that pre-dates South Asian American women in the United States. However, in the hypersexual media of the United States, the sexless South Asian woman is perpetuated. While "black sexual stereotypes are rendered virtually invisible by their ubiquity"[28] in the mass media, the almost complete absence of South Asian American women as sexual beings in the media has a different effect. Fareena notes that the first time she saw a South Asian woman in a sex scene was in a 2008 episode of *ER*, with the actress Parminder Nagra.[29] Both she and her father were shocked. Fareena notes that when women of South Asian (and even Middle Eastern) descent are given sexual roles in TV or Hollywood movies, there is a certain pattern followed. Janina Gavankar, who is half-Indian and half-white, played a sexually promiscuous lesbian in Showtime's *The L Word*. However, her character Eva "Papi" Mendes was Latina. There is a dearth of strong, independent, East, Southeast, or South Asian

American characters in the media in control of their own bodies and sexuality.

White women then become the obvious choice as ideal sexual partners. While there are a number of problems with the portrayal of white women in the media, where they are sexually exploited and violence against them is still prevalent in all forms of media, upper- and middle-class white women possess just the "right" amount of sexuality. Constructions of masculinity encourage all men to be sexually experienced. Since white women have been historically restricted and "off limits" to men of color, dating white women enhances Asian American men's "standing within the existing system of hierarchical masculinities." [30]

Even with all these difficulties dating South Asian American men, Fareena thought that was what she was "supposed to do." It seemed like an epic challenge to find a partner who shared a similar background and cultural experience. She very much wanted to date South Asian American men her first year of college. She said, "That's all I wanted to do. So I'm going to date only brown dudes because that's what I'm supposed to be doing. All these other people are meeting brown people. Why can't I?" Initially, one major barrier for Fareena finding a South Asian American partner was a lack of sheer number of partners. However, when she found a sizeable population in college, they were not the best matches based on personality. While other South Asian American women were finding partners, they were not close friends of Fareena's. Her critical perspective on social issues alienated her from them, and most of her female friends were other politically active students, mostly East and Southeast Asian Americans.

Jessica had a much easier time finding partners with a similar ethnicity, but her sisters "love white guys" which is annoying to her because she believes it is a "fetish" of theirs. She has never dated any whites because they just "didn't get it." She grew up in a metropolitan city with a large, racially diverse population. This made it easier to find men of color who understood her life experiences:

> I've never dated somebody who wasn't a person of color. When I was little, I wasn't that aware of oppression and the symptoms of racism. So it wasn't that. They [whites] just didn't get it. Of all different races that aren't Asian, I'm like particularly attracted to men that are Latino, and I think that's because of all men that are not Asian, they're the ones whose experiences most closely parallel mine, especially if they come from an immigrant family. Right there, if they're bilingual, they understand it, they get it. Like having to eat your kind of food, all these little things that were so traumatizing when you were little and now are so funny, they get it. And it's harder when they're white.

Empathy and shared perspective are the key elements that make the relationship work for Jessica. Jessica prefers these men because they share a counter-frame. Even if the home-culture frames are not rooted to the same country or even continent, they share an understanding of the immigrant experience. They can both share anti-oppression frames because they know what it is like to be a racial other.

Similar to Ann, an understanding non-Asian partner is essential to Jessica. While she does not say it overtly, issues with language, food, and immigration as "traumatizing" memories from youth are connected to white racial framing. Children of color, not just children of Latinos and Asians, face stigma from white peers for the way they talk (accents and language) and eat. Jessica does draw lines of differences between African American men and Latino/Asian American men:

> Most black guys get the oppression. But do they get that my family is not from here? That I have these obligations to my family that they might not have? That I grew up in a completely skewed view of what is American? They grew up wary of cops, but we were wary of cops for a different reason. If you're bad, then the cops are going to come and kidnap you. It's stuff like that, like "Oh my God! I have a fear of police for a completely different reason than they did." Not the same. But, there's something about dating an Asian guy that's like being at home, which is kind of nice. I think back about my past relationships, because I'm not with somebody right now. The relationships that I've had when I was with an Asian guy, it felt comfortable.

There are obvious parallels of racial profiling of Latino/Asian American men with African American men. Although the treatment of Latino and Asian American men can be disguised as a question of citizenship and protection of the nation-state, it resembles the same racist treatment that is older than the nation-state itself. Jessica identifies a common fear of police, but argues that there is something unique about the immigrant experience. For her, having an anti-oppression counter-frame may not be enough; the combination of anti-oppression and home-culture framing as an immigrant is more appealing to her.

The anti-immigrant sentiment is at a heightened level right now, with the passage of laws like SB1070 in Arizona and even more restrictive ones in Alabama and showing up on ballots in many different states (e.g., Georgia and South Carolina). The fear of being targeted for being Latino or Asian can be overwhelming because the cost is so great for these families.[31] Dealing with a traumatic event such as deportation (whether done legally or illegally by U.S. government) has lasting effects on the deportee but also the family and community left behind. Hagan and Rodriguez argue that deportation can have painful psychological and emotional ramifications. Many respondents stated that family separation was the specific cause of their emotional suffering.[32]

The psychological and emotional consequences are the least visible consequences of racism. These internal struggles with racism are unac-

counted for when looking at the health disparities between racial categories. Latino, Asian, and African Americans all face notable health disparities compared to whites.[33] This psychological and emotional suffering as
a result of racism cannot be discounted when looking for explanation.
Whites do not have to live in a state of constant threat. Recent white
immigrants are rarely stopped and questioned about their citizenship by
authorities. By incarceration or deportation, racial profiling is destructive
not only to the individual, but also the families and communities in
which these individual live. White officers develop a disdain for an entire
community of color.[34] This antipathy is felt in the community, and a fear
of law enforcement develops. Immigrant communities can feel as though
they are constantly on the run,[35] just as Jessica describes. Her comfort
with men of color is likely connected to their understanding of this complex racist relationship with whites and the law. They share similar
frames that counter the white racial frame.

Jessica's experience as a Southeast Asian American aligns her more
closely, class-wise, with African and Latino Americans. What about the
East Asian American who is constructed as the "model minority"? Charlene, who dated the abusive white man who fetishized her, stopped being interested in white men altogether. She has also had difficulty finding
East Asian American men who have not bought into the "model minority" myth:

> I also don't find myself attracted to East Asian men much anymore.
> East Asian men are kind of self-righteous and they buy into "white-
> ness." I guess I shouldn't accuse my own community of doing that, but
> I get that sense when there is no tie to an ethnic community. Maybe this
> is unfair because members of our community are always typified as
> "honorary whites." And I realize that people who are buying into
> "whiteness" are really just doing the best that they can with the path
> that they think will be the best for them.

Charlene's critical racial standpoint prevents her from buying into the
white racial frame. There are still many Asian Americans who believe in
meritocracy and that Asian Americans have achieved many things in the
United States by "pulling up their bootstraps,"[36] especially East and
South Asian Americans whose immigration cohorts after the civil rights
movement have brought highly educated or middle- to upper-class individuals and families. With this different perspective from potential East
Asian American partners, Charlene found relief with a Southeast Asian
American:

> I dated a Vietnamese guy, and that was such a healing relationship. He
> was really into Asian American issues, social justice, and community
> organizing. And I was like, "oh my gosh, you're perfect." He was so
> gentle, and he cared about the same things I cared about. He had been
> through similar things, like his family was an immigrant family. He

read me really well, and it was so beautiful and lovely. I felt so validated in my [Asian American] identity and I learned a lot about what it means to be in a caring relationship or at least to have a partnership. I feel like he's my first love. If you can call it that, and he had no expectations about what it meant to be the female kind of our relationship and what it meant for him to be the male part, which is super nice.

Charlene and her boyfriend met during a summer internship and tried to have a long-distance relationship when the summer was over; but it proved difficult as they lived thousands of miles away from each other. The therapeutic aspects of the relationship proved to be very beneficial to Charlene. She has not given up entirely on East Asian American men. Currently, she is interested in a man who is Taiwanese American.

Sharing Counter-Frames: When It Works with Other Men of Color

Amanda and Fareena have African American male partners. Their partners identify closely with the immigrant experience and "model minority" stereotyping because they are second-generation Nigerian Americans. The rates of educational attainment for Nigerian Americans are higher than all Asian American ethnicities.[37] One respondent noted a similar "model minority" connection with Jewish American men and Asian American women. Sociologists Noah Levitt and Helen Kim, a Jewish–Asian American married couple, saw this coupling so often that they performed a research study on the pairing.[38] They interviewed over forty couples and found that they were "very compatible" and "share similar values." Some of the compatibility could be explained through sharing similar aspects of counter-frames.

These relationships are not without obstacles. Amanda, a second-generation Filipina American in her twenties from the Southwest, finds that she and her boyfriend often get strange stares and facial expressions directed toward them when they are out in public. Fareena and her boyfriend, Allen, have also had problems with gendered and racial stereotyping. A manager of a local grocery store was attempting to ask Fareena out on a date. When she informed him that she had a boyfriend, he asked follow-up questions to determine her race (she's often misidentified as Latina) and the race of her boyfriend. When the manager found out that her boyfriend is black, he responded, "You're too pretty to date a black guy." Fareena was furious at the manager of the store.

Fareena is mindful of how difficult the interracial relationship is for both her Asian American community and his African American community. She makes sure they do not go to soul food or Indian restaurants together, for fear of upsetting other patrons. In the mall, a man stared at them and he pulled her aside to ask, "Does your dad know?" Fareena responded back, "I'm twenty-six years old," insulted by the condescending patriarchal inquiry. Fareena elaborates on other public responses to her boyfriend:

> Every time I was with him, in the beginning, he would always get pulled over. You know, you would read about it [racial profiling of African Americans], but it could have been because he was driving the car he was. I don't know. Or that it's [the city]. At that time, he was training to play football. He was never a football player, but he was training. So he was really muscular at the time. He looks menacing if he's not smiling. I can't even try to justify it. People are really threatened by him frequently.

Racial profiling is a reality for all people of color, but especially for African Americans. Fareena got a first-hand look at the racist practice while Allen was "driving while black." The fear and assumptions made about Fareena's partner were not reserved for strangers. Her family was initially hesitant in accepting him. With very little knowledge about Nigerians and Nigerian Americans, Fareena's father was skeptical. The white-constructed stereotypes of African American men, whether they are eighth- or second-generation like Allen, are woven into the fabric of U.S. society. When her father found out that he was Nigerian, he responded, "Why couldn't he be a regular black guy? Why did he have to be Nigerian?" Her father associated Allen with all the spam he received from "Nigerians" and "Nigerian Banks." As a first-generation American, Fareena's father has adopted xenophobic notions about Nigerian Americans. Her own brother, who knew Allen before introducing him to his sister, has stereotypical notions about him as well.

> My brother makes a lot of assumptions about me and Allen. Those things make me more aware of how the world really sees us. My brother thinks he's a buff, threatening dude, but he's not. Anytime he wants to tell his friends or his girlfriend how liberal my parents are, he says, "They're cool with my sister dating a black guy." That's the ultimate test. Apparently, it's a declaration. He's like, "My sister dates a black dude. I know they're having sex." So, without even saying it, there's that stereotype that black men are really sexual. If you're going to get with one, it's going to be a really sexualized relationship. People want to know if there is a sexual fetish in that way. Even with people I don't talk about my sex life with. It's the weirdest thing.

Fareena's involvement with a black man is automatically sexualized because of hypersexual constructions of African American masculinity. When Fareena dated Desi men, these same assumptions were not made about the couple.

Allen's family also struggles with the interracial union:

> No one in his family has ever dated outside their race, so his dad doesn't talk to me, doesn't acknowledge me. All his younger brothers have only dated black women and will always do so. I'm pretty sure

Allen would too if not for me. I messed things up. I made him a sell-
out.

A black man partnering with a non-black woman, in symbolic terms, can
easily be seen as a rejection of his community.[39] An argument can be
made that men and women should be free to fall in love with whom they
please; however, it is difficult to separate notions of love as a "state independent of history, politics, and cultural conditioning."[40] Sexual relationships are so intimately tied to racial identity. Fareena and Allen must deal
with discomfort and varying amounts of disapproval from both of their
families.

ASIAN AMERICAN MEN ON RELATIONSHIPS

Asian American men face their own unique experiences with courtship,
dating, and relationships. The vast differences in the construction of
Asian American men and women as sexual bodies are reflected in the
narratives of my male respondents. Many of them express that they were
ill-equipped and unprepared to interact with girls and women they
found attractive, whether they were Asian or non-Asian American. They
compare themselves to a Western hegemonic masculine standard for
courtship. When some of the men were involved with interracial relationships, it was not without difficulties. Many of the men found most success in their relationships when they could relate to a partner who did
not proscribe to Western hegemonic standards of men.

Unrequited Love

There was quite a range of ages at which the male respondents started
dating. Some of them were pressured to focus on school until the end of
college, so they did not spend any time going on dates and pursuing
relationships. Charlene's brother met his first girlfriend at age twenty-
four. Jeremy's brother-in-law is a second-generation Bangladeshi
American and at thirty years old has never dated. Even without parental
pressure to concentrate on studies, some of my male respondents simply
had a hard time finding dates in high school.

Chance, a second-generation Filipino American, did not date in high
school and hardly dated in college. He largely blames his shyness, trig-
gered by being teased in elementary and middle school. With women, he
finds it difficult to read whether or not he's in the "friend zone."[41]
Chance has a strong desire to be connected to Filipino culture and would
want to share that with a partner. He says that he may have a better
connection to it with a Filipina partner. Ray, a third-generation Chinese
American in his thirties, is another example. He did not date at all in high
school and made attempts in college and graduate school:

That was really rough. I was pretty timid, really shy. I didn't know how to talk to a girl in the way that I would want to lead up to I want to ask them out. I still have that problem now. I mean, I can make friends with girls and ladies. If my whole point was to be friends with them, that was pretty easy. But that's the only thing I knew how to do, to be a friend, and I didn't know how to ask girls out. From undergrad to grad school I probably asked, like, seven girls out and none of them ever said yes. It was always friend mode.

Some male respondents stressed that they received little to no training on how to talk with girls and women. Their families wanted them to concentrate on school, and this inability to talk to women as possible romantic partners did not bode well for them. Robert, a second-generation Chinese American, notes that there are racial/ethnic/cultural differences on how white men speak to women compared to Asian American men. Robert notes that a lot of his white male peers speak sarcastically and condescendingly to women they find attractive, but that it is laced in confidence. It baffles him why women would want to be spoken to in that way, but he acknowledges that white men with the air of confidence meet the ideal masculine construction. White men have also had few institutional barriers to women of all races.

Historically, African American boys and men received both overt and covert controlling messages about their sexuality. Antimiscegenation laws were institutionalized prohibiting African American men from forming relationships with white women. These laws were not in place to prohibit white men from sexually assaulting African American women. There are residual effects from centuries of controlled sexuality. There are still emotional responses to black-white relationships in both the white and African American communities. Similarly, as discussed in chapter 1, there is a long history of specific laws and policies that controlled Asian American male sexualities. Respondents who attended schools with smaller populations of Asian Americans and largely white populations found it much harder to find dates.

Brent, like Ray, went to a high school that was largely white. Dating was very difficult for him in high school. He shares his experience:

The first two years of high school I stayed in my hometown. The last two years I went to this math and science school. So those first two years I had an interest in girls but dating was just not an option. First of all, because of my parents. They kept blasting on the education thing and not having a social life. Second of all, I guess the girls just weren't interested. The very popular [white] girls were, of course, pretty; you can't deny that, but I just didn't get a sense that they were interested in who I was or want hang out more after school. Dating just wasn't really an option those first two years.

His junior year, he attended a public boarding school. There were no problems with racial taunting but not more dating opportunities either.

The failure of empirical studies is to fully capture how systems of oppression affect our everyday lives. Sociologists often limit the significance of racism in their research.[42] It is difficult to discern how much lack of interest that girls and women had for Brent was due to race. There are times when people have said overtly to respondents that they never considered them sexually because of their race.

Irwin is familiar with the cold shoulder from women he is sexually attracted to and the signals he picks up look "like nothing, just nonchalance or treating someone like a friend or stranger or acquaintance, anything but interest." He's had "a lot of white women who have told me, 'I've never even considered going out with an Asian guy.'" As a response to women's indifference, Irwin now makes his interest very clear to women:

> It's almost instinctual that if I find someone attractive, I'm going to have to do something. Otherwise I'm assumed to be asexual. They just won't think, "Hey, this guy's a potential sex partner or partner." I've actually felt the need to like tell women that I don't have a small penis. It's assumed. Actually, I don't know how assumed it is, but I'm so caught up in my own feelings of anxiety and insecurity sometimes. I just want to let them know, "hey, don't buy too much into the stereotypes." I think that's one sentence that I've used. It's ridiculous that I have to say that.

Few respondents who had difficulty with dating responded in this assertive manner. Irwin states that his physical height, which at 5'11" is taller than the average East Asian American, gives him some advantages. But even with his height advantage Irwin still has trouble with those stereotypes.

Jeremy attributes the Asian American male dating difficulties to parenting and the community:

> We lack experience dating women, and we have the whole arranged marriage thing going. So if all else fails, mom and dad are just going to hook us up. They're always networking to hook us up. Especially when we get to a certain age. When I had no relationship, my mom was always looking around. I didn't want that but they couldn't help it. That being said, we're not really smooth with the ladies. It's the man's duty to approach the girl most the time. So we kind of lack the Casanova game, so to speak.

There are certain sociohistorical and cultural factors that do have some impact on how individuals approach dating and courtship. However, stereotyping all Asian and Asian American men as shy or unskilled romantically inaccurately essentializes a group that is vastly diverse. Not all Asian cultures are the same. Sexism manifests and operates differently in different regions of the world. Essentializing Asian American men as shy removes any context of power and domination from the situation. It also implies that some characteristics are innate by race (timidity) when they are, in fact, not biologically determined. There are hierarchies of masculinities and emphasized femininities that have an effect on who individuals choose to date. There are Indian cultural traditions tied to the home-culture frame that may conflict with how marriage and dating is largely practiced in the United States. Jeremy perpetuates the anti-Asian stereotype by painting South Asian men as asexual or romantically inept.

These framed shortcuts can create obstacles for Asian American men when they seek out partners of any race. Some male respondents see media portrayals and racialized stereotypes as making it difficult to relate to Asian American women as well. Irwin explains:

> I think I have more of a complex about Asian women now than before. I've come to this conclusion, right or wrong, that I have a harder time trying to make a connection with an Asian American woman than other women.

Irwin argues that some of the difficulty making a connection with Asian American women has to do with a number of factors. First, there are few Asian American men for Asian American women to choose. He figures that 96 percent of the men they will meet are non-Asian American, which is pretty close according to U.S. Census data. Second, Irwin contends that Asian American women "are less interested in foreign-born Asian men than Asian men are interested in foreign-born Asian women" so that reduces the population of Asian American men by half. As mentioned earlier, Irwin has had non-Asian American women openly stereotype him as an unlikely partner, so his work to legitimize Asian American women's disinterest as unrelated to race is quite contradictory. However, later in the interview, Irwin implies that media constructions and racism are also factors; and as demonstrated by interviewees, they do make a difference in how they choose partners.

Interracial Dating and Relationships

Many Asian American men do date interracially, but not always without disapproval from others. Asian American men, gay, bisexual, and straight, were also exoticized. Irwin has dated white, African American, and Latina women in addition to Asian American women. He details one negative experience with a white girlfriend:

> I definitely have come up against people who didn't like the idea that I was with a woman who wasn't Asian. That fear [of interracial relationships] was very palpable. I was in [a city in the Southwest] in the car with my blonde girlfriend, and these guys pull up wanting to start trouble. They pull up on the passenger side where she's sitting and start making gestures at us. If I had had a gun I might have waved it at them or something. And that's why I don't carry a gun, because I know I would have used it by now.

These public threats to interracial couples are impossible to predict. In November of 2011, Gulnare Freewill Baptist Church in Pike County, Kentucky, banned interracial couples from attending their church following a visit from twenty-four-year-old Stella Harville, the daughter of the church's secretary and clerk, and her twenty-nine-year-old fiancé, Ticha Chikuni, a native of Zimbabwe.[43] In some places whites still continue to try and control with whom their children romantically intermingle, like the racially segregated proms that continue in Montgomery County, Georgia.[44] New research from the Pew Research Center suggests that there is a geographic and generation gap regarding attitudes on interracial marriage.[45] Older whites, especially in the South, are more likely to oppose interracial marriage. Those known as the Millennials[46] overwhelmingly approve of interracial marriage.[47] There were also gendered racial differences. Black men were more likely to outmarry than black women, and Asian American women more likely than Asian American men.[48] The constructions of hegemonic masculinity and emphasized femininity arguably play a role in that differentiation.

While attitudes toward interracial partnerships seem to be changing over time, people of color and whites who choose to partner with them can never be sure if they come across an overt incident of discrimination based on race. While Irwin's incident happened in the Southwest, Ann's problems mentioned earlier in the chapter occurred in the Northeast in an area where the population of Asian Americans is very large. There is an assumption that racism is a problem of the South, but racism is systemic and increasingly a global issue with the export of the white racial frame.

When Irwin dates white women, he has problems with their families as well:

> One white woman told me "I could never take you home to see my parents. It just wouldn't happen." And other women basically said that it would be too difficult. That it wouldn't be "smooth." Her family used to use the word "Chink" and stuff when they were kids. Her parents probably still do.

In 1967, *Loving v. Virginia*[49] granted formal rights to people of color to marry whites. However, the denial of realistic opportunities to do so, coupled with pernicious gender and racial ideologies that derogate Asian American manhood, has meant that a proportion of heterosexual Asian American men lack opportunities to exercise this "freedom of choice." My Asian American female respondents have not run into these same problems with the white families of their partners.

Brent is married to a white woman, and they have not had any problems with overt racism from strangers. Most of their difficulties have been with family and extended family. Brent met his wife's family for the first time at a Fourth of July get-together. He was nervous because it's "the pinnacle of Southern white holidays." "I treated everyone with as much respect as I could." Brent had to be very mindful of the white space. Brent shares his experiences with his wife's family:

> We knew it was going to be difficult for both us with our families meeting each other and getting them to accept us. She told her mom that she was dating me, a Chinese guy, and, it didn't help that I had long hair. Not only was I Chinese, but I was some wacky-looking guy. Someone in her family said, "You're dating a Chinaman? Why can't you date someone white?" Sometimes I would hear some really crazy shit come out of their mouths, like whenever we were afraid of North Koreans. They would start talking about North Koreans and Asians like "I just don't trust them." And here I am, just standing there. I'm like "Man, that's messed up." And every so often one of her family members would stop and look at me and say, "Oh, but we don't mean you, Brent. You're totally cool." I'm thinking, "What the fuck, man? Probably these Koreans are pretty cool for the most part. You don't know anything about them!"

Brent was able to witness backstage racism because he was seen as an "exception." Brent did not publicly challenge them, and it's unclear if they fully accept him or if they are just backpedaling because they forgot he was there.

His relationship with his wife's parents and brother improved a great deal over time. However, the extended family continues to make racist comments:

> Her uncles and aunts . . . there are a lot of Vietnamese fisherman on the [Gulf Coast area] and if we get seafood, it's always, "You didn't go to that Vietnamese guy, did you?" They're convinced the food they get from Vietnamese is somehow worse, even though they fish the same bays. Another really strange thing they said: "We respect hard-working people, but these Vietnamese fisherman are going out on Sundays and fishing, and that's not right." What? Why can't you fish every day of the week if you're trying to support your family? I would hear things like that and think, "Dude, if you didn't know me, you'd probably think I was a damn "gook" too!"

His wife has been an amazing support and stands up to family members when they make racist remarks. She told her family "if they want anything to do with her they need to accept that fact. That she's going out with me." Brent thinks after the initial meeting, her white family was not as accepting as his parents were to her, but it continues to improve.

One drawback for some Asian American families is a sense of loss when one of their family members marries a white spouse. As mentioned in chapter 4, Brent has a cousin who has completely abandoned his Chinese family after marrying a white woman. Both of Josh's sisters prefer relationships with white men, so he has a similar sense of loss.[50] Josh prefers dating women who are not East Asian American. He has struggled because some are "trying too hard to be something they're not." In Josh's experience, the East Asian American women have tried too hard to match the image of emphasized femininity, like middle- to upper-class white women.[51]

When Relationships Work: Birds of a Feather?

When my male respondents found relationships that worked, there were very specific characteristics of the relationship that made them successful.[52] As some of the women noted, there was comfort in sharing similar backgrounds and experiences, specifically similar counter-frames. If their partner was white, then he or she had to be supportive and understanding when dealing with racial matters. John and Henry found partners in Asia. Henry, who is seventy-four, explains his choice:

> Well, at that time, I had been working about ten years trying to find a woman. It was rough, not enough women around at that time. [Because of] the [Chinese] Exclusion Act, most of the women weren't allowed to come over. I went back to Hong Kong to find a wife. That was rough.

There were clear structural obstacles for Henry when he sought a wife in the late 1950s, early 1960s. John, while born in the United States forty years ago, feels a strong connection to China. He faced a great deal of painful discrimination growing up and found a wife from Taiwan.[53]

Samir, a second-generation Asian Indian American in his thirties living in the Southwest, met his girlfriend of six years in his first semester of college. Up until that point, he dated white women because "there wasn't anything else available." In a partner, Samir wanted "everything to match up as best as possible. And we're both South Indian, both come from similar families." Jeremy also prefers a partner with a similar background:

> Having been born in Bangladesh and raised there the first ten years of my life, seeing my parents, and learning from all the people that I have dated, you have taught yourself that it just *works* when you're with someone who is somebody that's South Asian or even Asian. We have a different culture in the Eastern world than the Western world does. And even though we're very Westernized, I'm just in a better place. Especially if I stick to someone of South Asian descent, preferably my religion too, preferably my country, which happens to be the case now. I've dated some women from India and Pakistan. It was very good, but it wasn't as good as it is now being with a Bangladeshi person. Dating white, Hispanic, and African American is fine when you're young. But when you get older, you realize that being with someone of your kind works out well. As Americanized as I am, I don't think I'd ever end up with someone outside my race.

Jeremy's honesty in selecting a partner of the same race is antithetical to the current discourse of color-blindness and the older but still popular discourse of the United States being a melting pot. If we examine it further, there are many similarities with other communities of color. This conscious choice of seeking a partner that has had similar experiences is about seeking out a partner who can understand what it is like to be racialized in the same manner. Charlene mentioned earlier in the chapter that when she admits that she prefers dating Asian Americans, to other men, she is accused of being a "reverse racist." Terms such as "reverse racism" are problematic and are often poor attempts at masking or denying social inequality. When choosing a partner, whether inter- or intraracial, there are negotiations individuals have to make. Some parents encouraged same-race unions because they would preserve culture or face fewer problems. But these concerns only become important issues because of racial inequality. If immigrant and nonwhite ethnic cultures were valued or normalized as much as white culture, then this may not be a concern for parents. The acknowledgement that racism is a problem is veiled in vague comments like "less problems" or "easier on the children." The key issue is that racist reactions to multiracial children are a realistic threat.

Jeremy has distinct memories of being an outcast when he left his all-black high school for one that was all-white. That left a significant impression on him, but he was still open to dating women of all races in high school. He says that he would be open to settling down with a woman who was Latina, white, or African American, but he "would definitely have to date them for awhile and be really sure." Like many other respondents, Jeremy finds comfort with a partner who understands the Asian American experience.

THE GREAT INTERRACIAL DEBATE

In my interview with Erin, she recalled a discussion in college with an Asian American male friend who was very interested in identity politics. He was interested in law and civil rights, but expressed something that stuck out to Erin as a "disgusting sexist" moment. He insisted that Asian American men "have it really bad" and "haven't really arrived" until they are able to "go out with the pretty white girls." Erin's male friend was making a poorly delivered sociological point. Asian American women are finding white partners at a much higher rate than their male counterparts. There is a racist aspect to this disparity. Asian American men are portrayed as the undesirables in the white racial frame and Asian American women are the exotic bodies.

The gender imbalance of white–Asian American relationships is an ongoing debate within the community. As mentioned in an earlier chapter, there are some bitter Asian American men. There are some geographical limitations. The migration patterns for African Americans after the Civil War affected how communities developed and thus influenced family life and gendered expectations.[54] Similarly, Asian Americans have specific migration and immigration patterns, which helped or hindered the development of communities. One result of Asian American immigration patterns is that the immigration reform of the 1960s created more isolated pockets of Asian Americans. In those areas, there are less concentrated Asian American communities. Lack of close proximity to other Asian Americans can also affect marriage patterns.

However, a strong factor in these disparities is that colonial regimes routinely manipulated ideas about sexuality in order to maintain unjust power relations.[55] White women were objects controlled and protected by white men. White women were out-of-bounds for men of color. It was institutionally enforced. It is still very much reinforced today, ideologically. There is a similar disparity in the African American community. Black men are much more likely to have a white partner then black women. In the African American community there is a double standard regarding intermarriage.[56] Collins argues:

> The rule of 'marry within your race' is more easily enforced for black women. . . . This double standard and the reality of so many African American women without partners is bound to lead to friction in how black men and women interpret the interracial marriages that do exist.[57]

As the group that is left alone without a partner, African American women "remain the group most bothered by this situation."[58] The crux of the problem is posed in the question that Collins asks, "If black women were as worthwhile as white ones, why wouldn't black men choose them?" African American women are constructed as "ugly" and "undesirable" to define white women as beautiful and desirable.

There is a similar situation in the Asian American community, but the prevalent gender of outmarriage is reversed. Of the white–Asian American intermarriages, 75 percent are Asian American women with white men. This double standard (acceptability and frequency of Asian American women to marry white men) and the reality of so many Asian American men without partners is bound to lead to friction in how Asian American men and women interpret the interracial marriages that do exist. It further exacerbates the strained relationships among heterosexual Asian American men and women. African American women and Asian American men face a serious problem in this supposed postracial America that cannot be resolved simply by branching out and pursuing white partners.[59]

The real issue at hand is that gendered racism constructs African American women and Asian American men as the bottom of an "ideal partner" hierarchy. White men have to retain their position as the normal or perfect male. In order to retain that central position, two poles have to be created. African American and Latino men are positioned at one pole as the extreme, dangerous, hypermasculine figures, and Asian American men are positioned at the other pole as the weak, nonthreatening hypomasculine figures. White masculinity depends on these extreme constructions. Without Asian American men, there would be no appropriate bottom for white masculinity. That hypomasculine position makes it more challenging for Asian American men to access the women that meet the standard of beauty exemplifying emphasized femininity, the "clean," "virginal," upper- or middle-class, "pretty" white woman.

Who's to Blame for the Disparity? He Said, She Said

Asian American men and women voice various reasons for the intermarriage disparities. Some respondents are more broadly critical of social constructions in their views, while others take a more microlevel look. Amanda, a Filipina American, used to be attracted to Asian American men in high school but she was "mistreated by them." For a while, she would attribute negative connotations to all Asian American men. Alice is a third-generation Japanese American in her fifties who lives on the West Coast. She has a South Asian American partner[60] and has had many discussions with Asian American women about their problems with Asian American men:

> A lot of Asian women say that Asian men raised by Asian mothers have a lot of macho expectations, especially if they are from China, Korea, or India. They find that relationships with white men is much more on equal footing, meaning that there are no men screaming about their wife, and that they have much more power about where they want to live, how they want to live, how they share their money, and they are treated better. So I think going back to Asian men, some of them are really angry. They complain that Asian women say no to them. And I say, "Look at you guys; look at what you guys do. Do you ever treat your wife or your girlfriend out?" [They respond,] "No – it's too expensive. It costs some money." I said, "Well, think about it. You can't be that mad if they end up going for a white guy." I don't know. It's an interesting dilemma to me because I see the seething Asian man. You have the angry Asian man, and they are so outspoken about why, and so enraged about why. But nobody ever comes to any conclusions except that it's just happening.

There is very little research on the relationship dynamics between Asian American men and women. One study found that Asian American men who acculturate to cultural patterns of the "host culture" had lower rates of gender conflict in their homes.[61] Basically, the more an Asian American man conformed to white American values the fewer spousal conflicts they had. However, the study was never clear on how it defined "traditional Asian values" and how they differed from "host" (i.e., white) "cultural values." The study fails to incorporate white hegemonic Western masculinity into the frame of "traditional Asian values." Hierarchies become intertwined with love and sexual expression.[62] Asian Americans' relationships, whether inter- or intraracial, can uphold prevailing hierarchies of race, class, gender, and sexuality.[63]

Irwin asserts that the interracial marriage disparity between Asian American men and women has a connection to white power and domination. He argues:

> I do think that there's a sad thing that has occurred between Asian American men and women. A lot of the resentment on these message boards is overblown on the part of Asian American men. Just yesterday an Asian American woman told me, "I would especially treat the Asian American boys badly when I was in school because I wanted nothing to do with them, I didn't want to be associated with them. I was ashamed of [Asianness]." She said she didn't like to use chopsticks either. She wanted to avoid things that made her look bad, and to her it was Asian American boys. I think that that happens a lot. And it's not a coincidence that that is precisely what historically and in the present a lot of what white men prefer. Either consciously or subconsciously, they want to separate the Asian man from the Asian woman. That's what happens with the immigration laws. Bring in the men, but don't bring the women. Or bring in the women, but don't bring in the men. Someone was telling me that he was at a party where they [the white men] were trying to get all the Asian men out of the party and keep the Asian women in the party. People don't want to believe this but this is history. If you're a man and you have the power, you're gonna tend to want to divide and conquer. You know, if it's a black woman, separating their families and the white master raping the black women as they wish and making babies that they can even keep or do whatever they want with the baby. They can set it up so they can do whatever they want to do, whoever has the power.

Irwin does specifically name whites as having a historical and contemporary role in this interracial debate between Asian American men and women. He is on point, as demonstrated with the historical discussion of immigration and labor laws in chapter 1. However, he backs off at the end, referring to power more generally, or normalizing the "racial morphology." Colonizers have justified their oppression by making social Darwinism a "naturalized" given, justifying their exploitation and eliminating the role of whites in maintaining the racist order.

Irwin's resentment is noteworthy because it demonstrates the alienated relationships that can be created between Asian American men and women because of systemic racism. In a keynote speech to an Asian American student organization, activist Ryan Takemiya asked the crowd,

"Who hates Asians the most? Asians." He was speaking in a humorous way about how the students in the audience all had friends who, when asked about participating in such an event would respond, "No, too many Asians." Systemic racism alienates people of color not only from whites and other people of color but also from themselves. The woman Irwin interacted with had learned as a girl to distance herself from boys of her own race. Irwin's feelings, while still weighted with a twinge of sexist ownership of women and who should have access to them, acknowledged the historical roots of this.

Asian Americans have been exploited for their labor. Asian American men faced racist, emasculating treatment throughout their time in the United States. The framing of Asian American men in the media and imbalanced outmarriage rates can have a cumulative effect on the psyche of Asian American men. Irwin says that because of all of these factors, it becomes a very difficult subject to breach with Asian American women.

> What compounds the resentment is that some of us feel like Asian women don't understand where we're coming from or, worse, resent us for being these male chauvinists or sexists for pointing out certain things that we think are wrong.

Irwin's observation about the difficulty in broaching the subject with Asian American women is an example of how the blatant racist assault on Asian American men strains the heterosexual gender relationship between the two. Asian American men are the targets of a unique gendered racism where many feel emasculated. Seeing Asian American women with men of non-Asian descent can feel like a stab in the back from someone they hoped would understand their perspective. Some Asian American women have been verbally harassed by Asian American men when out in public with a partner who is not of Asian descent. While verbal assault by strangers is unacceptable, the emotions tied to the event are real and related to racist relations causing a strain between Asian American men and women.

Irwin has an instant emotional reaction to seeing Asian American women with non-Asian men. He portrays this reaction as an instinctual, biologically tied response:

> Because every man has that visceral response. When they see some type of woman, whether it's by genotype or phenotype, who they feel like she's part of their ethnic group or class, going out with someone else, it brings an automatic response. I think it's caveman-esque. If a woman of my tribe or group is going out with someone else, there's some reaction there. I'm not going to lie to you or pretend like I'm this perfect left-wing writer on race. Of course there's a response.

While those relationships may be happy and egalitarian, Irwin's visceral response is really a response to how he has been treated his whole life and the deep understanding and connection he shares to Asian American history. He describes it as "caveman-esque," but oppression creates real emotional and physical responses. Irwin normalizes the white-created racial hierarchy of dating and partnership by saying that any man would be mad if women of their race were dating someone outside of the group. White men partnering with Asian American women become a form of symbolic violence. White men are constructed as the most ideal partner in a number of ways and for Irwin to see these types of partnerships becomes another microaggression, adding to his collection of racialized experiences throughout his lifetime.

Even with an understanding or connection to the past, Asian American men may not have the words to articulate the deep feelings of injustice in the act. But that is the purpose of the message boards, blogs, and websites like *Bitter Asian Men* and *I Am S.A.M.* These sites serve as a safe place for the strong emotional reaction connected to a systemically racist society where white supremacy is so skillfully hidden in every nook and cranny. The treatment and harassment from all social institutions is latent and repetitive but still damaging and effectively maintains the racial status quo.

Through colonial conquests, there were narratives of white men sexually exploiting women of color by raping slaves and "going native." This concept of "going native" paints a romantic picture of white men assimilating into the native culture and falling in love with a native woman. In reality, "many white sexual advances were not welcomed by native people, but were accepted as acts of desperation."[64] Sacagawea's history has been completely rewritten through the eyes of the colonizer. In today's globalized economy, white men do not have to submerge themselves into the native culture and stay. Instead, they can visit sexual tourist destinations and remain in control of how long they stay and if they will take a native woman home with them. They can even personally pick one out on the Internet before they travel.[65]

The myth of our post-racial world is exposed when we see the disparity in intermarriage rates. There is a general increase in Asian Indian–white American unions, but Asian Indian American women marrying white men is most frequent. There are messages that are internalized from this. Jeremy argues that if South Asian American men do have the chance to marry white women, it is because they "settle."

> I don't see that many South Asian men with other races. There are a few of us. Most of us date East Asian women, but it's weird because when a South Asian man dates a white person she's below average in appearance. Because some of us are darker, and so white is marrying up. Indian women, they're clearly *way more attractive* than we are on a large scale. And you'll see them with all races. You'll see them with African American, white, East Asian, everything. But Indian men in our culture, there's no dating. If you're at a party, you can't go across the room and make a pass at some girl. I think Indian men don't out-

marry because they don't have the confidence to approach people of another race. We feel like it's out of our league.

Jeremy, while jovial throughout the interview, was not being light-hearted. He repeated a few times that he "truly believed" the statements he was making about attractiveness. Asian American women, whether South, East, or Southeast Asian in origin, were just "naturally" more attractive. These constructions of beauty do not come from the home. Jeremy was not raised in a household that touted women's beauty over the men in the home. His concepts eerily match the constructions of Asian men in American media. Asian and Asian American men are un-desirable partners and the women are beautiful. While intraracial mar-riage is encouraged, you get a pass if you marry someone lighter skinned. Whiteness is acceptable. Additionally, he said that women outside of his race were "out of his league." Here he is placing clear boundaries, or conjuring images of a hierarchy of women to which he has access to some, but not others. Jeremy has internalized the constructions of exotic Asian female beauty and the lack of attractiveness of Asian men, making "attractive" women of other races unapproachable. Jeremy continues:

> I have two uncles who married white women and they're pretty *gross*. I have one uncle that married three times, and this computer [points to computer on the table] is more attractive than my uncle's wives. That's just the truth. When we pick white, they're not white—they look *busted*. I'll give it to East Asians; when they pick white, they're at least halfway decent.

In essence, Jeremy is stating that beauty *is* whiteness. He considers the women his uncles have chosen as partners unattractive and thus "they're not white—they look *busted*." While his statement is sexist and proble-matic, he again highlights the racial boundaries when it comes to dating and partnerships. Jeremy has internalized these white supremacist con-cepts when he makes sweeping statements about "all Indian men." The adoption of the white racial frame further complicates Asian American sexual politics. The stereotypes of Asian American men leads to political-ly charged conceptions of self and others.

"GAYSIANS?"

Of my sixty respondents, seven openly self-identified as gay, lesbian, or bisexual. In their attempts at dating and relationships, the men have had difficulty with rigid stereotypes affecting their dating possibilities. The constructions of asexuality that are imposed on straight Asian American men are also imposed on gay and bisexual Asian American men.

Sexual tourism in Southeast Asia effectively commodifies Asian bod-ies, both male and female. Transsexual Asian women, aka "lady boys," are hot commodities for white Western men. There is a discourse that Southeast Asian transgender women, like the Thai lady boys, are more appealing than the Asian women at these sexual tourist destinations. Straight-identified white men love the "lady boys" because they get a "beautiful Asian female body" combined with the "sex drive of a man." There was similar commodification of Asian American bodies in the Craigslist ads discussed in chapter 2. The commodification alienates people from their own bodies, and people who are alienated "from their own honest bodies become easier to rule."[66] My LGBTQ respondents have their own experiences with commodification and alienation. The gay men have had a more difficult time finding partners. The gendered beauty constructions are intertwined with sexuality.

Rice Queens[67]

As discussed earlier by Glenn, he finds that Asian American heterosexual men are burdened with weak media constructions. Those stereotypes extend into the LGBTQ community. He used to almost exclusively be romantically involved with "rice queens." Rice queens are gay men who prefer dating Asian men. He sees the same problems that Asian American women have with fetishism among Asian American gay men:

> Asian gay men are screwed in some way, too. Even though there is a small community of "rice queens," non-Asian gay men who like Asian men. They are gay, so they are called "queens" and they like "rice." But there are stereotypes about them, too. Some stereotypes are that rice queens are losers and they can't find partners of their own race, or any non-Asian gay men. That's why they are like, "I'll just be with Asians because they are easier." Another stereotype is that all gay Asian men are bottoms, so the assumption is that they are easy targets because they are the leftovers. So if you can't find your own type or a more macho gay man, go to the Asian gay men. They're submissive. Easy targets. I think these two assumptions draw gay men to Asian men, which I totally reject. That has been my experience about what has been portrayed in both the traditional mainstream media as well as in gay media—that Asian men are portrayed as feminine, weak, passive bottoms. And in a way, asexual.

Again, Asian American men are the undesirable leftovers. The assumptions are very similar to the ones that exist for straight Asian American men: they are weak, passive, and effeminate. For Asian American men, the emasculating stereotypes just become exaggerated in the LGBTQ community, whereas African American gay men are often construed as antithetical to the hypermasculine straight African American man.

Often gay men are stereotyped as hypersexual as well, but Glenn did not find this to be true. Glenn has a gay friend of many years whom he mentored as a resident assistant in his college dorm. Glenn served as a support while the friend was coming out. Even though his resident knew that he was gay, Glenn was never seen as a sexual being:

> Basically, he very honestly told me, "I've always seen you as asexual. I don't see you as anything else in the gay world. I would just walk right past you. When I go to the gay club, looking for targets, looking for a one-night stand, a date, a boyfriend, whatever, I would probably just walk right by you. I wouldn't register anything because Asian men are asexual to me." He's a white American, born and raised in Nebraska.

It's clear that the symbolic castration of Asian American men crosses the lines of sexuality. This racist stereotyping has had an impact on Glenn's self-esteem and his choice of partners. He colluded with the system and internalized that he was not capable of getting partners other than rice queens. Glenn explains:

> You usually get a lot of attention from rice queens. It's not really what I want, because I want to fit in. I'm still hoping for that ideal situation where my race and my color don't factor in. Or the assumption of my penis size doesn't get in the way. I think things have become better. When I was younger, I was contributing to that cycle, to those assumptions, that the only types of people that you can date or sleep with are rice queens, who are losers. Now I am consciously breaking out of that and having other types of successes.

While Glenn is finding other successes, he still has to contend with an LGBTQ community that may or may not see him as an equal man or potential partner. Daniel, a second-generation Vietnamese American introduced in earlier chapters, also identifies as gay. He recognizes that the intersection of his identities as a gay Asian American man can exponentially reinforce gender stereotyping:

> I do recognize that people see me as an Asian, so there's obviously racism intersected in the gay culture. I feel like I do get turned away sometimes because I'm Asian. Personally, I don't care. Well, I do care, but I get over it real quick. I think being gay plus being Asian, having those two together, actually reinforces another stereotype. It gets deeper and more complex.

Daniel vocalized earlier that he could use his race to hide his sexuality because he was not expected to talk about women. However, in gay spaces, it was not clear if his race became a deterrent to some potential partners. His queerness intensifies the already negative racial stereotyping. Gay men are considered a marginalized masculinity; men of color are subordinate masculinities. Asian American men are constructed as hypomasculine, so an Asian American gay man is a combination of all of these categories.

We Are (Still) Family, Aren't We?

The Asian American women I have interviewed share that they have more overt pressure to meet gender expectations and that their families make clear attempts to control their sexuality. As bi-sexual and lesbian women, their families have struggled to accept them. These women received both overt and covert messages that they were expected to marry a member of the opposite sex. Some families saw that marriage as a preservation of culture. The queer Asian American women in this sample had to face disrupting cultural or racial expectations when they came out to their families. Erin explains,

> My mom completely freaked out. There was a lot of "Are you sure? Do you need to see a doctor?" Oh, and then the funniest question, the funniest and saddest question and the most indicative of them not understanding at all was, "Do you think you're a boy? And would you rather be a man?" (Laughing) Me trying not to laugh and going, "No. I am completely comfortable and accepting of being a woman. It's just that I happen to be also attracted to women." And for me to tell my parents, to tell them the difference between queer, trans, bisexual, and gay, that is not going to fly. So, I didn't bring those things into the conversation at all. I'm not even going to start with like ranges.

Erin, and other lesbian or bi-sexual women I spoke with, said that their families associated gayness with whiteness. Lily and Yuan share that no language or public discourse existed when they lived in Taiwan. They were not aware of non-hetero sexualities before immigrating. The shorter history of LGBTQ social movements in the non-Western[68] (or global South) nations restricts the public empowerment of those organizations. There are public LGBTQ organizations in the global South that assert their issues openly, for example, lesbians in Nicaragua.[69] However, the strong public backlash makes it more difficult for individuals and organizations to work in the public limelight.[70] Even with constitutional protections of LGBTQ in South Africa, the social stigma attached to same-sex sexuality as deviant and un-African creates great problems for openness and resistance. The LGBTQ populations in non-Western nations must deal with the added stigma of being un-authentic in their identity, as if colonialism imposed "deviant" sexuality upon them.

Phan, a Vietnamese American, has felt discrimination because of her lesbian identity. Strangers and acquaintances have mistreated her, and her family lacks understanding.

> I'm queer and a minority and a female, and I think that might be more of a problem for me. It's difficult to tell the reason why people would have a problem with me. I think it would be more based on sexual orientation—with my family definitely; they still don't accept it. So, in a way, I'm glad to be in the States. If I were in Vietnam, this would not even be an option. I'd be married and have kids. And I'm definitely

glad to be in [a major metropolitan city in the Northeast] because it's much more open, accepting, liberal, and all that. I'm sort of afraid to go to certain parts of the country.

The parents of Phan and Erin may have difficulties with their daughter's sexuality because of the strong tie to the home-culture frame. If their home countries did not accept LGBTQ communities, there can be great conflict. While homophobia is still a systemic problem in the United States, Phan appreciates the freedom she has in the United States.

CONCLUSION

This chapter serves as a starting point to discuss and analyze Asian American sexual politics. Asian Americans first receive messages about relationships and sexuality within their homes and communities. Parents have distinct racial partner preferences for their children that are tied to the home-culture and white racial frame. The home-culture frame can clash with anti-oppression frames and inhibit development of counter-narratives, sometimes further marginalizing Asian Americans. Many parents articulate an acceptance of white partners over African and Latino Americans. In some cases, they prefer white partners to Asian. They may base these preferences on preserving culture, but also may be influenced by white hegemonic ideals and the existing white racist structure that stretches the globe.

Partnerships are political. The way we choose partners or even have the ability to "choose" is based on a number of sociopolitical factors tied to our identities. Although media portrayals sell us ideas about romantic love that knows no bounds, we are, in fact, bound by conscious and unconscious meanings and definitions that affect our decisions for partnership. Reality television shows like *The Bachelor* and *Millionaire Matchmaker* are crude yet sociologically significant examples of how the search for love is based on class, age, race, constructions of beauty, ability, and weight. Individuals who have an element of freedom to choose a partner must contend with these dimensions of attraction that are not necessarily based on animal urges but on economic and sociopolitical hierarchies.

The white racial frame can place psychological boundaries on what partners Asian American men think they can access. This ideology tells them how they should think about their own bodies, relationships, and sexuality.[71] We can never be free from these influential factors. We can only work to be conscious of them and make the best decisions with our partnerships. In the next chapter, I discuss strategies to combat hegemonic ideology both on a personal and structural level.

NOTES

1. Sut Jhally, *Dreamworlds III: Desire, Sex, and Power in Music Video* (North Hampton, MA: Media Education Foundation, 2007).

2. Patricia Hill Collins, *Black Sexual Politics: African Americans, Gender, and the New Racism* (New York: Routledge, 2005).

3. Loving v. Virginia, 388 U.S. 1 (1967).

4. Collins, *Black Sexual Politics,* 249.

5. For in-depth discussion of Lee, see Rosalind S. Chou and Joe R. Feagin, *The Myth of the Model Minority: Asian Americans Facing Racism* (Boulder, CO: Paradigm, 2008), chapter 5.

6. Nadia Y. Kim, "Patriarchy Is So Third World": Korean Immigrant Women and 'Migrating' White Western Masculinity, *Social Problems* 53, no. 4 (2006): 519–36.

7. Joane Nagel, *Race, Ethnicity, and Sexuality* (New York: Oxford University Press, 2003).

8. Nagel, *Race, Ethnicity, and Sexuality.*

9. Nagel, *Race, Ethnicity, and Sexuality.*

10. Annie Gowen, "Immigrants' Children Look Closer for Love: More Young Adults Are Seeking Partners of Same Ethnicity," *Washington Post,* March 8, 2009, http://www.washingtonpost.com/wp-dyn/content/article/2009/03/07/AR2009030701841.html, accessed February 4, 2010.

11. Gowen, "Immigrants' Children."

12. For extensive discussion of Asian Americans and stereotyping of other Americans of color, see Chou and Feagin, *Myth of the Model Minority,* 170–80.

13. Kristen Lee and Simon Ho, "Asian American Sexual Politics" (unpublished manuscript, 2011).

14. Joe R. Feagin, *The White Racial Frame: Centuries of Racial Framing and Counter-Framing* (New York: Routledge, 2009).

15. Feagin, *White Racial Frame.*

16. Feagin, *White Racial Frame.*

17. Vickie Nam, *YELL-Oh Girls!* (New York: Quill, 2001).

18. Nam, *YELL-Oh Girls.*

19. Nam, *YELL-Oh Girls,* 132.

20. For a detailed account, see Chou and Feagin, *Myth of the Model Minority,* 39–40.

21. Kristen Lee, Simon Ho, and Rosalind Chou. "The Myth of the Model University" (unpublished paper, 2011).

22. Feagin, *White Racial Frame.*

23. Feagin, *White Racial Frame.*

24. Claire Jean Kim, *Bitter Fruit: The Politics of Black-Korean Conflict in New York City* (New Haven, CT: Yale University Press, 2003); Mia Tuan, *Forever Foreigners or Honorary Whites? The Asian Ethnic Experience* (New Brunswick, NJ: Rutgers University Press, 2003).

25. Chou and Feagin, *Myth of the Model Minority.*

26. Richard Lapchick, Eric Little, Colleen Lerner, and Ray Matthew, "The 2008 Racial and Gender Report Card: College Sport," report for the Institute for Diversity and Ethics in Sport, February 19, 2009.

27. Collins, *Black Sexual Politics,* 54.

28. Collins, *Black Sexual Politics.*

29. A British actress of Indian ancestry, Parminder Nagra is most famous for her roles in *Bend It Like Beckham* and *ER.*

30. Collins, *Black Sexual Politics,* 262.

31. Collins, *Black Sexual Politics,* 198.

32. Collins, *Black Sexual Politics,* 198.

33. Thomas Laveist, *Minority Populations and Health: An Introduction to Health Disparities in the United States* (San Francisco: Jossey-Bass, 2005).

34. Joe R. Feagin and Melvin P. Sikes, *Living with Racism: The Black Middle-Class Experience* (Boston: Beacon Press, 1995), 64.

35. Jaqueline Hagan and Nestor Rodriguez, "Resurrecting Exclusion," in *Latinos: Remaking America*, ed. Marcelo M. Suarez-Orozco and Mariela M. Paez (Berkeley: University of California Press, 2002), 193.

36. Chou and Feagin, *Myth of the Model Minority*.

37. US Census Bureau,http://www.census.gov/population/cen2000/stp-159/STP-159-nigeria.pdf(2000).

38. Noah Levitt and Helen Kim are assistant professors of sociology at Whitman College studying Jewish-Asian American married couples.

39. Collins, *Black Sexual Politics*, 264.

40. Collins, *Black Sexual Politics*, 264.

41. "Friend zone" or "friend mode" refers to the situation where the female has begun to view a male as a friend only and not a potential suitor, a psychological classification supposedly exceptionally difficult to undo.

42. Tufuku Zuberi and Eduardo Bonilla-Silva, *White Logic, White Methods: Racism and Methodology*, (Lanham, MD: Rowman & Littlefield, 2008), 137–52.

43. *The Huffington Post*, November 30, 2011, http://www.huffingtonpost.com/2011/11/30/interracial-couple-banned-from-kentucky-church_n_1121582.html, accessed December 28, 2011.

44. Sarah Corbett, "A Prom Divided," *New York Times*, May 21, 2009.

45. Jeffrey S. Passel, Wendy Wang, and Paul Taylor. "Marrying Out: One in Seven New U.S. Marriages Is Interracial or Interethnic" Pew Research Center, http://www.pewsocialtrends.org/2010/06/04/marrying-out/, 2012.

46. Also known as Generation Y, the Net Generation. These are people born in the mid-1970s through early 2000. Pew Research report 2010 http://pewresearch.org/pubs/1480/millennials-accept-iinterracial-dating-marriage-friends-different-race-generations.

47. Passel et al., "Marrying Out."

48. Passel et al., "Marrying Out."

49. Loving v. Virginia, 388 U.S. 1 (1967).

50. For a detailed account of Josh and his sister, see Chou and Feagin, *Myth of the Model Minority*, chapter 5.

51. Chou and Feagin, *Myth of the Model Minority*, chapter 5.

52. Twenty-four of the respondents are men. At the time of the interviews, only one had a white partner. The age range of this group of men is twenty years old to seventy-three, with a mean age of thirty-six.

53. For a detailed account about John's experiences, see Chou and Feagin, *Myth of the Model Minority*.

54. Chou and Feagin, *Myth of the Model Minority*.

55. Collins, *Black Sexual Politics*.

56. Collins, *Black Sexual Politics*.

57. Collins, *Black Sexual Politics*, 263–64.

58. Collins, *Black Sexual Politics*, 263–64.

59. Collins, *Black Sexual Politics*, 263.

60. Alice and her partner have had problems with their racial discrimination from their white neighbor. For more details, see Chou and Feagin, *Myth of the Model Minority*.

61. William Liu and Derek Iwamoto, "Asian American Men's Gender Role Conflict: The Role of Asian Values, Self-Esteem, and Psychological Distress," *Psychology of Men and Masculinity* 7, no. 3 (2006): 153–64.

62. Collins, *Black Sexual Politics*.

63. Collins, *Black Sexual Politics*.

64. Nagel, *Race, Ethnicity, and Sexuality*.

65. Sheridan Prasso, *The Asian Mystique: Dragon Ladies, Geisha Girls, and Our Fantasies of the Exotic Orient* (New York: Public Affairs Books, 2006).

66. Collins, *Black Sexual Politics*, 249.

67. A gay man of non-Asian descent who prefers Asian male partners.

68. I acknowledge the problematic use of Western and non-Western to describe various geographic regions with a diversity of political positions. I prefer the use of global North and global South, but there is no adequate terminology to capture the effects of globalization and colonization.

69. Millie Thayer, "Identity, Revolution, Democracy: Lesbian Movements in Central America," *Social Problems* 44, no. 3 (1997): 386–407.

70. Thayer, "Identity, Revolution"; Sylvia Tamale, "Out of the Closet: Unveiling Sexuality Discourses in Uganda," in *Africa after Gender?* ed. Catherine M. Cole, Takyiwaa Manuh, and Stephan F. Miescher, 17–29 (Bloomington: University of Indiana Press, 2007).

71. Collins, *Black Sexual Politics*.

SEVEN

Now What?

Resistance, Empowerment, and Counter-Frames

Since 2008, I have been traveling to different cities to discuss my work and the nature of it brings Asian Americans from different backgrounds to my talks. After detailing the racial experiences of Asian Americans, I often get affirmations from Asian American audience members. Reactions usually entail newer stories with similar themes dealing with oppression at varying levels of severity. One woman shared that her world "finally made sense" after reading a chapter on identity, and I was truly awed and humbled in that moment. Yet, after every talk I have given, I have been met with the same question over and over again: "how do I fight against racism?" Starkly different for many Asian Americans, compared to their African American counterparts, is what seems like an absence of counter-narratives and resistance. Some regions have more Asian American visibility and political representation, and a new Asian American Renaissance[1] is taking place. On the West Coast and in Hawaii, some Asian American communities are thriving by creating new frames and new identities, even if discrimination continues and media representations are limited. About half of Asian Americans live outside of California, New York, and Hawaii and may be unfamiliar with resistance movements and empowerment campaigns and may have underdeveloped counter-frames.

However, Asian Americans and the situatedness of the diverse population and immigration patterns complicate having a collective voice. In many cases, Asian Americans know very little about Asian American history, and may not have a community or close family members to help them deal with racism, racialized sexism, or homophobia. So, many Asian Americans may find themselves unprepared to deal with the most

175

miniscule amount of racial teasing. Combined with stereotypes of passivity and the "model minority," Asian Americans become easy targets for teasing and taunting even among those who are in their inner circle of friends. It becomes so common that Asian Americans may joke about stereotypes themselves to fit in or "beat someone to the punch." However, whether you are Asian American or not, this chapter outlines some tools to fight oppression at an interpersonal level with some recommendations at a structural level.

Asian Americans have seemingly made it in the United States and are living the "American Dream." But gendered racist incidents are happening every day. And the construction of Asian Americans as relatively innocuous compared to other people of color has made it so that racist taunting and mockery is a low-risk activity. Strong Asian American counter-frames and counter-narratives are imperative to improve our lives.

Throughout the history of the United States there have been a number of resistance movements. Unfortunately, because of the diversity of the population, different waves of immigration patterns, generational differences, and various cultural/ethnic traditions, the term "Asian American" really represents vast groups of identities. Many respondents had families that drew from strong home-culture frames, but this varied by ethnicity, age, generation, geography, and family makeup. The collective anti-oppression frames that exist with African Americans do not have the same factors in their development. Asian Americans are not stereotyped as resisters in the same way as African Americans or even Latinos, who have been, in this hostile anti-immigration era, pictured most frequently protesting new anti-immigration laws. There is collective movement, especially in geographic regions like California and Hawaii where there is political activism and the development of Asian American anti-oppression frames. However, some Asian Americans are happy with being considered models and accept racial taunting as the price they pay to be treated "better" than African Americans or Latinos.[2]

This acquiescence to white racism and conformity to white standards can strain relations between Asian Americans and other groups of color. The white construction of the "model minority" has made Asian Americans into weapons to be used against other people of color.[3] "Model minority" stereotyping is a gross exaggeration of the Asian American experience and inflation of the facts.[4] All but one of the forty ethnic groups under the umbrella term "Asian American" have higher poverty rates than whites. While some East and South Asian Americans have high rates of educational attainment, strict racialized immigration laws have socially constructed this phenomenon. New African immigrants actually have a slightly higher rate of college completion.[5] Being deemed the "model minority" still upholds the boundaries of whiteness. Asian Americans, even if successful, are still othered and perpetually foreign.[6]

The "model minority" stereotyping provides no protection from racial discrimination.[7]

Race, class, gender, nationhood, and sexuality are tangled interlocking systems of power, domination, and oppression. Racial and gender inequality is maintained by everyday practices. For individuals, racialization and gendering begins before birth, and continues throughout the course of one's life. Asian American bodies are bombarded with ethnosexualized messages and images from both their most intimate familial relations and their surrounding environment. Cultural values are built into the gendering. My interviewees sometimes deal with family gender values that contrast with those of the outside world (i.e. peers, teachers, co-workers, and the media). They learn very quickly that they are inferior to whites, and assumptions are made about them not only based on race but also gender and sexuality.

The good news is that these hegemonic lessons can be unlearned. In this chapter, I offer concrete strategies on how to combat racism on both the structural and personal level. As I continue to create my own self-definition in opposition to hegemonic ideals, the more I understand that I have a responsibility to fight back against ethnosexualized stereotyping and to act as a mentor to others. I hope that the strategies that I suggest may be helpful, not only to Asian Americans but any person who wishes to fight against oppressive forces.

SOLUTIONS AND STRATEGIES

How is one person going to combat oppression that is embedded in social structure? If some Asian Americans choose to fight within these oppressive systems, are they colluding and participating in their own oppression? How can we keep from colluding in a system and keep our sanity?

When I teach undergraduates, the material in the class enlightens even the most unknowledgeable students about the hierarchical systems of domination. Unfortunately, the most empathetic and action-oriented students become overwhelmed with the size of the problem and do not know where to begin to fight. Besides large structural change, there are a number of strategies to deal with fighting injustice at the personal and communal level. What has to be understood first and foremost is that where power lies also lies resistance.[8] In order for hegemonic power to remain unchanged, resistance must be constructed as "unnecessary," "illogical," "crazy," and "over the top." Our lack of understanding racial oppression in the United States is shameful, and this is largely due to the hegemonic nature of the white racial frame. However, hegemonic ideology continues to thrive because of lack of resistance and the coercive normality as racial status quo being the "way it is and always should be." To combat the white racial frame, there are strategies to adopt at the larger community/structural level and personal level.

One thing to understand about battling gendered racism at a personal level is that changing racialized and gendered behavior is very unlikely to change the organization and structure of these social systems. People often ask me, "what good does it do for me to do work on a personal level when the social forces that perpetuate racism are so dauntingly large?" It's true that doing work at the personal level will not necessarily produce the change you seek in structure. However, it is imperative to do the personal work first. You have to take care of yourself, making sure you are emotionally and mentally healthy, so that you can do work at the structural level.

Two Strategies for Battling Oppression at the Structural Level

There are two very different approaches to fighting against oppression, and both require some critical understanding of social systems:

1. Reformative movement: This method primarily focuses on altering the norms of the existing systems, usually through law. [9] Examples of reformative organizations are the Asian American Justice Center (AAJC), the Asian Pacifica American Legal Center (APALC), and the Asian American Legal Defense and Education Fund (AAL-DEF).
2. Revolutionary/radical movement: This method focuses on fundamentally changing value systems. A major change in the structure is the goal of revolutionary/radical movements.

Reformative Movement

One strategy is to work within the system. I have spoken with many young Asian American law students who hope to use their discipline to better the lives of all citizens. They are members of Asian American law student associations and see the law as the appropriate vessel to create social change. While I applaud their efforts, reformative movement works within the boundaries set by the dominating hegemonic ideology. Students in law school are trained to think like lawyers when, in essence, that means to "think white." [10]

There have been visible changes to U.S. law throughout its history. African Americans' use of reformative movement to "obtain freedom, justice, and dignity is as old as this nation." [11] However, the problem with legal reform, especially regarding civil rights for people of color, comes in the enforcement. Critical race theorist Derrick Bell notes that "a judge can manipulate the law and arrive at an outcome based upon her worldview, to the detriment of blacks." [12] Bell's statement can be extended beyond the judge in the "justice system." The manipulation runs deeply through an entire system that has acted to the detriment of all people of color.

Systems of oppression (e.g., racism, sexism, classism, and homophobia) persist. Hegemonic ideologies shift in response to resistance against them. Hegemony is mutable and resilient. The "new racism"[13] and "color-blind" discourse[14] are strategies to maintain white supremacy, making racism no longer blatant and overt but tacit and covert. While there have been changes to policies and laws enacted to protect people of color, there has been little effort by whites to enforce them.

Revolutionary/Radical Movement

This method focuses on fundamentally changing societal structure and hegemonic value systems. Both reformative and revolutionary/radical movement require community organization and participation. They also require access to resources to financially support the efforts. Revolutionary/radical movements do not get as much widespread support because they are framed as extremist methods used by unstable individuals or factions. Whites often praise Martin Luther King Jr.'s use of non-violence, but he was actually very unpopular with whites until the time of his death.[15] His memory has been co-opted by whites to mythologize racial progress in the United States. Malcolm X and the Black Panther Party, on the other hand, are extremely vilified. Mohandas Gandhi and Martin Luther King Jr. are portrayed as the appropriate role models for social change: nonviolence in the face of even the most egregious injustice.

We have seen a resurgence of revolutionary/radical movement in the United States with the Occupy Wall Street movement. *Time* Magazine chose "The Protestor" as the person of the year. While the social change and ultimate result of the Occupy Wall Street movement remains to be seen, in the very early stages the movement is getting media coverage and some attention from political figures. When a revolutionary/radical movement gains momentum and enough support, great social change may result.

Strategy at the Personal Level: Counter-Framing

The persistence of the white racial frame, hegemonic masculinity, and continuing process of "white habitus" to socialize whites and people of color to normalize a white sexuality is a great barrier to social equality. Feagin theorizes that three types of counter-frames exist to combat the white racial frame. In this section, each counter-frame is discussed at length.

The Liberty-and-Justice Frame

Whites have utilized the liberty-and-justice frame since the American Revolution.[16] Over the centuries, some whites have taken this counter-frame very seriously in regard to the racial oppression of Americans of color. White abolitionists and civil rights activists invoked passages and promises of the Declaration of Independence and U.S. Constitution to highlight the hypocrisies of racist policies like slavery and Jim Crow laws. After the civil rights movement, it has become more difficult to identify racism that is embedded in social structure.[17] The new "color-blind" era or notion of the postracial U.S. society today has popularized the liberty-and-justice rhetoric so much so that white racism is perpetuated in the belief that the system is now fair and just with the dismantling of those racist legal practices. This is a major problem with this particular counter-frame.

For Asian Americans, this frame can be intertwined with "model minority" myth. There is great reliance on this particular frame in the belief that meritocracy exists, but that is a failed assumption. Some Asian Americans hope hard work will lead to opportunities in this free society and that Asian Americans merely need an equal opportunity to produce adequate change; however, this largely buys into the "abstract liberalism" frame of color-blind racism.[18] A number of my respondents had faith that performing well academically would protect them from discrimination, but that was not the case.[19] The concepts of liberty and justice are not in and of themselves flawed, but the belief that a level racial playing field exists and that institutions are color-blind is. The concepts about liberty, justice, and equality are great in a vacuum, but for them to be sufficient we would have to erase hundreds of years of white racial prejudice and eliminate an age-old white racist ideology. In discussing social equality for Asian Americans Irwin pulls from a liberty-and-justice counter-frame:

> We as Asian Americans deserve and want it all. All of it. All of what it means to be American including the dignity that many Americans are given the right to at birth. You know, I was born in the United States. I feel like that was not one of my rights—to live with dignity. Even from the second I was born, it wasn't worth their time to really analyze what to call me. For instance, I was labeled white on my birth certificate. I think that was on my driver's license, up until ten years ago. What are we, just an appendage to the white race? I'm not complaining about that in and of itself. I'm just saying that this idea that we deserve to be treated as equals, that should be an assumed, as they say, as a self-evident, natural right. That's something that we haven't had; that's something that we don't assume for ourselves. I think that when we take that step ourselves, that's going to be a major step for our own equality in America.

Irwin evokes notions of rights that are "self-evident" or "natural," but he also backtracks, noting that not all Americans are treated with dignity. He recognizes that he has not been seen or treated as an equal, but that Asian Americans deserve it. However, Irwin does not suggest that equality is something that is just awarded without effort. He critiques Asian Americans for not fighting for those rights. Asian Americans are not simply victims of oppression; they must be agents in the fight for equality. The use of the liberty-and-justice frame can certainly play a major role in bringing down systems of oppression, but the development of the two other counter-frames are vitally important to contend with the dominant white racial frame.

The Home-Culture Frame

Pulling from or taking actions out of the home-culture frame can counter the messages from a white racial frame. However, for Asian Americans who are often constructed as perpetually foreign, this can be detrimental in xenophobic political periods like the present. Major complaints and mythologies of immigrants in this openly hostile anti-immigrant era are that they "refuse to learn the language" and are not truly "American." Immigrants like Latinos and Asians have yet to be fully embraced as "real Americans," and their traditions, customs, and values can be targeted.

Yet, the home culture can also be a source of great strength. Indira, a third-generation Asian Indian, is a dean at a university. She found great strength in honoring her Indian identity after her mother shared that she felt "like a cartoon" and "primitive" when wearing traditional Indian clothing. Her mother's alienation fueled Indira to resist the white racial frame.

> That just made me so angry. I was like, "That will not happen." That [wearing traditional Indian clothing] is a legacy that I will carry with myself. In any space where I speak in public, I will always honor this identity, because of what you [her mother] felt.

Indira, while seemingly subtle, resists the ostracism her mother felt by making her culture visible in public spaces. Other respondents did not want to "stick out like a sore thumb," and tried to assimilate to whiteness. Indira was one of a few respondents that battled white racial stereotyping head on. Scholars have written that resistance to oppression is dependent on creating new self-valuation.[20] For Americans of color who are immigrants or a generation or two removed from a home-culture frame, self-valuation can be connected to this frame.

There can be a downside to pulling from the home-culture frame that complicates matters for multiframers, those individuals pulling from multiple frames at once. There is a complex relationship that the home-culture frame has when combined with both the white racial frame and anti-oppression frame. The home-culture frame can be a stigmatizing source for Asian Americans trying to fit into white or American culture. Already stereotyped as foreign, pressures from first-generation parents can be a burden. Additionally, some of the pressure to preserve their culture by avoiding interracial relationships can simultaneously be anti-black and anti-Latino. At times, those anti-Latino and black stereotypes are drawn from white racial framing, but it can also stem from a fear of different cultures. This complicates the development of multiracial coalitions.

Additionally, frames are not static; they transform over time. Some Asian Americans have begun to redefine the home-culture frame. In communities that allow for "Asian pride," younger generations of Asian Americans are finding strength from their Asian identity. This is evidenced in the popularity of imported Asian pop culture.[21] Korean pop (K-pop) is widely popular in the United States, as are a slew of emerging Asian American YouTube stars such as Bart Kwon, Clara Chung, Ted Fu, Megan Lee, Ryan Higa, and Joe Jo. Asian Americans are looking outside of mainstream media outlets to a plethora of self-affirming representations of Asians. These Asian Americans embrace their identity and are not ashamed of their culture. Building self-valuation from the "home-culture" frame can be a great asset for Asian Americans who may be struggling with identity.

The Anti-Oppression Frame

Asian Americans and African Americans have similar histories and experiences in the United States. Both groups have served white labor needs throughout U.S. history, reifying white supremacy. However, because of the fundamentally different patterns of immigration (forced vs. voluntary), large differences exist in media portrayals, the construction of ideologies and stereotypes, and how resistance movements have been both carried out and recorded in the history books. Asian Americans have been constructed as "solution minorities,"[22] and their history of racial oppression is often missing in standard history curriculum.

Because of the similarities with African Americans, Asian Americans can learn from their experiences. Lin, a first-generation Chinese American in her sixties, moved here in the 1960s and lived in the Northeast. She is a political activist and opened an Asian American community center a few years ago in the Southwest. She was inspired by the history of Asian American ancestors and social movements like the civil rights movement:

> We truly have our rightful place here because our ancestors have put down their lives here for us. They helped to build the railroad; they helped to really develop the economy and the future of this country. It

is up to us to take it [our rightful place]. In the past they could not do it, because they were not protected by the law, like the Chinese Exclusion Act and all of that. It was utterly racist, especially against us. But we have to thank the brothers, the black brothers and sisters and all the people that were in the Civil Rights Movement that they also claimed their space by working for fairness and justice of this nation, they also claimed the space for us. So, it's really up to us, to move into our rightful place.

Lin has developed an anti-oppression frame and acknowledges the parallels of the Asian and African American experience. Many Asian Americans often have little or no knowledge of racist legislation controlling and disciplining early Asian Americans. Asian Americans faced severe racist treatment quite similar to African Americans and also resisted in organized ways. Yet, the resistance movements of the past are largely unknown and invisible in the Asian American collective memory of racial oppression. African Americans most certainly faced brutal violence, kidnapped from their countries of origin and enslaved. From the atrocities of the slave system, with widespread brutality of all laborers and institutionalized rape of enslaved women, a white legacy exists of dehumanizing stereotypes of African Americans coupled with the reality of great political and economic racial disparity. African Americans have unceasingly resisted the racial degradation from the beginning, as have Asian Americans. Their counter-framing is well established and embedded in the African American psyche, but counter-framing for Asian Americans is disjointed and the "model minority" stereotype creates a myth that Asian Americans have it better than other Americans of color.

Jessica, a second-generation Vietnamese American in her twenties, comments on the lack of activism among her Asian American peers and its relationship to the "model minority" myth:

> When we don't learn about our history and we don't learn about our role here in this country and we're not even seen as Americans, I mean, we internalize all of that and we don't see it. A lot of times Asian Americans don't consider themselves people of color and other people don't consider them people of color either. So they don't understand it, they don't get it. Or they say, well yeah, I guess you're right, but it's not as bad as, you know, the black community or the Latino community, so we should shut up.

Occupying a middle place in the racial hierarchy complicates matters for Asian Americans. It can appear that Asian Americans are treated more fairly than other Americans of color. However, Asian Americans still face major discrimination in all facets of their lives.[23] From overt, violent hate crimes to more clandestine, subtler forms of exclusion, Asian American "success" has not provided a shield from racism.[24] Jessica began to construct an anti-oppression frame because she began to learn about the history of Asian American racial oppression in college; but the strength of the "model minority" myth persists.

While being used as justification to end affirmative action, a new change in the University of California state system admissions policy is unfairly targeting Asian American students.[25] The UC system has eliminated SAT subject tests, which Asians tend to do well on. On the surface, the UC administrators insist that the move will increase the African American and Latino enrollment in the system.[26] However, a study at UC Berkeley sponsored by the Board of Regents found that the only group to benefit from the change would be white students. Ignoring its own research study, the UC system has implemented the change. Asian Americans are a threat to white supremacy in these university systems with white-coined nicknames such as UCLA (University of Caucasians, Lost among Asians) and UC Irvine (University of Chinese Immigrants).[27] The new policy, while seemingly color-blind, is beneficial to whites. More importantly, the emphasis on Asian American success masks the economic disparities and racial discrimination that they experience.

African and Asian Americans have had similar difficulties being incorporated into the United States as full and equal citizens. Blatantly white racist legislation has been part of the United States throughout its history. African Americans have been able to create a strong collective identity and memory of racial oppression.[28] African Americans can rely on a community of peers to help deal with the burdens of racial discrimination. They have adopted their own "America" regardless of external pressures from whites to control every aspect of their lives. Asian Americans do not have the same collective identity. With such a great diversity of nations and ethnicities represented, the umbrella term is inadequate and externally imposed. Immigrants are coming from nations with their own unique histories, and some of the nations lumped together in the United States have been at war with each other for long periods of time. Even with varying histories from their nations of origin, Asian Americans share in the same racialized process in the United States. There are notable differences in the treatment of South Asians that is similar to Arab Americans and African Americans.[29] Yet, that different experience faced by South Asians highlights the arbitrary and constructed nature of race. Asian Americans are a mish-mash of peoples from similar geographic regions; collective group identity becomes based upon model minority stereotyping.[30] This creates great challenges in establishing counter-frames and resistance movements.

Asian American counter-framing and resistance are often missing from the history books. There were numerous labor strikes, boycotts, and lawsuits contesting racial discrimination brought on by Asian Americans. In 1867, two thousand Chinese railroad workers went on strike for a week. In 1870, Chinese railroad workers in Texas sued the company for failing to pay wages. In 1885, Chinese laundrymen won an important

legal victory in *Yick Wo v. Hopkins,* which declared that a law with un-
equal impact on different groups is discriminatory. In 1920, 10,000 Japanese and Filipino plantation workers went on strike. In 1924, 1,600 Filipino plantation workers went on strike for eight months in Hawaii.[31] Unfortunately, these strikes were often broken by bringing in other Asian
laborers, making it hard to coalesce as a group. Chinese men brought to
Mississippi to work on plantations after the Civil War protested their
practically enslaved positions and eventually carved their own niche by
opening stores in black neighborhoods.[32]

Also missing from both Asian and African American history is the life
of Richard Aoki. Aoki, a Japanese American, was one of the founding
members of the Black Panther Party. He attended Merritt College with
Huey Newton and Bobby Seale. His family was interned in the Topaz
Relocation camp in Utah from 1942 to 1945. Aoki became the coordinator
for the first Asian American studies program at UC Berkeley.[33] Interestingly, there were three Japanese Americans in the Black Panther Party,
and all three had experiences with overt racism during the internment of
Japanese Americans in World War II. Richard Aoki was four years old
when he was interned, and Mike Tagawa was born in camp. Guy Kurose
was born to a peace activist mother who suffered through internment.
Kurose's mother was unique because most Nisei who were interned
chose conformity and silence after camp. Kurose's mother was vocal
about the injustice, developing a collective memory of racial oppression
for her son Guy. Aoki grew up in an African American neighborhood in
California, where he was immersed in the resistance culture of the
1960s.[34] All three men were active in the movements to establish ethnic
studies in universities. I highlight these three men because there is a
direct link between their overt racist treatment, the development of a
collective memory of racial oppression, and their directly confrontational
forms of resistance. In 1968 and 1969 there were student strikes at San
Francisco State University and the University of California, Berkeley, for
the establishment of ethnic studies programs which included many Asian
American activists. The establishment of Asian American studies programs is one way of creating a collective memory of racial oppression.
These influential Asian Americans had experiences similar to those of
African Americans. The respondents that were exposed to Asian
American history all went through a sociopolitical transition. They were
able to see the racist structure in the United States.

There was a "Yellow Power" movement in the 1960s, and the political
involvement of groups on the West Coast is more prevalent than in other
geographic areas of the United States. But on the West Coast, different
ethnicities have drastic class and educational differences that make it
hard for them to coalesce as a political force.[35] This is key to systemic
racism; these groups have been constructed as a homogenous group.
They serve the same white interest for their labor and resources (not just

in the Pacific Islands but globally). They face the same exploitation, but differences in immigration patterns have created great imbalances in access to resources.

In the color-blind era of the twenty-first century, we face more a difficult challenge when fighting oppression. The question is "Who's the racist?" With "model minority" status, protest becomes less attractive and seemingly illogical, because there is material benefit in being considered higher on the racial hierarchy. Asian Americans may not be in the top position, but disrupting the racial order is seen as too much of a risk for many.[36] There are small pockets of resistance: student groups, community centers, and social justice organizations, for example. But Richard Aoki has been called "not your typical Asian." Some Asian Americans resist individually and privately by creating new self-definition and self-valuation.[37] There is a longstanding and visible history of resistance by African Americans. Their fights for racial justice have been in the public eye and embedded in the collective memory of racial oppression, not just for African Americans but Americans of every color. A strong collective memory is essential in creating counter-frames.

Besides direct confrontation, there are all the tactics used by slaves on plantation, breaking tools, doing work slowly, feigning illness, and developing strong kinship networks.[38] These are all strategies early African Americans used to help them survive. They have used more extensive and organized political movements to fight structural issues. Additionally, they have counter-frames to ideology. The promotion of a rich black culture and slogans such as "Black is beautiful" are examples of anti-oppression counter-framing. Newer African immigrants who may see many dissimilarities culturally with African Americans can still access the ideological counter-framing that has been strongly developed over centuries.

Asian and African Americans have been similarly exploited for their labor by white elites throughout U.S. history. Their different labor patterns shed light on their placement in the racial hierarchy. The selective and voluntary immigration of East and South Asian Americans explains the development of the "model minority" myth. Additionally, the differences among Asian Americans by waves of immigration and nation/ethnicity of origin create difficulties in forming coalitions. Asian Americans have been othered and deemed perpetually foreign, yet there is no strong development of shared collective memory. Instances of resistance have occurred throughout Asian American history, but it is largely unknown and absent from the mainstream media and history curriculum. There are Asian Americans with greater access to counter-narratives who have a stronger collective memory of racial oppression, but we can do better. This is why the scholarship on Asian American resistance has been so vital thus far. Many scholars have been doing the recovery work, and my hope is that it continues.

Further Development of Anti-Oppression Frames: Personal Coping Strategies

This next section is a departure from the rest of the book, and I see it as fulfilling a personal promise to Asian Americans looking for guidance on how to manage incidents of discrimination. As scholars, we are not trained to write a "how to" guide when dealing with oppression. I am, however, going to offer some coping strategies that I have passed along to students. I am focusing mainly on coping strategies for racial discrimination, but these strategies can certainly be used when dealing with sexism or homophobia. As demonstrated in earlier chapters, cumulative discrimination can take a toll. Respondents shared that their self-esteem, self-worth, and mental health can take a beating because of both overt and subtle discriminatory acts. Like Indira shared, we are containers and if we do not release some of what we bear, we can break. Studies have shown that racism takes a toll on health and well-being, and a recent study of 199 Filipino Americans confirmed that confronting racism boosts self-esteem.[39] Many of my respondents were not given lessons on how to deal with racist incidents; very few parents discussed this subject.

At the personal level, individuals must work diligently to construct their own identities and self-definitions. While Asian Americans are bombarded with messages of inferiority, inadequacy, and foreignness, we must refuse to accept these images as valid. The media are consistently projecting images and messages that are false. To fight the white racial framing, you must identify and understand the frame. Then construct a strong counter-frame so that you have a resource to fall back on when others challenge your counter-perspective. There are examples of counter-frames growing in strength and gaining some foundation in social movements, like "black is beautiful." Be prepared, when you stand up for yourself against hegemonic ideology, or against something that perpetuates racial stereotyping; even people you consider your friends might not understand.

When asked about how to combat "isms," I sense a great deal of fear from those who are asking for the advice. Some of the fear could be linked to the "model minority" myth or to new immigrant status. There are some ideological and material benefits in the short term for those people of color who are complacent with the racial hierarchy. That is the deceptive nature of "positive" stereotyping. The fear of rocking the boat is so strong and is further complicated by gender. Women and girls are discouraged from being too aggressive. The construction of Asian women as even more passive complicates attempts at assertion or aggression in defense of racial mistreatment. I find myself often trying to give tips. I myself struggle to stand up and fight without compromising the constructions I have of myself, asking myself "Is this how an Asian American woman should act?" How should an Asian American woman act and how have these constructions limited how free I feel to act? However, numerous health studies have concluded that assertiveness reduces stress, boosts self-esteem, and reduces the risk for depression.[40] Assertiveness could very well relieve some of the burden of racism.

A woman I met at one of my lectures told me that one of her close white friends repeatedly jokes that Asians eat dogs. This type of teasing, which seems innocuous to the white friend, has both larger sociohistorical meanings (Asians as barbaric) and personal meanings (Asians being easy targets for joking). The larger sociohistorical meaning may have no bearing on how hurtful this type of teasing may be to an eight-year-old Asian American; the child only sees that peers at school target them for looking different. The racial connotations of this type of taunting basically go unchallenged by adults who supervise these children.[41] I often spend time talking with young Asian American adults about techniques for dealing with racist incidents. In this era of color-blind rhetoric and the popularity of parody and comedians of color poking fun at their own race, legitimized by their membership, Asian Americans who do not find such humor funny often get accused of being "too sensitive" when they stand up for themselves against racial teasing. These experiences are deposited in the individual's collective racial memory. When a woman in law school has a close white friend who continues to joke that she eats dog after her repeated objections and her attempts to explain why it hurts her feelings, what should she do?

While I acknowledge that this section is highly prescriptive, I recommend a few coping strategies in dealing with these types of situations. These are merely suggestions that could act as a reference to particular individuals who seek advice in how to combat racism. These methods can be used singularly or in combination:

1. The "Diplomatic" Strategy: Try having an intelligent conversation, or even a heart-to-heart. Suggest some readings that may enlighten them.
2. The "Boundaries" Strategy: Retaining a "close" friend that thinks it is acceptable to demean you, for any reason, after you have explained that his/her actions are hurtful, is not a friend worth having.
3. The "This Ain't My Job" Strategy: It is a burden to try and convince people that racism exists. It is not your job to convince them, because hegemonic ideology will contradict your points, making them all look illogical. You can walk away from this discussion.
4. The "Structure Is Bigger than the Individual" Strategy: If you do care enough for the person to retain them as a friend, you think they have other retaining qualities, or they hold positions of power and influence that would make it costly to be on bad terms, then keep your sanity and maintain some forgiveness for their ignorance. Keep in mind that systemic racism and the white racial frame

are so powerful that whites *and* people of color will resist the truth about racial oppression. These ideologies are centuries strong and have been maintained because people believe them.

The "Diplomatic" Method

This method works for friends, family, and colleagues who are open to deconstructing both the world around them and their own personal beliefs. This method can also be effective with friends who possess a strong sense of empathy. They may not have had exposure to racial injustice. Hiding the truth about racial injustice is a key component to hegemonic whiteness, and educating an individual may work to alter someone's consciousness whether they are a white or a person of color.

Many of my Asian American respondents who became social activists were first exposed to critical writings about racist relations in the United States. These alternative voices struck a nerve with them and helped change their worldviews. This method is not foolproof, as some individuals are more invested in maintaining the white racial frame than others. Whites, for example, benefit psychologically by believing in meritocracy and white virtue. Deconstructing and destroying the myths of meritocracy and white virtue becomes a very uncomfortable process.

The "Boundaries" Method

This method is meant to work with people with whom you have an established relationship. Hold your friends and loved ones accountable for their actions, without negotiating your own principles. Relationships that are healthy allow for both individuals to openly share their thoughts and feelings with each other. If a friend or loved one continues to engage in hurtful actions based on race, gender, sexuality, and so on, you have every right to draw boundaries. If they are unresponsive to your attempts at having diplomatic conversations, you have a right to take some space for your own health. If a woman stayed with an abusive partner, most people would encourage her to leave that person. Why, then, do we fail to encourage each other to leave people who are racially abusive?

This can be a very difficult process, but also liberating. Fareena, a second-generation Bangladeshi American in her twenties, began to place boundaries on her relationships and became assertive when friends crossed a line. Fareena notes, "I had lost so many friends who were not brown. I guess they saw me as being immersed in this brown world, somehow losing me." However, Fareena was able to make friends who treated her as a full, equal human being. She did not have to carry the burden of maintaining relationships with people who saw her as a stereotype.

The "This Ain't My Job" Method

Perhaps you have expended energy trying to be diplomatic and have drawn clear boundaries. Also know that you do not have to make any attempts to convince anyone that your experience is valid. People of color are burdened with a "double consciousness," performing mental gymnastics in a white supremacist society. Your experience is real, regardless of how others may try and convince you otherwise. You do not have to expend excess energy trying to validate it.

The "Structure Is Bigger than the Individual" Method

I want to differentiate the last method, "Structure is Bigger than the Individual," from being a white apologist. Being a white apologist is buying into a version of "white virtue." Understanding that structure is bigger than an individual allows you to critique their racist stereotyping or discrimination, while allowing you to depersonalize it. While you may be the immediate target, these are racist scripts that have been in existence long before you. The white racial frame is powerful, and even people of color adopt the messages. Jessica identifies that Asian Americans often buy into racist stereotypes.

> In the African American community, somebody who wouldn't [fight racism] would be called an Uncle Tom, but in our community they would just be called *practical*. Don't you see? Our parents would just call them smart. Not rocking the boat, not causing trouble. And I think that it's just minority myths that we perpetuate within ourselves. And I mean even me, it's hard to think sometimes, "Why do I have to stop everything and worry about this? Because it doesn't have to do with me, it just has to do with other people who come after me. Why does it even matter?" And I could totally get by and not fight. Totally get by and be *mildly content*, but I don't want that.

Jessica articulates that there are certain rewards in the Asian American community to remaining silent about racial inequality. It is emotionally taxing to fight for equality when many others in the community do not see it as an imperative issue. Jessica can see structural issues at play, and this helps her understand why her Asian American peers are not taking up the fight. This method is a way for you to retain your sanity when individuals seem closed to critiquing their surrounding world.

Another Personal Strategy: Abandoning the "Model Minority" Image

For the most part, the four strategies I have suggested will not ruffle too many feathers when dealing with a racist situation. There is one last personal strategy that I urge Asian Americans to keep in their repertoire of resistance. Explode! Let your true emotions be released, unedited and uncut. Emotional management is a form of oppression.[42] Making fun of Asians and Asian Americans so publicly, like a "friend" joking to your face about eating dogs, says something about how Asian Americans are expected to respond—or, rather, not respond. Asian Americans have often been silent in these situations, providing a weak counter-narrative of resistance. African Americans are falsely constructed as dangerous, so a lot of anti-black statements get pushed into the backstage.[43] While that does not solve the problem of systemic racism, African Americans have a collective identity and a public history of resistance.

However, some Asian Americans have an underdeveloped anti-oppression counter-frame and are often unaware of examples of Asian American public resistance. Every time I do not speak up against racism, I feel as if I perpetuate stereotypes. I give the assailant a free pass and reinforce notions of Asian passivity. Then, I have another racial memory to add to my bucket. Instead of adding memories of racial oppression to that bucket, we can construct our own counter-frame, a frame in which Asian Americans are assertive and strong.

Iris, a third-generation Chinese American in her twenties, had a role model in her mother. She shares, "One time she was bartending at a Chinese restaurant, and a guy said, 'you have really small breasts' and my mom said, 'you probably have a really small dick.' So my mom is kind of ballsy." Iris was one of just a handful of respondents that spoke openly about her desire to confidently resist racism. Lessons from her mother and some personal experiences with discrimination had awakened something inside of her. She hates being stereotyped as agreeable. She asserts, "Oh, the one [stereotype about Asian American women] that is horrible is the agreeable. Oh my god, I hate that one. I just want to be, like, 'fuck you' to show them I'm not agreeable." Iris acknowledges that it is not always easy to fight against stereotyping, but she is willing to break the gendered racial stereotypes at times.

Fareena also abandons stereotypes of Asian American women. It has been a difficult process as she has lost friends in the process of developing anti-oppression frames but it has also given her much strength. She notes:

> I used to be a passive person in high school. Now I have this reputation as a big bad brown angry woman. And I was really resentful for that. If you see me as angry, you see me as someone who can't control their emotions; they're just a little firecracker and you just disregard them and just want to calm them down. You're not listening to their issues, and I didn't want to be invalidated in that way. But now I just embrace it, the "big bad brown mama" stereotype.

When individuals resist the white racial frame, they are often discredited and accused of "pulling the race card." African American activists are often painted as agitators and complainers, a consequence of countering the white racial frame. Fareena recognizes the negative consequences of battling racial oppression. People saw her as an "angry brown woman," which is quite similar to the constructions of the angry black woman or man. Resisting oppression can come with a price, the stigma of being emotionally out of control is one of them.

Since I have experienced being publicly insulted a number of times, I have resolved to abandon my often cool and collected demeanor, and let the assailant learn that insulting Asian American people in public is not tolerated by *this* Asian American. When I hold in my anger and rage, those emotions do not go away. Once I have gotten home, sometimes I am disappointed in myself for not making it clear to the assailant that he or she has messed with the wrong person. I do not encourage unnecessary violence. I am urging disruption. There are times when injustice should be met with physical force, but generally speaking my hope is to disrupt the assumptions made about me as an Asian American; as an Asian American woman; as a queer, Asian American woman.

The added stress for people of color dealing with racism negatively affects their health, and any strategies to lessen that stress are imperative for racial progress. Often, when I am enraged, I cry. Then I become angrier that I am crying. The rage turns to tears because I am trying to hold it in. As a woman, I have been taught that it is inappropriate for me to scream, curse, threaten, and beat when I am furious. However, this controlled rage is unhealthy. We must feel comfortable in allowing ourselves to be free with our emotions, even if they seem negative. We must disrupt oppression as it occurs.

A little disruption can go a long way. As mentioned in chapter 4, there have been numerous sexual predators targeting Asian and Asian American women specifically. At one of my talks, a Chinese American woman shared this experience:

> There was a time I was almost assaulted. There was someone, at that time, targeting Asian women and raping them. I was just coming home and he came onto my patio. He put on a black facemask over his head. He pretended he had a gun and said, "Just do exactly what I say." He didn't expect me to react the way I did. This rage came over my entire body. And this guy was not a professional; he was not a pro at this. I was holding all these bags in my arms and I raised my voice and said, "I do not have time for this right now!" [laughter] He was startled and then tried to pretend that he was trying to do something else. Finally, he just left.

While this woman was probably very lucky that her attacker was not more aggressive, she surprised him with her voice. She assumed that the attacker was used to women just doing as he said. Even small amounts of vocal dissent can go a long way. Guang is angered by the assaults of

Asian American women on the subway in his city and says that they are considered easy targets because it is assumed that they will remain silent.

Resistance does not always have to take the form of disruption. Paul Varghese uses his comedy as social commentary. He challenges white racism by incorporating material in his jokes. Other comedians that use self-deprecating, racialized humor in their acts bother him. Paul sees other Asian American comedians making karate and terrorist jokes as damaging. Through humor, Paul resists by wittily pointing out racist assumptions that are made about him without perpetuating racist stereotyping.

Humor is a healthy coping mechanism. Releasing rage is as well. Imagine fathers and mothers enraged when a predator has hurt their child. We empathize with their pain and excuse, even expect, emotions, which may include rage and thoughts of revenge. But every day, when people of color are abused by predatory and exploitative hegemonic whiteness, we call that rage pathological and unnecessary. We call that rage a product of an inferior violent culture or a culture of poverty. We praise the people of color who remain silent or collude with the system. Feeling enraged about being treated as a lesser human is not pathological. Rage is not sickness. It is "a potentially healthy, potentially healing response to oppression and exploitation."[44]

How does the treatment of Asian Americans in the United States relate to the global context of racial oppression? While many of us in the United States, unquestioningly, collude with white supremacy, even those who are critical of racist relations, we fail to question the continual colonial actions of the United States worldwide. There are women and children working in factories who look like us. Our families were selected or were able to immigrate here for the purpose of supporting the U.S. economy or because of U.S. involvement with wars in Asia. We conform and work to distance ourselves from those other Asians who have been constructed as different from us. Yet we are often still treated as just as foreign. Our lack of resistance, in many ways, aids in the further exploitation of Asians abroad and all peoples that are being affected by U.S. colonial projects.

I want all Asian Americans to feel comfortable having a voice, whatever that voice may be. I urge for stronger and more numerous counter-narratives from Asian Americans, and these counter narratives can take different forms. The way systemic racism is embedded into the structure, whites and people of color will not simply give up hegemonic racist ideology or the white racial frame. Racial progress in the United States has been the direct product of counter-narratives, resistance, and collective movements. Be brave. Be assured that you have a voice and it deserves to be heard.

194 *Chapter 7*

NOTES

1. Organizations such as RAMA, led by activist Ryan Takemiya, are trying to "forge a new Pan Asian identity"; they "value an identity that is inspiring and empowering without dehumanizing people based on race, culture, gender, or sexual orientation."

2. Rosalind S. Chou and Joe R. Feagin, *The Myth of the Model Minority: Asian Americans Facing Racism* (Boulder, CO: Paradigm, 2008); Mia Tuan, *Forever Foreigners or Honorary Whites? The Asian Ethic Experience* (New Brunswick, NJ: Rutgers University Press, 2003).

3. Chou and Feagin, *Myth of the Model Minority*; Feagin (2001); Vijay Prashad, *The Karma of Brown Folk* (Twin Cities: University of Minnesota Press, 2003); Claire Jean Kim, *Bitter Fruit: The Politics of Black-Korean Conflict in New York City* (New Haven, CT: Yale University Press, 2003).

4. Tim Wise, *Colorblind: The Rise of Post-Racial Politics and the Retreat from Racial Equity* (San Francisco: City Lights Publishers, 2010).

5. U.S. Census data, http://uscensus.gov, 2000.

6. Kim, *Bitter Fruit*; Prashad, *Karma of Brown Folk*; Tuan, *Forever Foreigners*; Frank Wu, *Yellow* (New Haven, CT: Yale University Press, 2004).

7. Chou and Feagin, *Myth of the Model Minority*.

8. Michel Foucault, *The History of Sexuality*, vol. 1 (New York: Vintage Press, 1984).

9. David Aberle, *The Peyote Religion among the Navaho* (Chicago: Aldine, 1966).

10. Wendy Moore, *Reproducing Racism* (Lanham, MD: Rowman & Littlefield, 2008).

11. Derrick Bell, "Racial Realism," in *Critical Race Theory: The Key Writings That Formed the Movement*, ed. Kimberle Crenshaw et al. (New York: The New Press, 1995), 302.

12. Bell, "Racial Realism."

13. Patricia Hill Collins, *Black Sexual Politics: African Americans, Gender, and the New Racism* (New York: Routledge, 2005).

14. Eduardo Bonilla-Silva, *Racism without Racists: Color-Blind Racism and the Persistence of Racial Inequality in the United States* (Lanham, MD: Rowman & Littlefield, 2003).

15. Boyce Watkins, "Would Martin Luther King Support Obama?" The Grio, http://www.thegrio.com/2010/01/would-martin-luther-king-support-president-obama.php, accessed February 25, 2010.

16. Joe R. Feagin, *The White Racial Frame: Centuries of Racial Framing and Counter-Framing* (New York: Routledge, 2009).

17. Leslie Houts Picca and Joe R. Feagin. *Two-Faced Racism: Whites in the Backstage and Frontstage* (New York: Routledge, 2007); Bonilla-Silva, Racism without Racists.

18. Bonilla-Silva, *Racism without Racists*.

19. For extensive discussion of academic achievement as a coping strategy against racism, see Chou and Feagin, *Myth of the Model Minority*.

20. Collins, *Black Feminist Thought*.

21. I am very thankful to an anonymous reviewer for bringing in insightful comments about the transformative nature of the "home-culture" frame.

22. Vijay Prashad, *The Karma of Brown Folk* (Twin Cities: University of Minnesota Press, 2003); Chou and Feagin, *Myth of the Model Minority*.

23. Chou and Feagin, *Myth of the Model Minority*.

24. Chou and Feagin, *Myth of the Model Minority*.

25. Lisa M. Krieger, "New UC Admissions Policy Gives White Students a Better Chance, Angers Asian-American Community," Mercury News, March 27, 2009, http://www.mercurynews.com/ci_12014954?IADID=Search-www.mercurynews.com-www.mercurynews.com, accessed March 2011.

26. Krieger, "New UC Admissions."

27. Chou and Feagin, *Myth of the Model Minority*.

28. Feagin, *The White Racial Frame*.

29. Chou and Feagin, *Myth of the Model Minority*.

30. Chou and Feagin, *Myth of the Model Minority*.

31. Ronald Takaki, Ronald, *Strangers From a Different Shore: A History of Asian Americans* (Boston: Back Bay Books, 1998).

32. James Loewen, *The Mississippi Chinese: Between Black and White* (Longrove, IL: Waveland Press, 1988).

33. Neela Banerjee, "Back in the Day . . .," Asian Week Magazine, http://asianweek.com/2001_04_27/feature_richardaoki.html.

34. Banerjee, "Back in the Day."

35. Chou and Feagin, *Myth of the Model Minority*.

36. Chou and Feagin, *Myth of the Model Minority*.

37. Chou and Feagin, *Myth of the Model Minority*.

38. Chou and Feagin, *Myth of the Model Minority*.

39. Alvin Alvarez and Linda Juang. "Filipino Americans and Racism: A Multiple Mediation Model of Coping." *Journal of Counseling Psychology* 57 (2010): 167–78.

40. Joseph Culkin and Richard S. Perrotto, "Assertiveness Factors and Depression in a Sample of College Women," *Psychological Reports* 57 (1985): 1015–20; Yen-Ru Lin et al., "Evaluations of an Assertiveness Training Program on Nursing and Medical Students' Assertiveness, Self-Esteem, and Interpersonal Communication Satisfaction," *Nurse Education Today* 24, no. 8 (November 2004): 656–65; E. Newby-Fraser and L Schlebusch. "Social Support, Self-Efficacy and Assertiveness as Mediators of Student Stress," *Psychology: A Journal of Human Behavior* 34, nos. 3–4 (1997): 61–69.

41. See Chou and Feagin, *Myth of the Model Minority*.

42. bell hooks, *Killing Rage: Ending Racism* (New York: Holt, 1995).

43. Houts Picca and Feagin, *Two-Faced Racism*.

44. hooks, *Killing Rage*.

Index

CPSIA information can be obtained at www.ICGtesting.com
Printed in the USA
BVOW080104220313

316048BV00001B/3/P